SONIA ALLISON'S HOME BAKING BOOK

SONIA ALLISON'S HOME BAKING BOOK

David & Charles

Newton Abbot   London   North Pomfret (Vt)

British Library Cataloguing in
Publication Data
Allison, Sonia
    Sonia Allison's home baking book.
    1. Cookery
    I. Title
    641.5   TX717

ISBN 0–7153–8159–8

First published 1983
Second impression 1987

Typeset by ABM Typographics Ltd, Hull
and printed in Great Britain
by Redwood Burn Ltd, Trowbridge, Wilts.
for David and Charles Publishers plc
Brunel House   Newton Abbot   Devon

Published in the United States of America
by David & Charles Inc
North Pomfret   Vermont 05053   USA

Contents

Introduction

Baking is subject to all manner of definitions and interpretations but my intention when writing this book was to gather together a bumper collection of cakes, breads, pastries and puddings under one roof and provide sufficient recipes for all potential bakers, whether they were seeking Hot Cross Buns for Easter, a traditional cake for Christmas, a lavish gâteau for special occasions or buttery biscuits for afternoon tea.

An art, a craft and a hobby best describes baking, a pleasant and soothing occupation which brings with it its own rewards; inviting aromas wafting out of the kitchen, personal satisfaction at the sight of a beautifully turned-out loaf or cake, and the appreciation of family and friends as they tuck into something homemade.

The recipes come from Britain and the USA, from Europe and the Middle East — and some of the most popular favourites have been included such as Black Forest Cherry Cake, Sachertorte, Strudels, Cheesecakes, Pizzas, Quiches, Chocolate Brownies and the Spicy Pumpkin Pie which is part and parcel of American Thanksgiving. Although not strictly baking, but for the convenience of readers, I have also given recipes for Refrigerator Cakes, Pancakes, Christmas Pudding, Suet Puddings, Dropped Scones and a handful of Savouries.

Knowing full well from correspondence that mistakes occur, I have described, where applicable, the likely reasons for these under the heading 'Mishaps'. Detailed hints and tips under 'Method' should also serve as a helpful guide.

Finally, I should like to express my special thanks to the home economists at the Flour Advisory Bureau in London whose expert and unfailing help and guidance over many years have made writing this book possible.

1
Plain Cakes
and Teabreads

These are what I term family or everyday cakes, the sort of cut-and-come-again efforts which seem to be everybody's favourite with a cup of tea, coffee, cocoa or chocolate. In a way, they are the simplest of all cakes, basically an extension of shortcrust pastry but somewhat less demanding to make. Nevertheless, it is important to bear in mind three pointers to success: correct proportions of ingredients, correct tin size and accurate oven temperature. Go wrong on any of these, and the cake could prove to be a disappointment. Compared with their richer relations made by the creaming method (see page 25), rubbed-in cakes go stale a little more quickly, are less moist in texture and do not lend themselves too happily to being dolled-up in fancy dress. A dusting of icing sugar, a simple filling or perhaps a topping of glacé icing and nuts, is all that is needed by way of decoration. Certainly I would never use one of these cakes as the basis for a luxurious gâteau or torte. The personality of these fairly plain cakes lies in their simplicity. Variations on this rubbed-in theme are used all over Northern and Middle Europe, nestling next to the extravaganza of ornate confections for which these areas are so famous. They should always be stored in airtight tins, separately from biscuits.

Ingredients

Flour
This may be plain white plus 4 level tsp commercial baking powder to every lb (450g), or self-raising only. Brown flour — again plain or self-raising — can be used if preferred, as can a mixture of half white and half brown flour. Plain flour without a raising agent should never be used, or the cake will not work at all.

Salt
I always class this as an optional extra in that some of the fats used contain a percentage of salt which is sufficient in quantity to bring out the flavour of the other ingredients. If a more pronounced salty taste is preferred, add ½-1 level tsp salt to every 1 lb (450g) flour.

Spices
The variety will depend on the recipe but it should always be sifted together with the flour and salt.

Fats
The choice here rests between butter (expensive), margarine, white cooking-fat and lard. For best results, opt for a mixture, such as half each butter and cooking-fat or half each margarine and lard. Ensure the fats are at kitchen temperature and therefore soft to the touch without being runny. The usual proportion of fat to flour is half, or just under half; in other words, 3-4oz (75-125g) fat to every 8oz (225g) flour.

Sugar
Fairly fine is best. The obvious choices are caster (never granulated), or soft brown sugar with a texture of fine sand. Do not use demerara or the cake texture might be spoiled.

Dry additions
These can be coconut, mixed chopped peel, grated orange or lemon peel, dried fruit such as raisins or sultanas, chopped nuts, or grated chocolate. Any of the additions chosen, be it one or several, should always be tossed into the rubbed-in ingredients after the sugar and before the addition of eggs and liquid.

Essences
The most popular are almond and vanilla. They should be beaten with the egg and other liquid before being added to the dry ingredients.

Eggs
Grade 3 is a good size to use for these cakes and usually 1 egg is adequate for 8oz (225g) flour. Using a Grade 2 egg instead will have no adverse effect on the mixture.

Cut fats into flour with a round-topped knife

Rub in fats until mixture looks like fine breadcrumbs

Liquid

Milk is the liquid most often recommended, although in some instances fruit juice or cold tea may be used. Again, this depends on the recipe instructions.

Method

1 Brush tin or tins with melted fat and line base and sides with greaseproof paper which should again be brushed with melted fat. If using non-stick parchment paper, a second brush with fat is unnecessary. For complete safety, line the tins, even if they are non-stick. For an average-size cake, made with 8oz (225g) flour, choose a 6in (15cm) deep, round, cake tin or a 1lb (450g) oblong loaf tin.

2 Set oven to temperature recommended in the recipe so that it has time to preheat. Omit this for fan ovens.

3 Sift flour, salt and spices, if used, through a fine-mesh sieve into a mixing bowl. This will ensure there are no lumps in the dry ingredients.

4 Add chosen fats, cutting them into flour with a round-topped knife until in pieces no larger than peas. Now let your hands

take over, and rub in the fats with fingertips until the mixture looks like a mass of fine breadcrumbs.

5 Toss in sugar — still with fingertips — and any dry additions, chopped or sliced or grated, depending on the recipe instructions.

6 Tip egg, or eggs, individually into a large cup to check for freshness, then beat in the essence if used, together with the recommended liquid.

7 Pour over dry ingredients *in one go* and, using a large fork (*not* a wooden spoon), stir to a softish consistency without beating. This should be done quickly to keep the texture of the cake light.

8 Spoon into prepared tin, then smooth top with a knife. Lift up tin and tap gently up and down 2 or 3 times to break up any air bubbles in the mixture, as they might cause holes through the cake.

9 Place in oven — on centre shelf unless otherwise directed or in any position in a fan oven — and bake for required length of time, usually 1¼ to 1½ hours in oven set to 350°F (180°C), Gas 4.

10 To check if the cake is done, gently push a thin metal skewer into centre of cake. If it comes out clean with no uncooked

12

mixture clinging to it, the cake may now be removed from the oven. If not, bake a further 10 to 15 minutes checking every 5 minutes.

11 Let the cake stand for 10 minutes, then carefully invert it onto a wire cooling-rack. When lukewarm, turn the right way up and leave until completely cold before storing in an airtight tin. If to be eaten the same day, remove lining paper while cake is still warm; otherwise leave on until ready for cutting, as this helps to keep the cake moist.

Mishaps

Texture solid instead of light

1 Plain flour used without enough baking powder, or baking powder stale.
2 Fat runny or not enough used, or both.
3 Mixture over-wet through addition of too much liquid.
4 Oven too cool.

Texture coarse and interspersed with holes

1 Fat insufficiently rubbed into flour etc.
2 Granulated or demerara sugar used instead of finer sugars.
3 Mixture beaten vigorously after egg and liquid were added.

Top crust shiny and hard

1 Proportion of sugar incorrect and too much was used.
2 Tin too large.
3 Cake cooked for too long.
4 Oven temperature too high and cake cooked too near top of oven.

Top peaks and/or cracks

1 Tin too small.
2 Too much baking powder used with plain flour.
3 Mixture too wet or too dry.
4 Cake baked too near top of oven.
5 Oven too hot.

Family Fruit Cake

serves 6-8

8 oz (225g) self-raising flour
¼-½ level tsp salt
1 level tsp mixed spice
4oz (125g) butter, margarine, white cooking-fat or lard or mixture of fats (at kitchen temperature and soft to the touch)
4oz (125g) caster sugar
4oz (125g) mixed dried fruit
1 Grade 3 egg
5 tbsp cold milk beaten with the egg

1 Grease and line a 6in (15cm) deep, round, cake tin or 1lb (450g) oblong loaf tin. Set oven to 350°F (180°C), Gas 4.
2 Sift flour, salt and spice into mixing bowl. Add fat or fats. Cut into dry ingredients, with a round-topped knife, until in pieces the size of small peas.
3 Rub in finely with fingertips until mixture resembles a mass of fine breadcrumbs.
4 Toss in sugar and dried fruit. Using a fork, mix to a softish consistency with egg and milk, stirring briskly without beating until ingredients are well combined.
5 Transfer to prepared tin, tap gently up and down to disperse air bubbles and bake 1¼-1½ hours, or until a thin metal skewer, pushed gently into centre of cake, comes out clean with no uncooked mixture clinging to it. If not ready, return to oven for a further 10-15 minutes. Cover top with a piece of greaseproof paper if it appears to be browning too much.
6 Leave in tin for 10 minutes then invert cake onto a wire rack. Store in an airtight tin when completely cold, separately from biscuits. (See Method for full directions.)

Marmalade Cake

serves 6-8

Follow recipe for Family Fruit Cake but omit spice and dried fruit. Reduce sugar by 1oz (25g) and replace with 1 rounded tbsp chunky marmalade and 1 level tsp finely grated orange peel. Add with the sugar.

Date and Walnut Cake

serves 6-8

Follow recipe for Family Fruit Cake but instead of mixed dried fruit, add 4oz (125g) chopped cooking dates and 1-2oz (25-50g) chopped walnuts.

Fig and Brazil Nut Cake

serves 6-8

Follow recipe for Family Fruit Cake but omit spice and sift ¼ level tsp nutmeg with the flour and salt. Instead of mixed dried fruit, add 3oz (75g) chopped dried figs, 1oz (25g) chopped brazils and 1 level tsp finely grated lemon peel.

Chocolate Cherry Cake

serves 6-8

Follow recipe for Family Fruit Cake but omit spice. Instead of mixed fruit, add 3oz (75g) quartered, well-washed and dried glacé cherries, and 2oz (50g) chopped plain chocolate. Include ½ level tsp vanilla essence with egg and milk.

Chocolate Walnut Cake

serves 6-8

Follow recipe for Family Fruit Cake but omit spice. Substitute ½oz (15g) *each* cocoa powder and cornflour for 1oz (25g) flour. Use fine soft brown sugar instead of caster. Omit dried fruit and add 2oz (50g) finely chopped walnuts instead. Increase milk by 1 tbsp, as cocoa powder absorbs a little more liquid than ordinary flour on its own.

Coffee Date Cake

serves 6-8

Follow recipe for Family Fruit Cake but omit mixed dried fruit and add 3oz (75g) chopped cooking dates instead. Mix with egg beaten with 5 tbsp cold, strong coffee instead of milk.

Lemon and Sultana Cake

serves 6-8

Follow recipe for Family Fruit Cake but omit mixed dried fruit and add 4oz (125g) sultanas

and 2 level tsp grated lemon peel instead.

Coconut Cake

serves 6-8

Follow recipe for Family Fruit Cake but omit mixed dried fruit and add 2oz (50g) desiccated coconut instead. Increase milk to 7 tbsp, as coconut soaks up extra moisture. Include also ½ level tsp vanilla essence.

Peanut Spice Cake

serves 6-8

Follow recipe for Family Fruit Cake but increase spice to 2 level tsp. Omit mixed dried fruit and add 2oz (50g) coarsely chopped, unsalted peanuts instead.

Ginger Cake

serves 6-8

Follow recipe for Family Fruit Cake but omit spice and sift 2-3 level tsp powdered ginger with the flour and salt. Do not add any fruit at all.

Rock Cakes

makes 10

A variation of the basic recipe. Follow the directions for Family Fruit Cake, but reduce milk by about half as the mixture should be fairly stiff. Spoon 10 rocky heaps on to 2 lightly greased baking trays (5 on each to allow for some spreading) and bake 15-20 minutes in oven set to 400°F (200°C), Gas 6. Cool on a wire rack and store in an airtight tin, separately from biscuits, when cold.

Choc Chip Cakes

makes 10

Make as Rock Cakes but omit spice. Instead of mixed dried fruit, add 2-3oz (50-75g) chopped plain or milk chocolate, or chocolate dots. Include ½ level tsp vanilla essence with egg and milk.

Iced Cakes

Any of the cakes previously listed may be simply iced with glacé icing made as follows:
Sift 4oz (125g) icing sugar into bowl. Mix

to a stiff icing with 3 tsp milk, water, fruit juice or coffee. Spread over top of cake (or cakes) with a knife. Allow icing to set before cutting.

Decorating the cakes
When iced, the top may be decorated with cut-up glacé fruits, nuts, toasted coconut, chocolate vermicelli, crystallised flower petals, hundreds and thousands, or silver balls.

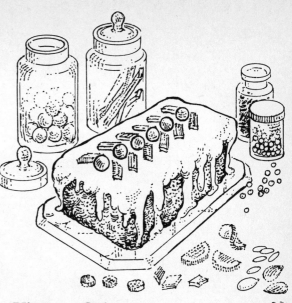

Fruited Soda Cake

serves 8

Originally from Somerset, this is a good old family cake made with lard or dripping and speckled with dried fruit.

8oz (225g) plain flour
1 level tsp bicarbonate of soda
1 level tsp mixed spice
3oz (75g) lard or dripping, at kitchen temperature
3oz (75g) caster sugar
6oz (175g) mixed dried fruit including peel
1 Grade 3 egg, at kitchen temperature and beaten
¼pt (150ml) milk, soured with 1 tbsp malt vinegar

1 Sift flour, bicarbonate of soda and spice into a bowl. Rub in fat finely.
2 Toss in sugar and fruit then mix to a fairly soft consistency with the egg and milk, stirring briskly with a fork.
3 Spread smoothly into a greased and lined 6in (15cm) round cake tin and bake 15 minutes just above centre of oven (any position in fan oven) set to 375°F (190°C), Gas 5.
4 Reduce temperature to 350°F (180°C), Gas 4 and continue to bake a further hour or until thin metal skewer, pushed gently into centre, comes out clean and dry.
5 Leave to stand 10 minutes then turn out on to a wire cooling rack. Store in an airtight container when cold.

Vinegar Cake

serves 10
(illustrated on page 90)

1lb (450g) plain flour
2 level tsp baking powder
1 level tsp mixed spice
6oz (175g) lard
8oz (225g) light-brown soft sugar
1lb (450g) mixed dried fruit
½pt (275ml) milk
1 level tsp bicarbonate of soda
2 tsp wine vinegar

1 Sift flour, baking powder and mixed spice into a bowl.
2 Add lard and rub into the flour until evenly distributed.
3 Toss in the sugar and mixed dried fruit.
4 Blend the milk with the bicarbonate of soda and vinegar, then pour the liquid into the dry ingredients.
5 Stir well together to make a fairly stiff consistency.
6 Spread mixture into a 7in (17.5cm) greased and lined round cake tin then make the centre slightly hollow so that the cake rises evenly.
7 Bake 1 hour in centre of oven (any position in fan oven) set to 350°F (180°C), Gas 4. Reduce temperature to 325°F (160°C), Gas 3 and continue to bake a further hour or

until a thin metal skewer, pushed gently into centre of cake, comes out clean and dry.

8 Leave cake to stand 15 minutes, then turn out on to a wire cooling rack. Store in an airtight tin when cold and leave 1 day before cutting.

Cinnamon Crumble Cake

serves 8-10

A winner of a cake with a crumbly centre and topping.

Crumble
2oz (50g) plain flour
2 level tsp cinnamon
2oz (50g) light-brown soft sugar
1½oz (40g) walnuts, finely chopped
1½oz (40g) butter, melted

Cake
5oz (150g) plain flour
1oz (25g) semolina
3 level tsp baking powder
2 level tsp cinnamon
1 level tsp ground ginger
4oz (125g) caster sugar
3oz (75g) butter or margarine, at kitchen
   temperature
1 Grade 3 egg, beaten
¼pt (150ml) milk

1 To make crumble, sift flour and cinnamon into a bowl. Using a fork, stir in sugar, walnuts and butter.
2 For cake, sift flour, semolina, baking powder, cinnamon, ginger and sugar into a bowl.
3 Rub in butter or margarine until mixture resembles fine breadcrumbs. Using a fork, mix to a softish consistency with the egg and milk.
4 Spread half the mixture smoothly into a 7in (17·5cm) greased and lined cake tin. Sprinkle with half the crumble mixture then spread with rest of cake mixture.
5 Sprinkle rest of crumble on top then bake 35-40 minutes in centre of oven (any position in fan oven) set to 400°F (200°C), Gas 6.

6 Leave to stand 10 minutes, then turn out on to a wire cooling rack. Cut into pieces when just cold and eat as fresh as possible.

Teabreads

These teabreads are not really 'bread' as they do not contain yeast. They are plain cakes, made by the rubbed-in method. Useful family fare, they keep well for up to 2 weeks.

Easter Bread

A simple, plain cake which is at its best when sliced and buttered.

8oz (225g) plain flour
2 rounded tsp baking powder
1½ level tsp mixed spice
3oz (75g) lard or white cooking fat, at kitchen
   temperature
3oz (75g) caster sugar
2oz (50g) cooking dates, chopped
2oz (50g) sultanas
1 Grade 3 egg
6 tbsp milk

1 Sift flour, baking powder and spice into bowl. Rub in fat finely.
2 Toss in sugar, dates and sultanas. Using a fork, mix to a softish mixture with unbeaten egg and milk, stirring briskly without beating.
3 Spread smoothly into a 2lb (1kg) loaf tin, greased and lined with greaseproof paper.
4 Bake about 1-1¼ hours in oven centre (any position in fan oven) set to 350°F (180°C), Gas 4. Cake is ready when a thin metal skewer, pushed gently into centre, comes out clean and dry. If not, return to oven for 10 minutes or so.
5 Leave 10 minutes then turn out on to a wire cooling rack. Store in an airtight container when cold.

(right from top) Quick Wholemeal loaf page 19; Banana Bread, page 19; and Cheese and Walnut Loaf, page 21 *(Pura Advisory Service)*

Banana Bread

(illustrated on page 17)

Another moist and appetising cake based on bananas. It's ideal for hungry schoolboys, self-catering holidays and picnics.

12oz (350g) self-raising flour
4oz (125g) butter or margarine, at kitchen temperature
4oz (125g) caster sugar
2 Grade 3 eggs, at kitchen temperature
4 medium bananas
2 tsp lemon juice
1 tsp almond essence
1 tbsp milk

1 Sift flour into a bowl. In second bowl, cream butter or margarine and sugar until light and fluffy.
2 Beat in eggs singly, adding 1 tbsp of flour with each.
3 Mash bananas finely with lemon juice and essence then stir into creamed mixture.
4 Fold in flour alternately with milk then spread mixture smoothly into a greased and lined 2lb (1kg) loaf tin.
5 Bake in oven centre (any position in fan oven) for 1 hour at 375°F (190°C), Gas 5. Cake is ready when a thin metal skewer, pushed gently into centre, comes out clean and dry.
6 Leave to stand 10 minutes, then turn out and cool on a wire rack. Store in an airtight container when cold. Cake may be eaten plain or served sliced and buttered.

Nutty Citrus Bread

A very easy American-style cake which can be made speedily and successfully.

12oz (350g) self-raising flour
3oz (75g) caster sugar
2oz (50g) walnuts, finely chopped
2oz (50g) mixed chopped peel

(left) Sweetheart Cake, page 33, *(Pura Advisory Service)*

2 Grade 2 eggs, beaten
¼pt (150ml) milk
2oz (50g) butter or margarine, melted

1 Sift flour into a bowl. Toss in sugar, walnuts and peel.
2 Mix to a soft consistency with the eggs and milk then stir in the butter or margarine.
3 Pour into a 2lb (1kg) greased and lined oblong loaf tin. Bake 1 hour in oven centre (any position in fan oven) set to 350°F (180°C), Gas 4.
4 Cool in tin 10 minutes then turn out and cool on a wire rack. Store in an airtight container when cold. Serve plain or sliced and buttered.

Nutty Raisin Bread
Make as Nutty Citrus Bread but use raisins instead of mixed chopped peel. Add 1 level tsp finely grated lemon peel at the same time.

Glazed Cinnamon Bread
Make as Nutty Citrus Bread but sift flour with 3 level tsp cinnamon and substitute 2oz (50g) chopped walnuts for mixed chopped peel. As soon as it comes out of the oven, brush with glaze made by dissolving 1 rounded tbsp caster sugar in 1 tbsp milk and boil briskly for 3 minutes or until syrupy.

Quick Wholemeal Loaf

(illustrated on page 17)

2 level tsp golden syrup
8fl oz (225ml) warm water
1 tsp lemon juice
8oz (225g) plain white flour
¼ level tsp salt
1 level tsp bicarbonate of soda
1 level tsp cream of tartar
2oz (50g) soft lard
8oz (225g) wholemeal flour
¼pt (150ml) milk

1 Dissolve the syrup in the warm water, add the lemon juice and leave to cool.
2 Sift the white flour, salt, bicarbonate of soda and cream of tartar into a mixing

bowl. Rub in lard and when it is evenly distributed, mix in wholemeal flour.

3 Stir in milk and cooled syrup liquid to make a fairly wet consistency.

4 Transfer to a 2lb (1kg) greased and lined oblong loaf tin and spread evenly with a damp knife.

5 Bake 15 minutes just above centre of oven (any position in fan oven) set to 400°F (200°C), Gas 6. Reduce the temperature to 350°F (180°C), Gas 4 and continue to bake a further 20-30 minutes or until the loaf is well-risen and cooked.

6 Cool on a wire rack, then sprinkle the surface with a little plain flour before cutting. Serve sliced.

Malt Loaf

An old-time favourite, as delicious as it ever was when served sliced and buttered. This is a fairly easy recipe.

8oz (225g) wholemeal flour
2 level tsp baking powder
1oz (25g) margarine or vegetable cooking fat
2oz (50g) caster sugar
3oz (75g) mixed dried fruit
1 level tbsp malt extract
1 level tbsp golden syrup
1 level tbsp black treacle
¼pt (150ml) milk

1 Toss flour and baking powder together in a bowl. Rub in fat, then add sugar and fruit.

2 Melt the malt, syrup and treacle together in a saucepan over a low heat.

3 Add to flour mixture with milk, and stir briskly without beating until all ingredients are well-combined.

4 Spread evenly into a greased and lined 1lb (450g) loaf tin and bake just above centre of oven (any position in fan oven) set to 375°F (190°C), Gas 5. Allow about 45 minutes or until firm and golden.

5 Turn out on to a wire rack to cool. Store in an airtight tin when cold and leave 2-3 days before cutting.

Fruited Bran and Banana Loaf

A tasty, healthy, low-fat loaf.

1oz (25g) bran
2oz (50g) cooking dates, chopped
3oz (75g) light brown soft sugar
¼pt (150ml) cold milk
1 medium ripe banana
1 tsp lemon juice
6oz (175g) self-raising flour

1 Put bran, dates and sugar into a mixing bowl. Add milk and stir well.

2 Peel and mash banana. Mix with lemon juice. Add to bran mixture then gently work in flour by tossing over and over with a large metal spoon.

3 When well-combined, spread evenly into a well-greased and lined 1lb (450g) loaf tin.

4 Bake about 50-60 minutes in centre of oven (any position in fan oven) set to 350°F (180°C), Gas 4. Cool on a wire rack and store in an airtight tin when cold.

Marmalade Tea Loaf

A good keeper with a fine flavour. It's especially appetising served sliced and buttered.

10oz (275g) plain flour
3 level tsp baking powder
4oz (125g) easy-cream margarine, at kitchen temperature
6oz (175g) golden syrup
3 Grade 3 eggs, at kitchen temperature and beaten
8oz (225g) coarse-cut orange marmalade
2oz (50g) chopped walnuts

1 Sift flour and baking powder into a bowl. In separate bowl, beat margarine until very creamy then beat in syrup, eggs, marmalade and walnuts.

2 Fold flour mixture into beaten ingredients then spread evenly into a greased and lined 2lb (1kg) loaf tin.

3 Bake 1½-1¾ hours in oven centre (any position in fan oven) set to 350°F (180°C), Gas 4. Cake is ready when a thin metal skewer, pushed gently into centre, comes out clean and dry.

4 Leave in tin 10 minutes then turn out on to a wire rack. Store, with lining paper for protection, in an airtight container when completely cold. Allow to mature 1 day before cutting.

Lemon Marmalade Tea Loaf
Make as above, using lemon marmalade instead of orange.

Iced Tea Loaf
Make as above. Leave until cold then cover top with glacé icing by mixing 6oz (175g) sifted icing sugar to a thickish paste with lemon or orange juice, adding it tsp by tsp.

Cheese and Walnut Loaf
(*illustrated on page 17*)

8oz (225g) self-raising flour
1 level tsp baking powder
1 level tsp dry mustard powder
Salt and pepper to taste
2oz (50g) lard, softened
1oz (25g) walnuts, chopped
3oz (75g) Cheddar cheese, grated
1 Grade 2 egg
¼pt (150ml) milk

1 Sift the flour, baking powder, dry mustard and salt and pepper into a bowl.
2 Add the lard, walnuts, cheese, egg and milk.
3 Using a fork, stir all the ingredients together then beat thoroughly until they are smoothly combined.
4 Spread evenly into 1lb (450g) greased and lined oblong loaf tin. With wetted hands, press the mixture into the sides and level the surface.
5 Bake the loaf for 50 minutes just above oven centre (any position in fan oven) set to 375°F (190°C), Gas 5. Loaf is ready when it is well-risen and golden and when metal skewer, pushed gently into centre, comes out clean and dry.

6 Leave 10 minutes, then turn out and cool on a wire rack. Store in an airtight tin when cold. Serve sliced and buttered.

Farmhouse Loaf
(*illustrated on page 35*)

4oz (125g) smoked streaky bacon
4oz (125g) plain flour
1 level tsp bicarbonate of soda
½ level tsp cream of tartar
4oz (125g) wholewheat flour
½-1 level tsp dried mustard powder
2oz (50g) butter
4oz (125g) mature English Cheddar or Derby cheese, finely grated
½ small onion or 4 small spring onions, finely chopped
1 Grade 3 egg
¼pt (150ml) milk

1 Preheat the oven to 200°C (400°F), Gas 6.
2 Grill or fry the bacon slowly until brown and crisp.
3 Meanwhile, sift the flour, bicarbonate of soda, cream of tartar and mustard powder into a bowl. Stir in the wholewheat flour.
4 Rub the butter in until the mixture resembles fine breadcrumbs. Stir in 3oz (75g) of the cheese and all the onion. Chop the bacon finely and add. Beat the egg and milk together, stir into flour mixture, mix well.
5 Spread mixture smoothly into greased and paper-lined 2lb (1kg) loaf tin. Sprinkle the remaining cheese over the top. Bake in oven centre for 35-40 minutes, or until a thin metal skewer, inserted into centre, comes out clean and dry.
6 Allow to cool for 5 minutes, then turn out onto a cooling rack. The loaf can be sliced and eaten warm or cold.

2
Rich Cakes

These popular cakes have a relatively high proportion of fat, sugar and eggs to flour, as you will see later on. The most typical examples are Victoria Sandwich and Madeira Cake, although from one basic recipe endless variations are possible, ranging from a fairly simple teatime classic to an ornate after-dinner gâteau, or a white-iced Christmas Cake with all its trimmings.

Shallow cakes, like the Victoria Sandwich, can be made very successfully with self-raising flour, but as the cake mixture deepens in height and the ratio of fat, sugar and eggs to flour increases, the flour *must* be plain with variable amounts of baking powder. This is to prevent the cake from rising up too much initially through excessive raising agent (be it baking powder and/or air) and then, being unable to support its own weight, collapsing in the middle while baking — or as soon as it comes out of the oven.

The advantage of creamed cakes is their durability. Given correct storage conditions, they will keep their moist and velvety texture up to a week or even longer. However, if filled and covered with fresh cream or butter cream, they should be eaten within a few days. Another aspect of these cakes is their firmness. They are, when correctly made, beautifully light, yet rarely do they break or fall apart. They are therefore easy to handle and can be sliced with ease, provided the knife has a large non-serrated blade. (A serrated blade might snag the texture.) When baked in a flattish tin, such as the type used for a Swiss Roll, the cold cake — or cakes — can be cut into all manner of shapes to suit the occasion; when my own son was small, I remember making ships, planes, picture-books and funny-faced clocks from a basic Victoria Sandwich mixture baked in oblong tins. They took time and patience but were great fun and very rewarding, providing me with a change from some of the more fanciful elaborations presented to adult guests at the end of a dinner party.

Ingredients

Flour
White is the one usually used but be guided by individual recipes as to whether it should be plain or self-raising.

Salt
Allow ½-1 level tsp to every 1lb (450g) flour.

Fat
Half butter and half block margarine, both at kitchen temperature but neither oily nor runny, give the best texture, flavour and colour. Lard makes the cake taste a bit fatty and produces a heavy and greasy texture. White cooking fat is passable but contributes little positive flavour. Unless the cake is packed with fruit and destined for a wedding, for Christmas or for some other celebratory occasion, avoid using all butter, as the texture might well be lethargic.

Sugar
Never granulated. Caster, sifted icing sugar or fine brown soft sugar (the kind looking like sand) are the only choices. Avoid demerara sugar.

Flavouring
Essences and grated fruit peel should be creamed with the fat and sugar. (See Method below.)

Eggs
Cold eggs play havoc with the creamed mixture in that they can cause curdling and subsequent loss of air, resulting in a heavy texture. Therefore make sure the eggs are the same temperature as the kitchen. If you are 'impulse baking' and need eggs from the fridge in a hurry, warm them up by standing them, unshelled, in a bowl of hand-hot water. Leave them 10-15 minutes or until they feel comfortable to hold — neither hot nor cold. *Never* use boiling water, as the white nearest the shell will begin to cook and coagulate. Al-

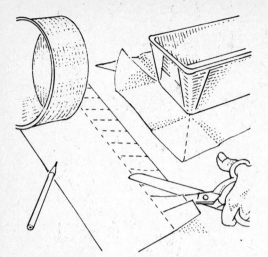

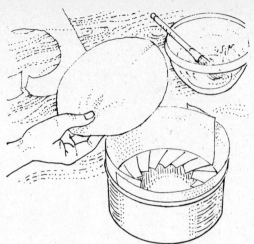

Grease and line tins

though egg sizes do vary and cookbooks make different recommendations, I have found Grade 3 the most satisfactory for baking. Grades 2 and 4 will suffice without causing too many problems, but obviously the larger eggs will give more mixture and the smaller eggs less. Never crack eggs, one after the other, directly into creamed fat and sugar, as the last one could be 'off' and then the whole lot has to be thrown away. It is better to break eggs individually into a cup before adding, so that you have the chance to check for freshness.

Dry additions
Nuts, fruits, etc should be added *after* the eggs have been beaten into the creamed ingredients.

Liquids
For some mixtures, additional liquid is necessary. The most usual for rich cakes is milk, although it can be wine, sherry, fruit juice, cold strained tea or cold coffee. Individual recipes will advise.

Method
1 Grease and line tin or tins as directed in

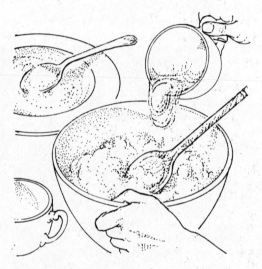

Beat in whole eggs one at a time

the recipe. Check that eggs are at room temperature.
2 Sift flour, plus salt, spices etc, through a fine-mesh sieve into a bowl or deep plate.
3 Put chosen fats into a separate bowl. Add sugar. Cream both together (with flavourings used) until light and fluffy, pale in colour and the consistency of softly whipped cream. The mixture should billow up to at least twice its original volume, so do not skimp on this part of the action. Use a wooden spoon (which will

take the longest), or a balloon whisk, or hand-held electric beaters or an electric mixer.

4 When the fat and sugar have been creamed sufficiently, beat in whole eggs (out of their shells), one at a time, adding a scant tablespoon of sifted dry ingredients with each to prevent curdling and subsequent loss of air.

5 When all the eggs have been incorporated, gently stir in the rest of dry ingredients with the metal spoon, flipping the mixture over and over on itself until smooth and evenly combined. *Do not beat.*

6 Spread smoothly into cake tin, then tap gently up and down on work surface to disperse air bubbles which can, if left, create holes throughout the texture. Bake as directed in individual recipes.

Mishaps

Top peaked and badly cracked

1 Excess baking powder and/or self-raising flour used.
2 Tin not big enough.
3 Mixture either too wet or too dry.
4 Oven too hot.
5 Cake baked neat top of oven.

Cake sunk in centre

1 As point 1 above.
2 Excess creaming of fat and sugar.
3 Excess beating after eggs were added.
4 Mixture too wet.
5 Tin not large enough.
6 Cake under-baked.
7 Oven too cool.
8 Opening and banging shut oven door early on during baking.

Fruit cake sunk in centre

1 All above points in addition to . . .
2 Fruit washed and then inadequately dried.

Cake or cakes pale

1 Not enough sugar or eggs used.

2 Mixture over-wet.
3 Oven too cool and/or cake undercooked.

Top of cake speckled

1 Flour and baking powder not sifted evenly together.
2 Coarse sugar used, such as granulated or demerara.
3 Fat and sugar under-creamed.

Texture heavy with look of matted wool

1 Fat and sugar under-creamed.
2 Eggs cold and/or insufficiently beaten into creamed ingredients.
3 Not enough baking powder used with plain flour.
4 Dry ingredients beaten in, instead of being gently stirred or folded in.
5 Oven too hot or too cold.
6 Cake undercooked.

Texture full of holes

1 Dry ingredients beaten into mixture instead of being stirred or gently folded in.

Texture rubbery

1 Dry ingredients added to creamed mixture in a heavy-handed way.
2 Too much liquid — either/or eggs and milk — added.

Texture very crumbly

1 Mixture too dry.
2 Fat and sugar under-creamed.
3 Too much baking powder used with plain flour.
4 Cake baked for too long in too cool an oven.

Victoria Sandwich Cake

serves 6

4oz (125g) self-raising flour
Pinch of salt
2oz (50g) butter or margarine or mixture, at
  kitchen temperature, soft but not runny
2oz (50g) caster sugar
2 Grade 3 eggs, at kitchen temperature
Jam
Extra caster sugar

1 Brush base and sides of two 7in (17.5cm) sandwich tins with melted butter or margarine. Line bases with rounds of greaseproof paper. If preferred, use non-stick parchment paper. Set oven to 350°F (180°C), Gas 4.
2 Sift flour and salt through fine-mesh sieve into deep plate or bowl.
3 Cream butter or margarine and sugar together until light and fluffy. Break eggs, individually, into a cup.
4 Tip eggs into creamed mixture, one at a time, adding 1 tbsp of dry ingredients with each to prevent the mixture curdling and losing air. Beat in thoroughly.
5 Fold in remaining ingredients with a large metal spoon, taking care not to beat. When smooth and evenly combined, spread into prepared tins.
6 Place in centre of oven (any position in fan oven) and bake 25-30 minutes or until well-risen and golden brown.
7 Remove from oven and leave to stand 5 minutes. Carefully turn out onto a wire rack and leave until cold. Gently peel away paper.
8 Sandwich together with jam, then sprinkle top with sugar.

Jam and Cream Sandwich

serves 6

Follow recipe for Victoria Sandwich Cake but sandwich together with both jam and 5 tbsp double cream, whipped until thick. Dust top with sugar.

Vanilla Sandwich

serves 6

Follow recipe for Victoria Sandwich Cake but cream ½ tsp vanilla essence with fat and sugar. Sandwich together with jam and/or cream. Dust top with sugar.

Almond Sandwich

serves 6

Follow recipe for Victoria Sandwich Cake but cream ½ tsp almond essence with fat and sugar. Sandwich together with raspberry or apricot jam. Dust top with sugar.

Lemon or Orange Sandwich Cake

serves 6

Follow recipe for Victoria Sandwich Cake but cream 1 level tsp finely grated lemon or orange peel with the fat and sugar. Sandwich together with a light-coloured jam and/or cream. If preferred, replace jam with marmalade or curd such as lemon or orange. Dust top with sugar.

Coffee Sandwich

serves 6

Follow recipe for Victoria Sandwich Cake but cream 3 level tsp instant coffee powder with the fat and sugar. Sandwich together with lightly sweetened whipped cream. Dust top with sugar.

Coffee and Nut Sandwich

serves 6

Follow recipe for Victoria Sandwich Cake but cream 3 level tsp instant-coffee powder with fat and sugar then stir in 2oz (50g) chopped hazelnuts or walnuts after beating in the eggs. Sandwich together with lightly sweetened whipped cream. Dust top with sugar.

Chocolate Sandwich

serves 6

Make as Victoria Sandwich Cake but substitute ½oz (15g) each of cocoa powder and cornflour for 1oz (25g) flour. Cream 1 tsp vanilla essence with fat and sugar. Fold in dry ingredients alternately with 1 tbsp milk. Sandwich together with whipped cream. Dust top with sugar.

Black Forest Cherry Cake 1

serves 10-12

Make up The All-chocolate Cake (page 32), using 6oz (175g) flour, fat and sugar and 3 Grade 3 eggs. Bake in two 8in (20cm) greased and base-lined sandwich tins for about 25-30 minutes. Turn out onto a wire cooling rack and leave until cold.

Use 1 large can of cherry pie filling or tip 1 can (15oz or 425g) cherries (stoned for preference) into a saucepan and stir in 3 level tbsp cornflour, smoothly mixed with some of the syrup. Bring to boil, stirring constantly. Remove from heat and stir in 1 tbsp kirsch (traditional) or cherry brandy. Leave to cool completely.

Whip ¾pt (425ml) double cream with 2 tbsp milk until thick. Stir in 2 tbsp kirsch or cherry brandy and 3 level tbsp sifted icing sugar. Put a quarter aside for decoration.

To assemble, split cakes in half horizontally then sandwich together with cherry filling and cream. Spread more cream over top and sides. To decorate, grate up 1 bar (3½oz or 100g) plain dessert chocolate in blender or food processor. Press grated chocolate thickly against sides of cake. Using reserved cream, pipe a border round top edge then stud with halved glacé cherries.

Black Forest Cherry Cake 2

serves 8

This is a simplified version, once made by Black Forest housewives for Sunday tea.

Make up The All-chocolate Cake as given on page 32. When cold, halve each layer horizontally and sprinkle with kirsch or cherry brandy. Sandwich together with ¼pt (150ml) sweetened whipped cream and 1 can (15oz or 425g) canned and drained stoned cherries. Traditionally, Morello cherries are the favourite, so use if you can find them as they have a very distinctive flavour. If preferred, use cherry jam or cherry pie filling.

Small Cakes

All the following are variations of the basic Victoria Sandwich Cake. The mixture should be spooned equally into 18 paper cases standing in 18 ungreased bun tins and baked 20-25 minutes in oven set to 375°F (190°C), Gas 5.

Fairy Cakes
makes 18
Make as Victoria Sandwich Cake but stir in 2oz (50g) currants after beating in eggs.

Ginger Cakes
makes 18
Make as Victoria Sandwich Cake but stir in 2 rounded tbsp chopped stem ginger (the kind preserved in syrup) after beating in eggs.

Coconut Cakes
makes 18
Make as Victoria Sandwich Cake but cream 1 tsp vanilla essence with fat and sugar. Stir in 1oz (25g) desiccated coconut after beating in eggs. Fold in dry ingredients alternately with 2 tbsp milk.

Cinnamon Crumble Cakes
makes 18
Make as Victoria Sandwich Cake but sift 2-3 level tsp cinnamon with flour and salt. (Amount of cinnamon used will depend on how pronounced you want the flavour to be.) After spooning into paper cases, sprinkle with a crumble made by rubbing 1½oz (40g) butter into 3oz (75g) plain flour and then tossing in 2 level tbsp light-brown soft sugar. (For a large Cinnamon Crumble Cake, see page 16.)

Chocolate Flake Cakes
makes 18
Make Victoria Sandwich Cake but stir in 3 crushed chocolate flake bars (small size) after beating in eggs.

Chocolate Chip Cakes
makes 18
Make as Victoria Sandwich Cake but cream 1 level tsp vanilla essence with fat and sugar. Add 2oz (50g) chopped plain chocolate after beating in eggs.

Double Chocolate Cakes
makes 18
Make as Victoria Sandwich Cake but reduce the flour by ½oz (15g) and substitute same amount of cocoa powder. Sift with dry ingredients. Cream 1 tsp vanilla essence with fat and sugar, then stir in 2oz (50g) grated dairy milk chocolate after beating in eggs. Fold in rest of dry ingredients with 1 tbsp of cold milk.

Fruit and Nut Cakes
makes 18
Make as Victoria Sandwich Cake but cream 1 level tsp finely grated orange or lemon peel with fat and sugar. Stir in 2oz (50g) sultanas and 1oz (25g) coarsely chopped, unsalted peanuts after beating in eggs.

Date and Walnut Cakes
makes 18
Make as Victoria Sandwich Cake but sift flour and salt with 1 level tsp mixed spice and use soft light brown sugar instead of white. Stir in 2oz (50g) finely chopped dates and 1oz (25g) finely chopped walnuts after beating in eggs.

Figgy Cakes
makes 18
Make as Victoria Sandwich Cake but sift flour and salt with ¼ level tsp ground allspice. Cream 1 level tsp grated orange peel with fat and sugar. Stir in 2oz (50g) chopped dried figs after beating in eggs.

Cherry Cakes
makes 18
Make as Victoria Sandwich Cake but cream 1 level tsp finely grated lemon peel with fat and sugar. Stir in 2oz (50g) chopped glacé cherries, washed and thoroughly dried, after beating in eggs.

Tutti Frutti Cakes
makes 20
Make as Victoria Sandwich Cake but cream 1 level tsp vanilla essence with fat and sugar. Beat in 2 level tbsp *each* glacé pineapple, glacé cherries, angelica (all chopped) and seedless raisins after beating in eggs.

Butterfly Coffee Cakes 1
makes 18

Make as Victoria Sandwich Cake without any additions. Cut a slice off the top of each cake, then cut the slice in half to form 2 wings. Make up Butter Cream by creaming 2oz (50g) softened unsalted butter with 4oz (125g) sifted icing sugar and 1 tbsp very strong cold coffee. Pipe 3 bands of Butter Cream on top of each cake then angle wings on either side of centre line so that they stand up slightly. Dust each with icing sugar.

Butterfly Rose Cakes 2
makes 18

Make as Butterfly Coffee Cakes but flavour and colour the Butter Cream with 1 tbsp Ribena.

Madeleines
makes 12

Follow recipe for Victoria Sandwich Cake but divide mixture equally between 12 well-greased and lightly floured dariole or castle-pudding tins: these look like chimney pots, one end wider in diameter than the other. Bake as small cakes, allowing about 20-25 minutes. Turn out and cool on a wire rack. Cut a thin slice off base of each (wide end) so that the Madeleines stand upright without toppling. Brush all over with melted apricot or seedless raspberry jam, allowing about 2-3 rounded tsp for each. Afterwards, toss in desiccated coconut tipped onto a piece of greaseproof paper or foil. Decorate top of each with ½ glacé cherry, and 2 small diamond shapes cut from a length of green angelica.

Decorated Small Cakes

Cover tops with Glacé Icing, made by mixing 8oz (225g) sifted icing sugar with a few tsp of water or fruit juice to form a thickish icing. Alternatively, decorate with Butter Cream or a dusting of sifted icing sugar.

Quick-whip Victoria Sandwich
serves 6

Follow recipe for Victoria Sandwich Cake but use easy-cream or whipped-up margarine or white cooking fat (or a mixture of the two). Sift 1 level tsp baking powder with the self-raising flour and salt. Put *all* the ingredients into a mixing bowl with 2 tsp cold milk. Beat 3-4 minutes or until well-mixed and very creamy looking. Divide between 2 tins and bake as previously directed.

Variations of Quick-whip Recipe

Add chosen additions with all the other ingredients as given under the first Victoria Sandwich. Beat all together as the Quick-whip Victoria Sandwich above. Even if other milk is recommended in the recipe, still include the 2 tsp.

Victoria Sandwich Cake Flan
serves 8

Make up Victoria Sandwich Cake as directed on page 28 or the Quick-whip version above. Spread mixture into an 8in (20cm) greased and lightly floured flan tin (raised middle, deep sides, which when reversed, gives you a hollow for fillings). Bake for 35-40 minutes in centre of oven (or any position in fan oven) set to 325°F (160°C), Gas 3. Leave to stand 5 minutes, then turn out and cool on a wire rack. Fill with whipped cream and fresh or canned fruit, a chocolate or coffee mousse mixture, dessert toppings etc.

Black Forest Baked Alaska
serves 6-8

Stand Flan on heatproof plate and moisten with 3 – 4 tbsp of cherry brandy. Fill with scoops or slices of chocolate ice cream, then stud with fresh or canned black cherries, with stones removed. Cover with Meringue as described in recipe for Baked Alaska (page 94). Stud with chocolate buttons. 'Flash' bake as directed.

The All-chocolate Cake

serves 10-12

(illustrated on page 63)

6oz (175g) butter or margarine, at kitchen
temperature and slightly softened
6oz (175g) caster sugar
3 Grade 3 eggs, at kitchen temperature
6oz (175g) self-raising flour
1oz (25g) cocoa powder
1 tsp vanilla essence
2 tbsp milk

Filling

4oz (125g) butter, at kitchen temperature
and slightly softened
6oz (175g) icing sugar
2oz (50g) cocoa powder
2 tbsp cold milk

Decoration

3 large chocolate flake bars, crushed
1/2 bar (size 31/2oz or 100g) plain dessert
chocolate
1/2oz (15g) butter
1 or 2 packets chocolate buttons

1 Cream butter or margarine and sugar
together until light and fluffy. Beat in eggs
singly, adding 1 tbsp of sifted flour and
cocoa with each.
2 Stir in vanilla essence then fold in rest of
dry ingredients alternately with milk.
3 Divide equally between two 8in (20cm)
greased sandwich tins, their bases lined
with rounds of greaseproof paper. Bake
25-30 minutes in centre of oven (any
position in fan oven) set to 350°F (180°C),
Gas 4.
4 Turn out and cool on a wire rack then peel
off paper when cold.
5 For filling cream butter until light, then
gradually beat in icing sugar and cocoa
powder (sifted together) alternately with
milk. Sandwich cake together with filling
then spread remainder over sides.
6 Roll the cake in crushed flake bars (on a
piece of greaseproof paper) until sides are
completely covered.

7 To decorate, break up chocolate and put,
with butter, in basin standing over saucepan of hot water. Leave until melted,
stirring once or twice. Spread over top of
cake. When half set, mark in wavy lines
with a fork. Finally add a border of
chocolate buttons and chill lightly in the
refrigerator before serving.

Raspberry Cream Gâteau

serves 10-12

6oz (175g) solid vegetable oil
6oz (175g) caster sugar
3 Grade 3 eggs, separated
8oz (225g) self-raising flour
1 level tsp cinnamon
1/4pt (150ml) water

Filling
1/2pt (275ml) double cream
8oz (225g) raspberry jam
8oz (225g) fresh or frozen raspberries

1 Place the solid vegetable oil in a bowl and
leave it in a warm place to soften.
2 Grease and line the bases of two 8in
(20cm) sandwich tins.
3 Cream the softened oil with sugar until
light and fluffy. Beat in egg yolks, then
fold in the sifted flour and cinnamon with
water.
4 Whisk egg whites until stiff then, using a
metal spoon, fold them into the cake
mixture lightly and quickly.
5 Divide mixture between the two tins then
bake the cakes 25-30 minutes in oven
centre (any position in fan oven) set to
375°F (190°C), Gas 5. Turn out and cool
on wire rack.
6 Split each cake into two to make four
layers in all.
7 Whip cream until thick and fluffy.
Spread one layer of cake with half the jam
and cover with a thin layer of cream.
8 Lift this layer onto the serving dish.
Spread the next layer with more cream
and place on top of layer on dish. Cover
with almost all the raspberries, leaving

about 15 for decoration. Spread next layer with the rest of the jam and another thin layer of cream. Place on top of raspberry layer.

9 Finally spread the top layer with a little cream and place on top of cake.

10 Put rest of cream into a piping bag filled with a large star pipe and use to decorate top of gâteau.

11 Chill lightly in the refrigerator, then stud with raspberries just before serving.

Sweetheart Cake

serves 8-10
(illustrated on page 18)

6oz (175g) soft lard or margarine
8oz (225g) light-brown soft sugar
3 Grade 3 eggs, at kitchen temperature
¼pt (150ml) milk
½ tsp vanilla essence
2 level tsp black treacle
8oz (225g) self-raising flour
1½ level tbsp cocoa powder
1 level tsp cinnamon

Decoration
About 12 rose leaves
6oz (175g) plain dessert chocolate, broken
    into squares
4oz (125g) soft lard or margarine
1lb (450g) icing sugar, sifted
1oz (25g) cocoa powder
1oz (25g) milk powder
6 tbsp boiling water
8oz (225g) apricot jam

1 Cream lard and sugar until light and fluffy. Beat in whole eggs, one at a time, adding 2 heaped tsp flour with each. Beat together milk, essence and treacle.

2 Sift rest of flour with cocoa powder and cinnamon. Using a metal spoon, fold alternately into creamed ingredients with milk mixture. When smooth and evenly combined and consistency is soft dropping, spread evenly into two greased and lined cake tins; one round tin of 6in (15cm) and a square tin of the same size.

3 Bake 40-45 minutes in centre of oven (any position in fan oven) set to 350°F (180°C), Gas 4. Leave to stand 10 minutes then turn out and cool on a wire rack.

4 On a piece of waxed paper (the inside of a cereal packet is ideal) mark out with a pencil a rectangle measuring 9 x 6in (22.5 x 15cm). Place the paper flat on a baking tray (Swiss-Roll tin).

5 Melt chocolate in a bowl over hot water, being very careful not to let it get too hot.

6 Select about 12 fresh rose leaves of varying sizes, wash and dry then, taking them one at a time, draw the leaf over the surface of the chocolate so that one side is covered.

7 Leave on the waxed paper to cool and harden. Spread the remaining chocolate over the waxed paper between the marked lines and the edge of the tray. Tap the tray to smooth the surface of the chocolate and leave to harden (see diagram overleaf).

8 For the icing, cream the lard until soft. Sift together the icing sugar and cocoa. Beat it into the lard with the milk powder and boiling water to make a smooth icing.

9 Trim the edges of the chocolate and cut it into 24 pieces, each 1½in (4cm) square. Cut each cake in half horizontally then sandwich together with the apricot jam.

10 Place the square cake on the board as a diamond. Cut the round cake into two half-moon shapes and place one on each side of the top point to make the heart shape. Hold in place with a little extra jam.

11 Spread the entire cake with icing and arrange the chocolate pieces round sides, slightly overlapping.

12 Put the remaining icing into the piping bag and pipe swirls along the inside top edge. If available, cut a red rose to size, strip off any extra leaves and position it in the centre of the cake.

13 Finally, carefully peel the rose leaves off the chocolate coverings and arrange along the rose stem.

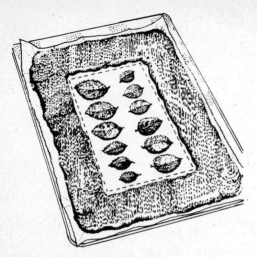

Spread the remaining chocolate over the waxed paper between the marked lines and the edge

Make up the heart shape

Madeira Cake

serves 8

8oz (225g) plain flour
1½ level tsp baking powder
¼ level tsp salt
6oz (175g) butter or best block margarine (not easy-cream for this recipe or the cake will over-aerate and fall)
6oz (175g) caster sugar
Finely grated peel of 1 small washed and dried lemon
3 Grade 3 eggs, at kitchen temperature
2 tbsp milk, at kitchen temperature
2 strips of citron peel (optional)

1 Well grease a 7in (17.5cm) deep, round, cake tin or 2lb (1kg) oblong loaf tin. Line base and sides with greaseproof paper (a good precaution even if the tin is non-stick), then brush paper with more melted fat. Pre-heat oven to 325°F (160°C), Gas 3.
2 Sift flour, salt and baking powder into bowl. In separate bowl, cream fat with sugar and lemon peel until light and fluffy.
3 Beat in eggs, one at a time, adding a tbsp of sifted dry ingredients with each.
4 Fold in rest of dry ingredients alternately with milk. When smooth and evenly combined, spread into prepared tin.

5 Tap tin gently up and down to disperse air bubbles. Place in centre of oven (any position in fan oven) and bake 1½-1¾ hours or until thin metal skewer, pushed gently into centre, comes out clean with no uncooked mixture clinging to it. At this stage, cake should be well-risen and golden-brown. If under-cooked, return to oven for a further 10-15 minutes.
6 At half-time, place citron peel (if used) on top of cake. Continue to cook for required amount of time. (If the peel were put on the cake at the beginning of the cooking time, it would sink straight to the bottom.)

Note *None of the variations below have citron peel on top.*
Lemon peel should be omitted unless otherwise specified.

Vanilla Cake
serves 8
Follow recipe for Madeira Cake but cream 1 tsp vanilla essence with the fat and sugar.

(right) Farmhouse Loaf, page 21 *(National Dairy Council)*

34

Almond Cake
serves 8
Follow recipe for Madeira Cake but cream ½ tsp almond essence with fat and sugar and stir in 2oz (50g) ground almonds after beating in eggs.

Walnut Cake
serves 8
Follow recipe for Madeira Cake but cream ½ tsp vanilla essence with fat and sugar, and stir in 2oz (50g) very finely chopped walnuts after beating in eggs.

Hazelnut Rum Cake
serves 8
Follow recipe for Madeira Cake but stir in 2oz (50g) coarsely ground hazelnuts after beating in eggs. Fold in dry ingredients with dark rum instead of milk.

Orange Cake
serves 8
Follow recipe for Madeira Cake, but cream the finely grated peel of 1 small washed orange with fat and sugar.

Orange Whisky Cake
serves 8
Follow recipe for Madeira Cake, but cream the finely grated peel of 1 small washed orange with fat and sugar. Fold in dry ingredients with whisky instead of milk.

Brazil Nut and Orange Cake
serves 8
Follow recipe for Madeira Cake but cream 2 level tsp finely grated orange peel with fat and sugar. Stir in 2oz (50g) chopped brazils after beating in eggs.

Lemon and Lime Cake
serves 8
Follow recipe for Madeira Cake but cream 1 level tsp *each* finely grated lemon and lime peels with fat and sugar.

Almond Sherry Cake
serves 8
Follow recipe for Madeira Cake but stir in 2oz (50g) chopped and lightly toasted blanched almonds after beating in eggs. Fold in dry ingredients with medium-sweet sherry (or port) instead of milk.

Seed Cake
serves 8
Follow recipe for Madeira Cake but stir in 1 level tbsp caraway seeds after beating in eggs.

Coconut Cake
serves 8
Follow recipe for Madeira Cake but cream 1 tsp vanilla essence with fat and sugar and stir in 1½oz (40g) desiccated coconut after beating in eggs. Fold in flour alternately with 4 tbsp milk instead of 2 (coconut absorbs more liquid than flour on its own).

Marble Cake
serves 8
Divide creamed mixture into 2 equal parts after beating in eggs. Fold 1 level tbsp sifted cocoa powder into one portion with half remaining dry ingredients and 1 tbsp milk. Fold rest of dry ingredients and last tbsp of milk into second portion. (You now have a white mixture and a brown one.) Drop alternate tablespoons of each into prepared tin and bake as directed.

Genoa Cake
serves 8
Follow recipe for Madeira Cake but cream 2 level tsp finely grated lemon peel with fat and sugar. After beating in eggs, stir in the following: 12oz (350g) mixed dried fruit including peel, 2oz (50g) chopped glacé cherries, 1oz (25g) blanched and chopped almonds.

(left) Christmas Cake Tropicana, page 47 *(Danish Agricultural Producers)*

37

Mixed Fruit Cake

serves 8

Follow recipe for Madeira Cake, but sift 2 level tsp mixed spice with dried ingredients. Stir in 1lb (450g) mixed dried fruit, including peel, after beating in eggs.

Sand Cake

serves 8

Follow recipe for Madeira Cake but use half flour and half cornflour instead of all flour. Cream 1 level tsp finely grated lemon peel with fat and sugar.

Cinnamon and Nut Loaf Cake

serves 8

Follow recipe for Madeira Cake but sift 2 level tsp cinnamon with the flour and salt. Use dark-brown soft sugar instead of caster. Stir in 2oz (50g) chopped walnuts after beating in eggs. Bake in a 2lb (1kg) greased and paper-lined loaf tin.

Dundee Cake

serves 10-12
(illustrated on page 61)
serves 10-12

Follow recipe for Madeira Cake but cream 2 level tsp orange peel with fat and sugar. After beating in eggs, stir in 1lb (450g) mixed dried fruit including peel, 2oz (50g) chopped glacé cherries, and 2oz (50g) ground almonds. Spread smoothly into prepared tin. Cover top with rings of blanched and split almonds, allowing 1-2oz (25-50g). Bake 2½-3 hours in oven set to 300°F (150°F), Gas 2. Leave 30 minutes before turning out and cooling on a wire rack.

Festive Dundee Cake

serves 10-12

When cake is cold, tie a red or green cake-frill round sides. Then it makes an ideal addition to the tea-table or a very acceptable seasonal gift.

Cherry Cake 1

serves 8

No cherry cake is, alas, perfect and the cherries have an irritating habit of sinking to the bottom. Hopefully, the selection below is better behaved than most but follow directions for preparing the cherries most carefully.

4oz (125g) glacé cherries
7oz (200g) strong plain white flour
1oz (25g) semolina
1 level tsp baking powder
6oz (175g) butter or half butter and half
   white cooking fat
6oz (175g) caster sugar
1 tsp vanilla essence
3 Grade 3 eggs, at kitchen temperature
2 tbsp milk

1 Quarter cherries and soak for 10 minutes in a bowl of hot water to remove syrup. This is essential or cherries will sink. Drain. Wipe dry in a clean tea-towel then toss in 3 tbsp of flour, taken from weighed-out amount. Sift rest of flour, semolina and baking powder into a bowl.
2 In separate bowl, cream the fat (or fats) with sugar and vanilla essence until light and fluffy.
3 Beat in eggs singly, adding 1 tbsp of sifted dry ingredients with each. Stir in cherries.
4 Fold in rest of dry ingredients alternately with milk.
5 When evenly combined, spread smoothly into greased and lined 7in (17.5cm) round cake tin.
6 Bake 1¼-1½ hours in oven centre (any position in fan oven) set to 325°F (160°C), Gas 3. The cake is ready when a thin metal skewer, pushed gently into centre, comes out clean and dry.
7 Leave 10 minutes in the tin then turn out on to a wire cooling rack. With the lining paper left on for protection, store cold cake in an airtight container.

Cherry Lemon Cake

serves 8

Cream fat and sugar with 2 level tsp finely grated lemon peel. Include vanilla essence.

Cherry Orange Cake

serves 8

Cream fat and sugar with 2 level tsp finely grated orange peel. Include the vanilla essence as well.

Cherry Almond Cake

serves 8

Substitute 1 tsp almond essence for the vanilla.

Cherry Cake 2

serves 8

4oz (125g) glacé cherries
8oz (225g) self-raising flour
2oz (50g) semolina
3oz (75g) butter
2oz (50g) block margarine
4oz (125g) caster sugar
2 Grade 3 eggs, at kitchen temperature
3 tbsp milk
1 tsp vanilla essence

1 Prepare cherries exactly as directed in Cherry Cake 1.
2 Sift flour into bowl. Add semolina. Rub in butter and margarine finely. Toss in caster sugar and cherries.
3 Using a fork, mix to a stiffish consistency with eggs, milk and essence. Stir briskly without beating.
4 Transfer to a greased and lined 7in (17.5cm) round cake tin and bake 1 hour in centre of oven (any position in fan oven) set to 350°F (180°C), Gas 4. The cake is ready when it is well-risen, golden brown and when a thin metal skewer, pushed gently into centre, comes out clean and dry.
5 Leave in the tin for 10 minutes then turn out and cool on a wire rack. Keep lining paper on for protection and store cake in an airtight tin when cold.

Spicy Cherry Cake

serves 8

Sift flour with 2 level tsp mixed spice.

Chocolate Cherry Cake

serves 8

Substitute 1oz (25g) cocoa powder for 1oz (25g) flour, and increase milk to 4 tbsp.

Guide to Cake Sizes for Rich Fruit Mixtures

Below is a brief guide based on a *total weight* of ingredients used and please note that eggs are roughly 2½oz (65g) each.

1 For a 6in (15cm) round cake tin or 5in (12.5cm) square tin: make up a mixture weighing approximately 28oz (1¾lb) or 825g.
2 For an 8in (20cm) round cake tin or 7in (17.5cm) square tin: make up a mixture weighing approximately 56oz (3½lb) or just over 1.5kg.
3 For a 10in (25cm) round cake tin or a 9in (23cm) square tin: make up a mixture weighing approximately 105oz (6½lb) or just under 3kg.

Guide to Almond Paste (ready-prepared)

For 1 above — 1lb or 450g
For 2 above — 1½lb or 675g
For 3 above — 2lb or 1kg
The above are generous amounts and less may be used for economy.

Guide to Royal Icing

For 1 above — 1lb (450g) icing sugar and 2 egg whites
For 2 above — 1½lb (675g) icing sugar and 3 egg whites
For 3 above — 2lb (1kg) icing sugar and 4 egg whites

Fruit Cakes based on Madeira Cake Mixture
Rich Fruit Cake 1

serves 12-14

Follow recipe for Madeira Cake but line tin with a double thickness of greased, grease-proof paper. Sift flour and salt with 1/4 level tsp baking powder and 3 level tsp mixed spice. Cream fat (butter only, please!) with finely grated peel of 1 washed and dried medium lemon and 1 tbsp black treacle. After beating in eggs, which should be increased to 4, stir in the following: 1½lb (675g) mixed dried fruit, including peel, 2oz (50g) washed and dried chopped glacé cherries and 2oz (50g) chopped blanched almonds. Fold in flour alternately with 1 tbsp brandy. Bake 3-3½ hours in oven centre (any position in fan oven) set to 300°F (150°C), Gas 2. (Outside of tin can be covered with brown paper if desired.) Cool at least 45 minutes before turning out onto a wire cooling rack.

Rich Fruit Cake 2

serves 12-14

Follow recipe for Madeira Cake but line tin with a double thickness of greased grease-proof paper. Sift flour and salt with 1/4 level tsp baking powder, 3 level tsp mixed spice and 1 level tsp cocoa powder. Cream butter with soft dark brown sugar, the finely grated peel of 1 small orange and 1 tbsp black treacle. After beating in eggs, which should be increased to 4, stir in the following: 1lb (450g) mixed dried fruit including peel, 4oz (125g) chopped dates, 2oz (50g) stoned chopped prunes and 2oz (50g) chopped walnuts. Fold in dry ingredients alternately with 1 tbsp Guinness. Bake 3-3½ hours in oven centre (any position in fan oven), set to 300°F (150°C), Gas 2. Cool at least 45 minutes before turning out onto a wire cooling rack.

Golden Rich Fruit Cake

serves 12-14

Follow recipe for Madeira Cake but reduce baking powder to 1/4 level tsp and cream 1 tsp vanilla essence and grated peel of 1 small washed and dried lemon with butter and caster sugar. After beating in eggs, which should be increased to 4, stir in the following: 12oz (350g) sultanas, 4oz (125g) chopped glacé pineapple, 3oz (75g) washed and dried chopped glacé cherries, 4oz (125g) chopped mixed peel and 2oz (50g) coarsely chopped angelica. Fold in dry ingredients alternately with milk. Bake for 3-3¼ hours in oven centre (any position in fan oven), set to 300°F (150°C), Gas 2.

Christmas Cake 1

serves 12-14

Make any of the three rich cakes as previously given. Leave in an airtight tin to mature for 2 weeks at least. Brush top with melted and sieved apricot jam, thinned down slightly with a little water. Cover with a round of Almond Paste made by tossing 4oz (125g) ground almonds with 4oz (125g) sifted icing sugar and 4oz (125g) caster sugar, then binding to a stiffish paste with 1 egg yolk (medium egg) beaten with 1 tsp vanilla essence, 1/2 tsp almond essence and 2 tsp sherry. The paste should be kneaded quickly until smooth on a sugar-dusted surface and then rolled to fit. Return cake to its airtight tin and leave to stand at least another week for topping to dry and set firmly in place.

Royal Icing
2 egg whites (small eggs)
1/2 tsp lemon juice
12oz (350g) icing sugar, sifted
1/2 tsp glycerine (available from chemists)
Beat eggs and lemon juice until foamy, then gradually beat in sugar. Continue beating until icing is *very* stiff and snow-white in colour. Stir in glycerine to prevent icing becoming too hard. Swirl over top of cake and, as the icing begins to set, flick up with the

back of a teaspoon for snow-like effect. Add Christmas ornaments. Leave, without moving, until icing has set and is hard. Tie a frill round sides before transferring to a serving plate.

Christmas Cake 2

serves 12-14

For a more ornate effect, make up double the quantity of Almond Paste given above. Spread top and sides of cake with melted apricot jam, then cover all over with the Almond Paste — a round on top and strip cut to fit for the sides. Press well on to cake with a rolling pin, jam jar or glass milk bottle. Leave to stand, loosely covered with a tea-towel, in a cool place for the paste to set, allowing between 10 days and 2 weeks.

To ice the cake, make up double quantity of Royal Icing, as given in Christmas Cake 1. Either swirl over cake and flick up for snow-effect or spread smoothly over top and sides. When completely set, pipe on decorations to taste, using a little extra freshly made Royal Icing. Add seasonal robins, holly, etc, and again leave to set.

Birthday Cake

serves 12-14

Make as Christmas Cake 2 and smooth-ice top and sides. Afterwards, pipe on appropriate decorations and greetings with freshly made icing, tinted to desired tone with edible food colouring.

Wedding Cake

serves 35-40

Make up double quantity of Rich Fruit Cake 1 or 2, and divide between a 9in (22.5cm) round tin and a 7in (17.5cm) round tin, both greased and lined. Alternatively, use an 8in (20cm) square tin and a 6in (15cm) square tin. Pre-heat oven to 300°F (150°C), Gas 2. Put small cake in oven centre and large cake one shelf below (any position in fan oven). Bake 2 hours. Reverse position of cakes. Bake small cake a further 45 minutes

and large cake a further 1¾-2 hours. Leave both to stand at least 30 minutes before turning out onto wire racks to cool.

When completely cold, wrap each cake with greaseproof paper and transfer to airtight tins. If you have no tins large enough, over-wrap with greaseproof paper and then with a double thickness of aluminium foil. Leave to stand at least two weeks for flavours to mature. Cakes should be stored in a dry, cool and dark pantry or larder, even if in airtight tins.

Almond Paste

Make up Almond Paste with 1lb (450g) ground almonds, 12oz (350g) *each* caster and sifted icing sugar, 2 well-beaten Grade 3 eggs, 2 tsp whisky or medium sherry and 1 tsp *each* almond and vanilla essences. Brush tops of cakes with melted and sieved apricot jam, thinned down with a little water, then cover top and sides with the Almond Paste as directed in the recipe for Christmas Cake 2. Leave to stand, loosely covered with a tea-towel, in a cool place for the Paste to set, allowing between 10 days and 2 weeks.

Marzipan

This is more extravagant than Almond Paste and may be used instead if preferred. To make, mix together *equal* amounts of ground almonds and sugar (half icing and half caster), then bind to a stiffish paste and either egg yolk or egg white. Work in a little almond and vanilla essence.

Royal Icing

Make up icing with 6 egg whites (Grade 4 eggs), 2lb (900g) sifted icing sugar and 1 tsp glycerine, following recipe given for Christmas Cake 1. Spread smoothly over top and sides of cakes, using a round-bladed palette knife dipped in and out of hot water. Leave without moving until set, allowing 5-7 days. Stand on silver boards, thinly covered with Royal Icing which has already set, then decorate to taste with extra piped Royal Icing, shop-bought horseshoes, angels, flowers, etc. Stand 3 or 4 pillars on centre of the large cake, holding them in place with dabs of Royal Icing. Top with smaller cake and add a bridal decoration to taste — anything from a small vase of fresh flowers to a miniature bridal couple.

Special Occasion Iced Cakes

Icing and decorating cakes is very much a specialist skill and there are many excellent books on the subject with more detail and descriptions than I can include. If you want to know about icing and piping in more depth, seek out a book on this subject alone.

Easter Simnel Cake

serves 12-14

Prepare a double quantity of Almond Paste as given in recipe for Christmas Cake 1. Wrap in cling film and leave on one side for the moment. Make up a Rich Fruit Cake mixture (either 1 or 2) and place half smoothly into an 8in (20cm) deep, round, cake tin, greased and double-lined with greased greaseproof paper. Divide Almond Paste into three equal pieces. Pat one piece into an 8in (20cm) round and place on top of cake mixture already in tin. Cover with rest of cake mixture, spreading it smoothly with a knife.

Bake about 3½-4 hours in lower half of oven (any position in fan oven) set to 300°F (150°C), Gas 2. Leave to cool in the tin for 30-45 minutes, then carefully turn out onto a wire cooling-rack and leave until completely cold.

Remove lining paper. Brush top of cake with melted and sieved apricot jam, first thinned down slightly with a little water, then press on second piece of Almond Paste, rolled into a round the same size as top of cake. Shape remaining portion of Almond Paste into 12 balls and arrange round edge of cake. Brush with a little beaten egg and quickly glaze

under the grill for a few minutes or, if preferred, in a hot oven set to 450°F (230°C), Gas 8. Fill centre with Glacé Icing, made by mixing 4oz (125g) sifted icing sugar to a thickish paste with a few tsp of water. Allow to set, then decorate with Easter chicks and tiny chocolate eggs. (This cake is supposedly named after a brother and sister team called Simon and Nell! It was always baked for Mothering Sunday.)

Speedy Simnel Cake

serves 8-10

Make up any of the Rich Fruit Cakes (page 40) and leave until cold. Prepare Almond Paste as directed in recipe for Simnel Cake. Halve the cake horizontally, brush cut sides with any jam to taste, then sandwich together with one portion of Almond Paste. Now proceed as for Simnel Cake.

A Christmas Cake Variety

There follows an assorted range of cakes which are all suitable for Christmas, though not perhaps entirely traditional. Some come from abroad and others cut down on certain ingredients, such as eggs or animal fats.

Festive Nut 'n' Fruit Loaf 1

serves 12

8oz (225g) plain flour
1 level tsp cinnamon
½ level tsp *each* allspice and ginger
1 level tsp baking powder
6oz (175g) butter or block margarine,
    softened
6oz (175g) light brown soft sugar
3 Grade 2 eggs, at kitchen temperature
1 level tbsp black treacle
12oz (350g) mixture of currants, sultanas
    and raisins
2oz (50g) mixed chopped peel
4oz (125g) hazelnuts, left whole
4oz (125g) brazils, thinly sliced

1 Sift dry ingredients onto a plate.
2 Put butter or margarine and sugar into a
  bowl. Cream until light and fluffy. Beat in
  eggs, one at a time, adding a tbsp of dry
  ingredients with each to prevent curdling.
3 Stir in treacle, fruits, peel and nuts.
  Finally fold in rest of dry ingredients with
  a large metal spoon.
4 Spread evenly into 2lb (1kg) loaf tin, first
  well-greased and completely lined with
  greased greaseproof paper.
5 Bake 1½ hours in oven centre (any position in fan oven), pre-heated to 325°F
  (160°C), Gas 3. Reduce temperature to
  300°F (150°C), Gas 2, and continue to
  bake a further 1¼-1¾ hours or until a
  thin metal skewer, inserted into the
  centre, comes out clean and dry. Remove
  cake from oven, leave to stand for 15
  minutes then invert onto a wire cooling-
  rack. Store in an airtight tin when cold.
  Remove paper before slicing.

Festive Nut 'n' Fruit Loaf 2

serves 12-14

For a more pronounced fruity flavour, cream
fat and sugar with the grated peel of one
medium washed and dried lemon.

Festive Nut 'n' Fruit Loaf 3

serves 12-14

Make up a stiffish icing with 8oz (225g) sifted
icing sugar, mixed with a few tsp dry Martini
or pale sherry. Spread over loaf, allowing it to
trickle down the sides. When set, stud top
with halved glacé cherries and a mixture of
nuts to include walnuts, hazelnuts and
lightly toasted almond halves.

Portuguese-style Madeira Cake 1

serves 8-10

An unusual combination of flavours and tex-
tures, resulting in a cake which is not unlike
an enriched gingerbread. It is well worth
making.

9oz (250g) plain flour
4 level tsp cinnamon
½ level tsp allspice
2oz (50g) walnuts, chopped
2oz (50g) almonds, unblanched, washed,
    thoroughly dried then coarsely chopped
4oz (125g) raisins
3oz (75g) butter or margarine
2oz (50g) cooking fat
2oz (50g) golden syrup
5oz (150g) caster sugar
2 Grade 3 eggs
4 tbsp cold milk
2 level tsp bicarbonate of soda

1 Sift flour and spices into a bowl. Toss in
  nuts and raisins.
2 Melt fats, syrup and sugar in pan without
  allowing mixture to boil. Take away from
  heat. Beat eggs until foamy. Mix milk and
  bicarbonate of soda well together.
3 Make a well in the middle of dry ingredients. Pour in melted mixture, beaten eggs,
  then milk and soda.
4 Using a fork, stir briskly without beating.
  Spread smoothly into a 2lb (1kg) loaf tin
  first greased and then lined with greased
  greaseproof paper.
5 Bake in oven centre (any position in fan

oven) set to 325°F (160°C) Gas 3. Allow 1-1¼ hours or until a thin metal skewer, pushed gently into centre, comes out clean and dry. Leave to stand for 15 minutes then invert cake onto a wire cooling-rack. Store in an airtight tin when cold. Remove paper before slicing.

Portuguese-style Madeira Cake 2
serves 8-10

Make exactly as previous recipe but add 1 level tsp finely grated tangerine peel and 1 tsp vanilla essence to the beaten eggs.

Mincemeat Christmas Cake

serves 12

For those who want to economise and still have a splendid, quick-to-make cake for Christmas, I cannot recommend a better recipe than this one with its luscious, fruity flavour and succulent texture. The only fat comes from the mincemeat itself, and of course the condensed milk.

1lb (450g) mincemeat
1lb (450g) mixed dried fruit, including chopped peel
4oz (125g) quartered glacé cherries, washed and dried
4oz (125g) brazils or hazelnuts, coarsely chopped
8oz (225g) cornflakes, crushed
3 Grade 3 eggs, beaten
1 tsp vanilla essence
½tsp almond essence
1 large can sweetened condensed milk
2 level tsp mixed spice

1 Put mincemeat into a large bowl. Gradually work in rest of ingredients until evenly mixed.
2 Spread into an 8in (20cm) deep, round, cake tin, well-greased and lined completely with greased greaseproof paper.
3 Bake 2-2¼ hours in oven centre (any position in fan oven), pre-heated to 300°F (150°C), Gas 2 or until a thin metal skewer, pushed gently into centre, comes out clean and dry. Leave to stand 20 minutes, then

invert onto a wire cooling-rack.
4 Store in an airtight tin when completely cold and leave at least 1 week before removing lining paper and cutting.

Iced Mincemeat Cake
serves 12

The top, or top and sides, may be covered with Almond Paste and Royal Icing in the same way as cakes on pages 39-41.

Eggless Christmas Cake

serves 12-14

There are some people who do not eat eggs for reasons of diet, and others are allergic to them; hence this cake. It is less rich and dark than its relations, but it has a festive flavour all the same, and keeps very well.

10oz (275g) self-raising flour
1 level tsp salt
1 level tsp mixed spice
½ level tsp cinnamon
½ level tsp allspice
8oz (225g) ground rice
8oz (225g) softened butter or block margarine (kitchen temperature)
8oz (225g) dark brown soft sugar
1lb (450g) mixed dried fruit including chopped peel
4oz (125g) chopped cooking dates
½pt (275ml) boiling milk (skimmed if desired)

1 Sift dry ingredients into a deep plate. Cream fat and sugar until light and fluffy.
2 Stir in fruits then gradually fold in dry ingredients alternately with the boiling milk. Avoid beating.
3 Spread evenly into an 8in (20cm) deep, round, cake tin, well-greased then lined with greased greaseproof paper. Bake 1 hour in oven centre (any position in fan oven), pre-heated to 350°F (180°C), Gas 4.
4 Reduce temperature to 275°F (140°C), Gas 1, and continue to bake a further 1½-2 hours or until a thin metal skewer, inserted gently into centre, comes out clean and dry.

5 Leave in tin for 20 minutes, then turn out onto a wire rack. Store in an airtight tin when cold and leave at least two weeks before removing paper and cutting.

Eggless Cake with Nuts
serves 12-14
Make exactly as previous recipe but reduce mixed dried fruits by half, then add 8oz (225g) mixed chopped nuts to include brazils, hazels, walnuts and blanched, chopped almonds; even cashews if lightly toasted.

Eggless Iced Cake
Avoid Almond Paste and Royal Icing (both made with eggs), but either dredge top of cake heavily with sifted icing sugar, or cover with tangy Glacé Icing made by mixing 8oz (225g) sifted icing sugar to a stiff, spreadable icing with a few tsp fresh lime juice. When set, stud with pieces of angelica or green and yellow halved glacé cherries.

Christmas Corn Oil Cake

serves 12-14

For all those anxious about animal-fat intake, here is a rather delicious cake made with corn oil — Mazola, to be precise.

2 Grade 2 eggs
6oz (175g) dark brown soft sugar
¼pt (150ml) corn oil
10oz (275g) plain flour
1½ level tsp baking powder
1 level tsp cinnamon
1 level tsp mixed spice
3 tbsp Madeira or cherry brandy
½ tsp almond essence (Rayner's)
½ tsp sherry essence (Rayner's)
1½lb (675g) mixed dried fruit including chopped peel
2oz (50g) prunes, chopped (weight after stoning)
3oz (75g) walnuts, finely chopped
2oz (50g) glacé cherries, chopped

1 Break eggs individually into a bowl and add sugar and oil. Beat well together.
2 Sift flour, with next 3 ingredients, into

bowl over egg mixture. Add the Madeira or cherry brandy with the essences.
3 Using a metal spoon, gently fold in all remaining ingredients. When evenly combined, spread into 8in (20cm) deep, round, cake tin or a 7in (17.5cm) square one well-greased and lined with greased greaseproof paper.
4 Bake in centre of oven (any position in fan oven) set to 300°F (150°C), Gas 3, for 2½-3 hours or until a thin metal skewer, pushed gently into centre, comes out clean and dry.
5 Leave to stand for 30 minutes then invert onto a wire cooling-rack. Store in an airtight tin when completely cold and leave at least two weeks before covering with Almond Paste and Royal Icing as given on page 40. If preferred, do not ice but tie a cake frill round the sides of the cake.

Margaret's Christmas Cake

serves 10

Margaret is Australian, an ex-colleague and brilliant cook. She worked long and hard getting this recipe to work satisfactorily and I pass it on with pleasure, especially as it can be made just a few days before Christmas and still taste as though you had made it months before. It has a lovely warm flavour, deep colour and, considering the small amount of fat, a beautifully moist texture. (My adaptation is given after this recipe.)

8oz (225g) stoned dates, fairly finely chopped
3oz (75g) sultanas
½pt (275ml) boiling water plus 4 extra tbsp
2oz (50g) white cooking fat or lard
12oz (350g) caster sugar
2oz (50g) brazil nuts, coarsely chopped
2oz (50g) blanched and toasted almonds, coarsely chopped
1 Grade 3 egg, beaten
½ tsp *each* vanilla and almond essences
14oz (400g) plain flour
2 level tsp mixed spice
1 level tsp *each* bicarbonate of soda and cream of tartar

1 Put dates into bowl with sultanas, water and fat. Stir until fat melts.
2 Add sugar, nuts, beaten egg and essences. Mix well. Sift flour, spice, soda and cream of tartar over bowl of ingredients.
3 Stir in to begin with, then beat mixture vigorously with the back of a wooden spoon.
4 Spread evenly into a greased roasting tin measuring about 10 x 7 x 2in (25 x 17.5 x 5cm), with the base and sides lined with greased greaseproof paper.
5 Bake 1¼-1½ hours in centre of oven (any position in fan oven) pre-heated to 350°F (180°C), Gas 4.
6 To check if ready, gently push thin metal skewer into centre of cake; if it does not·come out clean and dry, return cake to oven for a further 10-20 minutes. Cool about 15 minutes, then invert onto a wire rack.
7 Store in an airtight tin when cold. If liked, cover with Almond Paste and Royal Icing as directed for other cakes.

Margaret's Christmas Cake by me
serves 10
Use half dates and half cut-up dried apricots (well-washed first) instead of all dates. Add 1 level tsp finely grated lemon peel with the sultanas. Use boiling tea instead of water.

'Boiled' Fruit Cake

serves 12

This is a real oldie and I have to admit it is one of my favourite Christmas cakes because of its simplicity of style. Just be careful with the bicarbonate of soda: too much and the cake rises and then sinks; too little and it's heavy. It's a rich, dark, moist and particularly festive cake.

8oz (225g) self-raising flour
3 level tsp mixed spice
1lb (450g) mixed dried fruit, including chopped peel
Finely grated peel and juice of 1 medium washed and dried orange and lemon
2oz (50g) walnuts, coarsely chopped
3oz (75g) caster sugar
4 level tbsp black treacle
2oz (50g) cooking fat or lard
¼pt (150ml) milk
¼ level tsp bicarbonate of soda (take care with this measurement)
1 Grade 3 egg, kitchen temperature

1 Well grease a 7in (17.5cm) square cake tin, and line base and sides with greased greaseproof paper.
2 Sift flour and spice into a mixing bowl. Tip dried fruit, grated peels, nuts, sugar, treacle, lard or cooking-fat and milk into a saucepan. Cook gently, stirring, until sugar dissolves. Bring to the boil.
3 Remove from heat and stir in bicarbonate of soda. Allow to cool until mixture is lukewarm. Beat in whole egg, then gradually fold in dry ingredients with a metal spoon, working gently and lightly.
4 Spread evenly into prepared tin and bake for 1 hour in centre of oven (any position in fan oven) set to 350°F (180°C), Gas 4.
5 Cool 15 minutes then invert onto a wire cooling-rack. Store in an airtight tin when cold. Leave at least 2 days before removing paper and cutting, or covering with Almond Paste, followed at a later stage by Royal Icing.

'Boiled' Dundee Fruit Cake
serves 12
Make exactly as previous recipe but after spreading smoothly in tin, cover top with 2oz (50g) blanched and split almonds. Do not cover wth icing.

'Boiled' Fruit Cake Exotica
serves 12
For a more glamorous version of the 'boiled' cake, use the following in place of the mixed dried fruit: 2oz (50g) chopped glacé pineapple, 4oz (125g) chopped dates, 3oz (75g) washed and dried quartered glacé cherries, 2oz (50g) diced angelica (in tiny dice), 3oz (75g) washed and cut-up dried apricots or dried peaches (again very small pieces), 2oz

(50g) sultanas and 1oz (25g) chopped preserved ginger, well-drained from its syrup.

Refrigerator Christmas Cake

serves 12-16

A sumptuous affair and I confess I'm stretching a point in giving it here at all, since it literally cooks in the refrigerator. But it's too
good to miss and the biscuits used in its making were, at some stage, oven-baked! (See
Chapter 13 for more refrigerator cakes.)

4oz (125g) unsalted butter
2oz (50g) pink and white marshmallows
1lb (450g) digestive biscuits (fairly finely
   crushed)
1½ level tsp allspice
Strained juice of 2 large lemons
14oz (400g) mixture of raisins, sultanas and
   chopped cooking dates
2oz (50g) flaked and toasted almonds,
   coarsely crushed in your hands

1 Put butter and marshmallows into a
   saucepan. Melt over a very low heat.
2 Tip biscuit crumbs and all remaining ingredients into a large bowl. Add melted
   butter and marshmallows. Draw together
   with fingertips, then spread smoothly into
   a 2lb (1kg) oblong loaf tin completely
   lined with foil.
3 Cover with another piece of foil, then
   refrigerate for about 12-24 hours, when
   cake should be firmly set. Turn out of tin,
   carefully remove foil, then cut cake into
   slices with a very sharp knife. Store
   left-overs in the refrigerator.

Glitter Refrigerator Christmas Cake
serves 12-16
Follow recipe above but instead of raisins,
sultanas and dates, use the following: 4oz
(125g) chopped dates, 4oz (125g) chopped
glacé pineapple, 4oz (125g) quartered glacé
cherries, 2oz (50g) angelica, cut into
diamonds, and 2oz (50g) pink marshmallows, each cut with wet scissors into 8 small
pieces.

Christmas Cake Tropicana 1

serves 12-14
(illustrated on page 36)

'Invented' by the Danish butter people I,
present you with two versions of the same
cake, one baked in a round tin and the other
in a ring mould. Both give a very pretty but
light fruit cake with an unusual frosting
based on pineapple juice and coconut.

6oz (175g) Danish butter, at kitchen
   temperature and softened
4oz (125g) caster sugar
2 Grade 2 eggs, at kitchen temperature
8oz (225g) self-raising flour, sifted
3oz (75g) glacé cherries
3oz (75g) mixed chopped peel
4oz (125g) sultanas
1oz (25g) desiccated coconut
1oz (25g) green angelica, chopped (or use
   chopped crystallised ginger)
1oz (25g) walnuts, chopped
1 small can (8oz or 225g) pineapple rings,
   drained and finely chopped
3 tbsp pineapple syrup from can of rings

Frosting
1½oz (40g) Danish butter
6oz (175g) icing sugar, sifted
1 tbsp syrup from can of pineapple rings
1oz (25g) desiccated coconut

1 Cream butter and sugar together until
   light and fluffy. Beat in eggs singly, adding
   1 tbsp flour with each.
2 Stir in cherries, peel, sultanas, coconut,
   angelica (or ginger), walnuts and pineapple.
3 Fold in remaining flour alternately with
   pineapple juice then spread mixture
   evenly into 8in (20cm) greased and lined
   round cake tin.
4 Bake 1 hour 20 minutes in centre of oven
   (any position in fan oven) set to 325°F
   (160°C), Gas 3. The cake is ready when a
   thin metal skewer, pushed gently into
   centre, comes out clean and dry. If not,
   return cake to oven for 10 minutes or so.
5 Leave to stand 15 minutes then turn out on

to a wire cooling rack. Peel away lining paper and leave until cold.

6 To make Frosting, melt butter in a pan, stir in sugar then beat in syrup and coconut. Spread over top of cake and decorate to taste. Tie a cake frill round sides.

Christmas Cake Tropicana 2
serves 12-14

Spread mixture smoothly into a 2½pt (1.5 litre) greased ring tin, brushed with melted Danish butter and lightly dusted with flour. Bake as round cake, allowing 1 hour. Frost and decorate to taste, then tie a cake frill round sides.

Golden Syrup Christmas Cake
serves 10

A wonderful cake that can be made in a few minutes by beating all the ingredients together.

12oz (350g) self-raising flour
½ level tsp *each* cinnamon, mixed spice and ginger
6oz (175g) easy-cream margarine (such as Blue Band)
4oz (125g) light brown soft sugar
3 Grade 3 eggs, kitchen temperature
6oz (175g) sultanas
4oz (125g) glacé cherries, cut into quarters
2oz (50g) walnuts, chopped
2oz (50g) lightly toasted cashews, chopped
3 level tbsp golden syrup (taken out of jar or can with a spoon dipped in hot water)

1 Sift flour into bowl with cinnamon, mixed spice and ginger.
2 Add all remaining ingredients. Beat briskly for 2 minutes, using a wooden spoon.
3 Transfer to a deep, 8in (20cm) round cake tin, greased then lined with greased greaseproof paper.
4 Bake 1-1½ hours in oven centre (any position in fan oven) set to 350°F (180°C), Gas 4. Cake is ready when it is well-risen and golden and a thin metal skewer,

pushed gently into centre, comes out clean and dry.

5 Leave to cool 15 minutes, then invert onto a wire cooling-rack. Store in an airtight tin when cold. If liked, ice and decorate as given for other cakes.

Honey-gold Christmas Cake
serves 10

Make as above but use clear honey instead of golden syrup.

Christmas Crown
serves 10

A pretty, light-textured cake which is ideal for any festive tea table. It is very easy to make and should be baked in a ring tin.

12oz (350g) self-raising flour
6oz (175g) butter, at kitchen temperature
6oz (175g) caster sugar
Finely grated peel of 1 small washed and dried orange
8oz (225g) mixed dried fruit including chopped peel
4oz (125g) chopped glacé cherries
½ tsp *each* vanilla and almond essences
3 Grade 3 eggs
5 tbsp cold milk
Icing sugar to decorate

1 Sift flour into a bowl. Cut in butter, then rub in finely with fingertips. Toss in sugar, orange peel, dried fruit and cherries. Beat eggs and milk well together.
2 Using a fork, mix flour and fruit etc to a softish consistency with essences, together with the beaten eggs and milk.
3 Spread evenly into a 4½pt capacity (2.5 litre) well-greased fluted ring tin lightly dusted with baking powder, a useful trick to prevent sticking.
4 Bake 1-1¼ hours in oven centre (any position in fan oven) set to 350°F (180°C), Gas 4, or until well-risen and golden and thin metal skewer, pushed gently into centre, comes out clean and dry.
5 Leave to cool 10 minutes then turn out onto a wire cooling-rack. Store in an air-

tight tin when cold and dredge icing sugar over the top after removing paper and before cutting.

Christmas Jewel Crown
serves 10

Make up Glacé Icing by mixing 8oz (225g) sifted icing sugar to a softish icing with whisky, dry sherry, dry cider or apple juice. Pour over crown, allowing it to trickle unevenly down sides. When set, stud top with halved glacé cherries and walnuts, or a mixture of well-drained red and green cocktail cherries.

Dutch Christmas Garland Cake
serves 10-12

I love this totally different idea of a festive cake which is cut on Christmas Day throughout Holland and eaten, day by day, to the end of the holiday. It is very rich and a little goes a long way.

8oz (225g) packet of frozen puff pastry, thawed (use home-made if preferred)
8oz (225g) home-made or shop-bought Almond Paste
1 small egg, beaten
2-3 rounded tbsp melted and sieved apricot jam
2 heaped tsp chopped and lightly toasted almonds
2 canned pineapple rings, cut into wedges

1 Roll out pastry into a thin strip measuring 19 x 4½in (47.5 x 11cm).
2 Shape Almond Paste into a long sausage about 1in (2.5cm) shorter than the pastry.
3 Stand the paste along middle of pastry, dampen edges with water then fold over to form an elongated 'sausage' roll, completely enclosing Almond Paste.
4 Put the roll on a wetted baking tray, brush with egg and bake until puffy and deep gold, allowing about 15-20 minutes in oven set to 425°F (220°C), Gas 7.
5 Cool on a wire rack for 10 minutes then brush with jam and decorate with nuts and fruit. Store in an airtight tin when cold.

Note If using home-made puff pastry, allow 1lb (450g) made-up weight and roll out more thickly than frozen.

Dutch-style Christmas Horseshoe
serves 10-12

This is my adaptation of the previous recipe. Make exactly as the Dutch Christmas Garland Cake, but use Walnut Paste instead of Almond. To make, finely grind 4oz (125g) walnuts in coffee mill or food processor, then combine with 4oz (125g) caster sugar, ½ tsp vanilla essence and sufficient beaten egg to bind to a paste. Shape the filled pastry into a horseshoe and bake as directed in previous recipe. When lukewarm, brush with clear honey and sprinkle with chopped walnuts.

Yeasted Christmas Cake 1
serves 20

Lightened and enriched by the inclusion of highly nutritious yeast, this is a splendid Yuletide party contribution with a warm and fragrant flavour and juicy texture.

½oz (15g) or 1 level tbsp dried yeast with 1 level tsp caster sugar *or* 1oz (25g) fresh yeast
¼pt (150ml) warm milk
¼pt (150ml) cold milk
½ level tsp bicarbonate of soda
8oz (225g) butter or block margarine, at kitchen temperature
12oz (350g) dark-brown soft sugar
2 Grade 3 eggs, beaten
14oz (400g) plain flour
1oz (25g) fine semolina
½oz (15g) cornflour
½oz (15g) cocoa powder
2 level tsp mixed spice
2lb (900g) mixed dried fruit including chopped peel
4oz (125g) cooking dates, fairly finely chopped
3 tbsp strong coffee

1 Well grease an 9in (22.5cm) deep, round, cake tin or 8in (20cm) deep square tin,

then line completely with greaseproof paper. Brush paper with melted fat.

2 Mix dried yeast and sugar with warm milk and leave to stand in a warm place for about 10-15 minutes, or until mixture foams up and looks like a glass of beer with a head. Alternatively, mix fresh yeast to a creamy liquid with the warm milk. Blend cold milk and bicarbonate of soda well together.

3 Cream butter or margarine and sugar till light and fluffy. Beat in eggs, one at a time, adding a tbsp of sifted dry ingredients with each.

4 Add all the fruits, then fold in rest of dry ingredients alternately with yeast mixture and coffee. Mix thoroughly.

5 Spread evenly into prepared tin then make a dip in the middle to prevent cake rising to a dome while it cooks.

6 Place in centre of oven (any position in fan oven) set to 300°F (150°C), Gas 2. Bake 3½-4 hours or until a thin metal skewer pushed gently into the centre, comes out clean and dry. If cake appears to be browning too rapidly, cover top with a double thickness of greaseproof paper or reduce temperature to 275°F (140°C), Gas 1 after 3 hours.

7 Leave to stand for 30 minutes, then invert on a wire cooling-rack. Leave until completely cold before overwrapping with greaseproof paper and storing in an airtight container for at least 1 week before icing as directed in previous recipes (pages 40-41).

Yeasted Christmas Cake 2
serves 20
Make as previous recipe but add 4oz (125g) chopped brazils or walnuts in addition to fruit, and use rum or whisky instead of coffee.

Barm Brack
serves 10

An Irish speciality, this falls under the category of bread in traditional Irish cookery books — and indeed some recipes do call for yeast. This version relies on plain flour and baking powder and is ideal for those who enjoy a less heavy and more economical Christmas cake.

5oz (150g) light-brown soft sugar
½pt (275ml) hot strong tea, strained
1lb (450g) mixed dried fruit including
    chopped peel
2oz (50g) butter or margarine, melted
1 Grade 2 egg, beaten
2oz (50g) glacé cherries, chopped
1oz (25g) blanched almonds, chopped
10oz (275g) plain flour
3 level tsp baking powder

1 Melt sugar in the hot tea. Add fruit and peel, mix well and cover. Leave to stand overnight in the kitchen.

2 Stir in melted butter or margarine, egg, cherries and almonds. Sift flour and baking powder over top then stir in with a metal spoon. When evenly combined, transfer to an 8in (20cm) deep, round, cake tin, well greased then lined with greased greaseproof paper.

3 Bake 1-1½ hours in oven centre (any position in fan oven) set to 350°F (180°C), Gas 4. When ready, Barm Brack should be well-risen and golden. To test, press a thin metal skewer gently into centre. If it comes out clean and dry, the cake is ready. If not, return to oven for a further 15-20 minutes.

4 Leave 15 minutes, then invert onto a wire rack. Make holes in base with a skewer then fill with whiskey. Store in an airtight tin when cold. Leave at least 2 days before cutting. The Barm Brack is excellent sliced and spread with butter.

Traditional Barm Brack

serves 10-12

This is the yeasted version. Make up 1lb (450g) bread dough, enriched with egg and/or milk for preference (see pages 180 and 189). Knead in 3oz (75g) caster sugar, 3oz (75g) chopped mixed peel, 12oz (350g) sultanas, 3 Grade 3 beaten eggs and 2oz (50g) softened butter or margarine. Put into well-greased 2lb (1kg) oblong loaf tin and leave to rise, covered with buttered foil, for 1-1½ hours in a warm place or until dough has doubled in size. Bake 10 minutes near top of oven (any position in fan oven) set to 425°F (220°C), Gas 7. Reduce temperature to 325°F (160°C), Gas 3. Bake a further 45-60 minutes. Leave in tin for 10 minutes, then turn out onto a wire cooling-rack. Store in an airtight tin when cold.

3
Sponge Cakes

Sponge mixtures produce light and airy cakes and form the basis of two-layer sandwich cakes and Swiss Rolls, in addition to many of the luxurious, multi-layered and richly decorated gâteaux and torten available from top pâtisseries in this country and in cafés, restaurants and cake shops abroad. The basic sponge mixture contains no fat at all; it depends for its success on careful handling and three main ingredients: eggs at kitchen temperature, caster sugar and flour which should be sifted at least twice, if not three times, to ensure there are no lumps and that it is as fine and as aerated as possible. The fact that these cakes lack fat means they quickly go stale; a simple two-layer sponge, sandwiched together with jam and/or cream should be made and eaten on the same day. When filled and completely covered wth cream, butter cream or other icing, they are given virtually an insulation or airtight seal and will stay moist and fresh inside for at least two days — if kept in the refrigerator.

When melted and cooled butter is added to the basic mixture it becomes a Genoese, another highly regarded foundation cake much appreciated by chefs; but it is less of a favourite with most of us at home, as it is more demanding of time, and fairly difficult to make successfully. I shall come to the Genoese later, but first let me describe what are commonly known in cookery circles as fatless sponges, bearing no resemblance at all — other than shape — to the classic Victoria Sandwich which has been with us for well over a century and is amply endowed with butter or margarine for extra richness and flavour.

Ingredients

Eggs
Use Grade 2 or 3 eggs and make sure they are at the same temperature as the kitchen. Cold eggs, straight from the refrigerator, take longer to beat up to the correct consistency (see Method, 6), so if you are making a sponge on impulse and have no time to allow the eggs to warm up, put the required number into a basin, cover with lukewarm water and leave to stand about 15 minutes. *Never* use hot water as the white nearest the shell will begin to coagulate and cook.

Sugar
Smooth caster sugar gives the best results. Granulated is too coarse. Sifted icing sugar may be used.

Flour
It makes very little difference to the finished result if shallow cakes, baked in sandwich tins, are made with plain or self-raising flour, but when that same mixture is baked in a deep tin, it is *essential* to use plain flour *only*. This is to prevent excessive aeration initially (from the baking powder in the flour) and then a subsequent collapse as the flour (a small amount in ratio to the eggs and sugar) finds it has insufficient gluten or elasticity to support a high-rise mixture.

Method

1 Prepare tins, bearing in mind that a sponge mixture made with three eggs is sufficient for two 7in (17.5cm) sandwich tins or one 7in (17.5cm) deep cake tin. Brush tin or tins all over with melted fat (white cooking-fat or unsalted butter for preference). Then line bases of sandwich tins with rounds of greaseproof paper. If using deep cake tins, brush all over with melted fat, then line base and sides with greaseproof paper. If tins are non-stick, I still advise lining bases. If using non-stick parchment paper, greasing is unnecessary.

2 Because sponges are delicate, they cannot be inverted, like sturdier cakes, directly onto a wire rack without protection. Therefore cover a rack or racks with a damp tea-towel, top with a piece of greaseproof paper, non-stick parchment paper or foil, and sprinkle with caster sugar.

Racks must be covered for sponge cakes

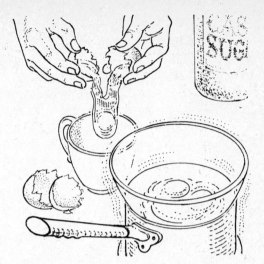

Place eggs and sugar in a bowl over a pan of hot water

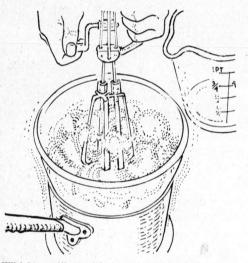

Whisk steadily until mixture reaches the required volume

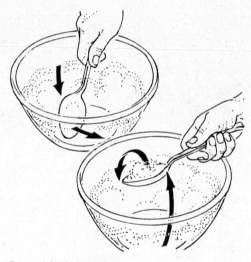

Cut and fold in the flour

3 Sift required amount of flour two or three times into a bowl. Do so through a fine-mesh sieve and from a height of about 6in (15cm) to give it maximum aeration.

4 Break eggs, one at a time, into a cup to check for freshness, then tip into a large bowl. Add sugar. Stand basin, whenever possible, over a pan of hot water as this speeds up mixing. Make sure the basin can tolerate the heat as some plastics will melt if in contact with hot metal. Also ensure the water is not boiling or the eggs will begin to cook and scramble.

5 Whisk steadily with a rotary or balloon whisk, or with hand-held electric beaters, until the mixture forms a light, aerated mass which looks like a cloud of softly whipped cream shaded a delicate yellow. One egg and 1oz (25g) sugar should build up to just over a ¼pt (150ml), so a 3 egg mixture should give you a minimum of ¾pt (425ml). Anything less indicates that

56

the mixture has been underbeaten, and therefore under-aerated and is less likely to rise satisfactorily.

6 When the mixture has reached the required consistency — thick but light — and also the required volume, tip in the flour *all at once*. Cut and fold it into the beaten eggs and sugar by drawing the edge of a metal spoon slowly across the bottom of the bowl and then quickly flipping it over. Repeat gently — taking your time as speed here is not of the essence — until the flour has been evenly incorporated into the eggs and sugar and no unblended bits stay at the bottom. *Do not beat* and work as rhythmically and as gently as possible.

7 Divide the mixture evenly between the tins if more than one used, bake as directed in the recipe, then turn out onto the prepared rack. Finish as directed.

Mishaps

Texture biscuity instead of spongy

1 Eggs and sugar insufficiently whisked — it can be a lengthy process.
2 Flour added with lack of finesse and a heavy hand!

Texture heavy and sticky

1 Proportions went astray and too much sugar used.
2 Underbaked.
3 Oven incorrect temperature — either too hot or too cool.

Deep sponge sinks

1 Self-raising flour used instead of plain.
2 Oven incorrect temperature — probably too high.
3 Sponge removed from oven too soon.

Swiss Roll brittle

1 Cooked for too long.
2 Oven too hot.
3 Not enough mixture for size of tin chosen.

4 Allowed to sit for too long before being rolled.
5 Crisp edges not cut off.

Basic Sponge Sandwich Cake

serves 6
(illustrated on page 61)

3 Grade 2 or 3 eggs, at kitchen temperature
3oz (75g) caster sugar
3oz (75g) plain or self-raising flour, sifted 3 times

1 Brush two 7in (17.5cm) tins with melted fat and line bases with rounds of greaseproof paper. Set oven to 350°F (180°C), Gas 4.
2 Break eggs into a cup to check for freshness, then tip into bowl resting over pan of hot, but not boiling, water. Add sugar. Whisk until very light, pale in colour, thick in consistency and almost ¾pt (425ml) in volume; allow about 10-15 minutes with a hand whisk and half that time if using electric beaters.
3 Add flour all at once. Cut and fold into whisked eggs and sugar with a metal spoon as described in the Method (point 6).
4 Divide equally between prepared tins. Bake 15-20 minutes or until well-risen and golden-brown. *Do not* open oven door until the last few minutes and then only if absolutely necessary.
5 Remove from oven. Allow to cool 5 minutes. Turn out onto a wire cooling-rack lined with a damp tea-towel, covered with a sugared piece of greaseproof, foil or non-stick parchment paper. Leave until completely cold. Remove lining paper.

Jam Sandwich
serves 6
Sandwich cold cakes together with red jam (traditionally raspberry) or apricot jam.

Lemon Sponge
serves 6
Whisk eggs and sugar with 1 level tsp finely

grated lemon peel before adding the flour. Fill cold cakes with whipped and sweetened double cream.

Orange Sponge
serves 6
Whisk eggs and sugar with 1 level tsp finely grated orange peel before adding flour. Fill cold cakes with whipped and sweetened double cream.

Almond or Vanilla Sponge
serves 6
Whisk eggs and sugar with ½tsp of almond or vanilla essence, before adding the flour.

Cinnamon Sponge
serves 6
Sift ½-1 level tsp powdered cinnamon with the flour. Fill cold cakes with apricot jam.

Ginger Sponge
serves 6
Sift ½-1 level tsp powdered ginger with the flour. Fill cold cakes with orange marmalade.

Spice Sponge
serves 6
Sift ½-1 level tsp mixed spice with the flour. Fill cold cakes with whipped cream mixed with chopped, preserved ginger.

Cream Sandwich
serves 6
Fill cold cakes with whipped and sweetened double cream.

Jam and Cream Sandwich
serves 6
Fill cold cakes with jam of your choice and then whipped and sweetened double cream.

Satin Sponge
serves 6
For a lighter, spongier mixture, replace ½oz (15g) flour with ½oz (15g) cornflour. Fill with whipped and sweetened double cream and/or jam to taste.

Chocolate Sponge
serves 6
Replace 1oz (25g) flour with ½oz (15g) *each* cocoa powder and cornflour. Sift 3 times with rest of flour.

Deep Sponge
serves 6-8
Make as Basic Sponge Sandwich cake, but turn mixture into 7in (17.5cm) round cake tin and bake 45 minutes in oven set to 325°F (160°C), Gas 3. *Use only plain flour*. Cool. Remove lining paper. Cut horizontally into 3 layers. Fill with whipped and sweetened double cream.

Deep Nut Sponge
serves 6-8
Make as Basic Sponge Sandwich cake, but finely grind (in food processor or blender) 1oz (25g) nuts — hazels, brazils, walnuts or unskinned almonds. Cut and fold into whisked mixture with the flour. (Make sure the nuts are ground and *not* finely chopped.)

Swiss Roll
serves 6-8

Make as Basic Sponge Sandwich cake (page 57), but transfer to greased and lined Swiss-Roll tin measuring 11 x 7in (27.5 x 17.5cm). Bake 10-12 minutes in oven set to 400°F (200°C), Gas 6. Leave to stand 2 minutes. Turn out onto a wire cooling-rack lined with a damp tea-towel, covered with a piece of sugared greaseproof, foil or non-stick parchment paper. Peel lining paper off Swiss Roll, then cut off crusty edges. Spread with about 4 rounded tbsp slightly warmed jam and roll up tightly. Hold in place for 1-2 minutes or until Swiss Roll 'sets' in position.
Note Should a few cracks appear, these can easily be camouflaged by a sprinkling of caster sugar.

Cream-filled Swiss Roll
serves 6-8
Follow directions for Swiss Roll above but

after trimming away crisp edges, roll up *without removing paper* to stop sponge sticking to itself. Cover with a damp cloth and leave until cold. Carefully unroll, remove paper then fill with whipped and sweetened double cream, then re-roll. Hold in position 2 minutes or until Swiss Roll 'sets'.

Chocolate Swiss Roll
serves 6-8
Follow recipe for Chocolate Sponge (page 58), then continue as for Cream-filled Swiss Roll as above.

Sponge Fingers 1

makes 12

Make as Basic Sponge Sandwich (page 57), using only 2 eggs, and 2oz (50g) *each* sugar and flour. Divide equally between 12 greased and lightly floured sponge-finger tins set into metal trays in the same way as bun tins. Bake about 10 minutes. Leave 1 minute. Remove carefully from tins. Cool on a wire rack.

Sponge Fingers 2

makes about 20

Cover 1 or 2 large baking trays with non-stick parchment paper. Make up Basic Sponge Sandwich (page 57), then transfer to a large piping bag fitted with a plain icing tube of about ½in (1.25cm) in diameter. Pipe about 20 fingers of mixture onto trays. Dust sifted icing sugar over each. Bake about 15 minutes in oven set to 300°F (150°C), or Gas 3. Leave 2 minutes, then carefully remove from trays. Cool on a wire rack.
Note These are fairly tricky to make and are not for novices.

Chocolate Rum Torte

serves 8

Prepare Butter Cream first to give it a chance to firm up. Gradually beat 8oz (225g) softened butter (unsalted for preference) to a light and airy cream with 1lb (450g) sifted icing

sugar, a large bar (100g) melted and cooled plain dessert chocolate and either 2 tbsp dark rum or 2 tbsp warm water and 1 tsp rum essence. Refrigerate about 30 minutes or until firm enough to spread. Make a Deep Nut Sponge exactly as directed on page 58, using shelled but unskinned almonds, finely ground in your food processor or blender. Cut into three layers when cold. Sandwich together and cover top and sides with Butter Cream. Put chocolate vermicelli on a round-topped knife then quickly press on to sides of cake. Then decorate top with a piped border of remaining Butter Cream and whole blanched almonds which have been toasted until golden.

Lemon Cream Gâteau

serves 6-8

Make up a Lemon Sponge as directed on page 57. Whip ½pt (275ml) double cream with 1 tsp cold milk and 2 level tbsp caster sugar until thick. Sandwich cakes together with about ⅓ of the cream. Swirl remainder over top and sides, then shower either with grated lemon peel or multi-coloured hundreds and thousands. Chill lightly before serving.

Coffee Walnut Torte

serves 8

Make a Deep Nut Sponge as directed on page 58. Whip ¾pt (425ml) double cream until thick with 3 level tbsp caster sugar. Add 2-3 level tsp instant coffee powder or granules dissolved in 6 tsp hot water, then left to cool completely. Cut cake horizontally into 4 layers. Sandwich together with coffee cream. Spread top and sides with more coffee cream, then press about 1½-2oz (40-50g) finely chopped walnuts against sides. Decorate top with piped rosettes of cream, then stud each rosette with a walnut half. Chill lightly before serving.

Cherry Cream Raspberry Layer

serves 6-8

Make up Basic Sponge Sandwich cake as directed on page 57. Whip ½pt (275ml) double cream until thick with 2 tbsp cherry brandy. Sandwich cakes together with about ⅓ cream and 4 oz (125g) fresh raspberries. Spread rest of cream over top and sides then stud top with extra 2 oz (50g) raspberries. Chill lightly before serving.

Strawberry Fayre Gâteau

serves 6

Make up a Basic Sponge Sandwich as directed on page 57. Sandwich together and cover top with ¼pt (150ml) whipped and sweetened double cream. Cover top with about 6oz (175g) halved strawberries, then decorate by studding with chocolate buttons.

Chocolate Yule Log

serves 6-8

Make up a jam-filled Swiss Roll as directed on page 58. Make up half Chocolate Butter Cream as given for the Chocolate Rum Torte on page 59, but omit rum. Cut a 1in (2.5cm) diagonal slice off one end of the Swiss Roll for a small log. Put on top of roll about one-third of the way along, holding it in place with jam. Cover Swiss Roll and baby log completely with Chocolate Butter Cream, then ridge with prongs of a fork to give a bark-like effect. Dust with sifted icing sugar for snow, then add Christmas decorations to taste, such as robins, holly etc.

Genoese Sandwich

serves 6

Melt 2½oz (65g) unsalted butter gently in pan. Leave until cool, then carefully pour into bowl, leaving behind any milky sediment that sinks to the bottom. Make up Basic Sponge Sandwich with self-raising flour as directed on page 57, but after whisking eggs and sugar, add half the butter and flour. Cut and fold in. When smooth and evenly combined, repeat with rest of butter and flour. Transfer to tins and bake as a sponge sandwich. Use in the same way as the other sponges in this section.

Deep Genoese Cake

serves 6

Make as Genoese Sandwich but *use plain flour only*. Transfer to greased and lined 7in (17.5cm) cake tin. Bake until well-risen and golden, allowing about 45 minutes in oven set to 325°F (160°C), Gas 3. Turn out and cool. Slice horizontally into three layers, then sandwich together with jam and whipped cream. Dust top with sifted icing sugar.

Assorted Gâteaux and Torten

Use Genoese mixture and follow recipes given in this section for Deep Sponge Cakes.

Petit Fours

makes about 12

Follow recipe for Genoese Sandwich but bake in Swiss-Roll tin as though you were making a Swiss Roll. When cold, cut into small squares and sandwich together with Vanilla Butter Cream made by beating 4oz (125g) unsalted butter with 8oz (225g) sifted icing sugar, ½ tsp vanilla essence and about 3-5 tsp cold milk. Spread each completely with coloured Glacé Icing, made by mixing about 1lb (450g) sifted icing sugar with enough warm water to make a thickish mix. Divide into four batches and colour each according to taste. When icing has set on cakes, decorate with silver balls, pieces of glacé fruits, chocolate vermicelli, nuts, toasted coconut and, if liked, a piped border of coloured Butter Cream.

(above right) Dundee Cake, page 38 *(Eggs Information Bureau)*

(below right) Basic Sponge Sandwich Cake, page 57 *(Eggs Information Bureau)*

(overleaf) Swiss Roll, page 58 *(Eggs Information Bureau)*

Raspberry and Cream Sandwich

serves 8
(illustrated on page 89)

A richly endowed Sandwich Cake which is perfect for summer eating. The one in the picture comes from Norway, where it is called 'soft' cake, the country's birthday cake made on 17 May.

½pt (275ml) double cream
1 tbsp cold milk
3 level tbsp caster sugar
4oz (125g) fresh raspberries
2 layers of Basic Sponge Sandwich (page 57)

1 Whip cream and milk together until thick. Stir in sugar.
2 Fold 2 level tbsp raspberries into 4 tbsp whipped cream and use to sandwich cake together.
3 Spread cream over top and sides of cake, then pipe on remainder in a decorative design (see picture). Stud with remaining raspberries and chill lightly in the refrigerator before serving.

Golden Swansdown Sandwich

serves 8

A Sponge Cake with a difference, lightened with custard powder. It can be simply sandwiched together with jam or converted into a fancy gâteau for special occasions.

2oz (50g) plain flour
2oz (50g) custard powder
2 level tsp baking powder
4 Grade 3 eggs, separated
4oz (125g) caster sugar

1 Sift flour, custard powder and baking powder into a bowl.

(previous page, above) The All Chocolate Cake, page 32 *(McCormick Essences)*

(previous page, below) William Chocolate Slice, page 65 *(Cadbury Typhoo)*

(left) Almond Crunch Cake, page 66 *(Cadbury Typhoo)*

2 In separate bowl, whisk egg whites to a stiff snow. Gradually add sugar and continue to beat until very thick and shiny.
3 Fold in egg yolks alternately with dry ingredients. Use a large metal spoon and work quickly and lightly.
4 When all streakiness has disappeared, spread evenly between two greased 8in (20cm) sandwich tins, base-lined with greaseproof paper.
5 Bake 15 minutes in oven set to 400°F (200°C), Gas 6. Turn out on to a tea-towel covered with a length of greaseproof paper or foil sprinkled with extra caster sugar. Leave until cold. Sandwich together with jam.

Spring Sunshine Gâteau
serves 8

Make Golden Swansdown Sandwich as above, then fill and cover top with ¼pt (150ml) double cream, whipped until thick with 2 level tbsp caster sugar. Sprinkle top with a border of finely grated lemon or orange peel.

Pineapple Gâteau
serves 8-10

Make Golden Swansdown Sandwich as above. Prepare Butter Cream by creaming 6oz (175g) softened butter with 12oz (350g) sifted icing sugar and 2 tbsp pineapple juice from can of pineapple rings. Leave in the refrigerator to firm up slightly then use about a quarter to sandwich layers together. Spread remainder over top and sides. Decorate top with well-drained pineapple rings, the centres filled with green glacé cherries.

William Chocolate Slice

serves 8-10
(illustrated on page 63)

3 Grade 3 eggs, at kitchen temperature
3oz (75g) caster sugar
3oz (75g) plain flour
1 rounded tbsp cocoa powder
2 tbsp hot water

65

Chocolate Butter Cream

6oz (175g) butter, at kitchen temperature
  and soft
12oz (350g) icing sugar, sifted
1 tbsp cold milk
1 rounded tbsp cocoa powder blended
  smoothly with 3 tbsp hot water and cooled

Decoration

2 ripe William pears
2 tbsp lemon juice
1 packet chocolate finger biscuits
Diamond cut from angelica or piece of green
  glacé cherry

1 Well grease a Swiss-Roll tin measuring 11 x 7in (27.5 x 17.5cm) then line with greaseproof paper. Brush paper with melted fat. Sift together flour and cocoa powder.

2 Whisk eggs and sugar together until they bulk up to almost 1 pt (575ml) and are thick and creamy in consistency.

3 Fold in flour and cocoa powder mixture gently, adding water last. Spread into tin and bake 15 minutes just above top of oven (any position in fan oven) set to 400°F (200°C), Gas 6, when cake should feel light and springy.

4 Turn on to a tea-towel covered with a large piece of greaseproof paper, sprinkled with caster sugar. Carefully remove lining paper and leave cake until cold.

5 For Butter Cream, beat butter, sugar and milk together until light and fluffy and the consistency of whipped cream. Put just over one-quarter on one side. Add cocoa and water to remainder to make Chocolate Butter Cream.

6 Peel pears, cut into slices and brush with lemon juice. Cut cake in half lengthwise and put one piece on a serving plate. Spread thickly with Chocolate Butter Cream, then cover with all but 3 slices of pears.

7 Top with second piece of cake and spread with more Chocolate Butter Cream. Place chocolate finger biscuits on top, as shown in the picture (page 63).

8 Pipe 2 rows of Chocolate Butter Cream round sides, then decorate top edge with the reserved White Butter Cream, also piped. Finally top with 3 pear slices and a piece of angelica or cherry.

Almond Crunch Cake

serves 8-10
(illustrated on page 64)

A chocolate crunch cake, 'frosted' with a novelty almond crumble.

2oz (50g) unsalted butter
2 Grade 3 eggs, at kitchen temperature
4oz (125g) caster sugar
4oz (125g) self-raising flour
1 rounded tbsp cocoa powder
2 tbsp single cream or top of the milk
Toasted breadcrumbs to coat tin

Frosting

2oz (50g) butter
2oz (50g) caster sugar
1 rounded tbsp plain flour
2oz (50g) flaked almonds
2 tsp milk

1 Brush a 7in (17.5cm) loose-bottomed round cake tin with melted butter or margarine. Dust base and sides with toasted crumbs.

2 Melt butter very gently and leave aside until cool. In large bowl, whisk eggs and sugar until they double in volume and look thick and creamy.

3 Fold in sifted flour and cocoa powder, the melted butter and cream or top of the milk. Do this as gently as possible, using a large metal spoon.

4 When mixture is smooth and evenly combined, spoon into prepared tin and bake 30 minutes in oven centre (any position in fan oven) set to 350°F (180°C), Gas 4. Meanwhile, prepare topping.

5 Melt butter in pan then stir in sugar, flour, almonds and milk. Stirring all the time, bring the mixture quickly to the sizzling stage then remove from heat.

6 Take cake out of oven. Spoon almond mixture over the top, then return to oven and bake for a further 15-20 minutes at same temperature.
7 Allow to cool, then carefully push up cake from underneath to remove from tin. Ease off its metal base when cold and transfer cake to a serving plate.

Pear Topsy-turvy Cake

serves 8
(illustrated on page 133)

A tea-time special or weekend dessert, whichever you prefer.

6 well-drained canned pear halves
2 Grade 3 eggs, separated
2oz (50g) caster sugar
2oz (50g) self-raising flour
1oz (25g) cocoa powder
1 orange, peeled and divided into segments

1 Arrange pears, cut sides down, in 8in (20cm) well-greased sandwich tin.
2 Whisk egg yolks and sugar to a thick cream. Gently stir in sifted flour and cocoa alternately with egg whites, whisked to a stiff snow.
3 Spread smoothly into tin over pears. Bake 30-35 minutes just above centre of oven (any position in fan oven) set to 350°F (180°C), Gas 4.
4 Turn out on to a wire rack and fill hollows of pears with orange segments. Serve warm or cold.

4
'Melted' Cakes

These cakes, usually gingerbread and family, fall into the category of 'melted' because some of the ingredients are warmed together in a saucepan and allowed to melt before being added to the dry ingredients; a technique which produces moist, mellow and easy-to-make cakes with a distinctive spiciness and dark, rich colour. Geared for winter, these cakes are especially popular at Hallowe'en, Guy Fawkes Night and Christmas when the cold, dark days call for robust-tasting foods.

Ingredients

Flour

Plain is the most usual, with the addition of bicarbonate of soda as the raising agent. Being an alkaline, the soda works in conjunction with the acids in the syrup/treacle/brown sugar mix to produce a lightened though firmish texture, with its own characteristic and distinctive stickiness.

Spices

Ground ginger is used liberally, together with mixed spice. I use 6 rounded tsp ginger and 2 rounded tsp spice to every 1lb (450g) flour.

Fat

White cooking-fat and lard are the two fats widely recommended, but I prefer the taste of block margarine or butter. A useful compromise, which gives a pleasing flavour, is to use half cooking fat or lard and half butter or margarine.

Sweeteners

The whole essence of a gingerbread is golden syrup, black treacle and soft brown sugar and the amounts will be specified in each recipe.

Eggs

Four Grade 3 eggs to every 1lb (450g) flour is the usual proportion.

Liquid

This is nearly always milk plus a little water. The proportion is about ½pt (275ml) milk and 2 tbsp cold water to every 1lb (450g) flour.

Method

1 Well grease a Yorkshire-pudding tin measuring about 11 x 9 x 1½in (27.5 x 22.5 x 4cm), then line base and sides with non-stick parchment paper or greased greaseproof paper. If using the latter, brush with melted cooking fat. The tin will probably have sloping sides and the measurements given are for the top of the tin. If you haven't the exact size of tin, you can use a slightly larger one without an adverse effect on the gingerbread.

2 Set oven to 300°F (150°C), Gas 2, as gingerbread mixtures need a coolish oven. Sift dry ingredients, through a fine-mesh sieve, into a mixing bowl.

3 Place fat, syrup, treacle and sugar in a pan and melt over a low heat. *Do not* allow mixture to boil.

4 Beat together eggs, milk and water.

5 Make a well in the centre of the dry ingredients, then pour in beaten eggs and milk, followed by the melted mixture.

6 Stir briskly to mix, using a fork, but *do not* beat. Remember to work in flour mixture from the base and around the sides of bowl as this sometimes tends to get left behind.

7 Pour into prepared tin and bake about 1¼ hours in oven centre (any position in fan oven). Remove from oven and leave 10-15 minutes.

8 Cool on a wire rack then store, when cold, for at least 1 day before cutting. Remove paper just before serving — not earlier, as paper helps to keep the cake moist.

Mishaps

Gingerbread sank

1 Too much bicarbonate of soda used.
2 Too much syrup and/or treacle used.
3 Oven temperature too high.
4 Tin placed too near top of oven.

Gingerbread heavy and top very shiny

1 Mixture beaten too hard and too long.
2 Mixture handled too slowly.

Gingerbread dry and cracked

1 Insufficient liquid added.
2 Too much bicarbonate of soda used.
3 Oven temperature too high.
4 Tin placed too near top of oven.

Gingerbread

serves 14-18

1lb (450g) plain flour
6 rounded tsp ground ginger
2 rounded tsp mixed spice
2½ level tsp bicarbonate of soda
8oz (225g) mixture of butter or margarine
   and cooking-fat
8oz (225g) golden syrup
8oz (225g) black treacle or molasses
4oz (125g) dark-brown soft sugar
4 Grade 3 eggs
½pt (275ml) cold milk
2 tbsp cold water

1 Well grease a Yorkshire-pudding tin of about 11 x 9 x 1½in (27.5 x 22.5 x 4cm) then line base and sides with non-stick parchment or greaseproof paper. If using latter, brush with melted white cooking-fat. Set oven to 300°F (150°C), Gas 2.
2 Sift first four dry ingredients into a bowl. Put fats, syrup, treacle and sugar into a pan and melt gently over a low heat. Do not boil. Beat together eggs, milk and water.
3 Make a dip in the centre of the dry ingre-dients. Pour in egg mixture followed by the melted mixture. Stir briskly without beating, making sure you work in all the flour, etc.
4 Transfer to prepared tin and spread evenly with a knife. Put into oven and bake 1-1¼ hours or until well-risen and deep brown, and a thin metal skewer, pushed gently into the centre, comes out clean and dry.
5 Leave in tin for 15 minutes then lift ginger-bread carefully out on to a wire cooling rack. Put into an airtight tin when cold and store in a cool place (warmth tends to turn a gingerbread mouldy). Remove paper just before cutting.

Small Gingerbread

serves 10
Halve all ingredients and bake 45-60 minutes in 8in (20cm) greased and lined deep, square, cake tin.

Marmalade Gingerbread

serves 14-18
Make as Gingerbread but halve the quantity of treacle and make up the weight with chunky orange marmalade.

Fruity Gingerbread

serves 14-18
Make as Gingerbread but after sifting dry in-gredients into bowl, toss in 4oz (125g) raisins or sultanas.

Date Gingerbread

serves 14-18
Make as Gingerbread but after sifting dry in-gredients into bowl, toss in 4oz (125g) finely chopped cooking dates.

Double Gingerbread

serves 14-18
Make as Gingerbread but after sifting dry in-gredients into bowl, toss in 4oz (125g) finely chopped preserved ginger, well-drained.

Chocolate Gingerbread

serves 14-18

Make as Gingerbread but use 14oz (400g) plain flour and 2oz (50g) cocoa powder. Increase water to 4 tbsp.

Chocolate Fruited Gingerbread

serves 14-18

Make as Gingerbread but use 14oz (400g) plain flour and 2oz (50g) cocoa powder. Toss 2oz (50g) mixed chopped peel into dry ingredients.

Iced Orange Gingerbread

serves 14-18

Make up any of the Gingerbreads previously given and leave at least 1 day for flavours to mature. Tie a band a greaseproof paper around the sides of the gingerbread to prevent icing trickling down. Mix 6oz (175g) sifted icing sugar to a thickish icing with strained fresh orange juice. Spread over top of gingerbread and leave until set. Decorate by sprinkling with finely grated orange peel then add a few halved glacé cherries in a decorative design. Remove paper before cutting.

Brandied Gingerbread

serves 14-18

After lifting gingerbread onto a wire cooling rack, make deep holes all over the cake with a thin metal skewer. Pour about 1 liqueurglass of brandy over the top and leave it to sink in. Store, when cold, as directed for other gingerbreads.

Parkin

serves 10

Parkin is closely associated with Yorkshire and is, essentially, a mildly spiced gingerbread containing oatmeal. It is not a light, airy-fairy cake by any means. Once cold, it should be left in an airtight tin for at least 1 week before cutting so that the flavours can meld together and mature.

8oz (225g) plain flour
1 level tsp ground ginger
1 level tsp mixed spice
1 level tsp bicarbonate of soda
8oz (225g) medium oatmeal
5oz (150g) butter
4oz (125g) light-brown soft sugar
7oz (200g) golden syrup
¼pt (150ml) milk
1 Grade 3 egg, beaten

1 Prepare a Yorkshire-pudding tin as given for Gingerbread (page 72). Set oven to 325°F (160°C), Gas 3.
2 Sift flour, spices and bicarbonate of soda into a bowl. Toss in oatmeal.
3 Put butter, syrup and sugar into a saucepan. Melt over a low heat. Draw pan aside, then add milk.
4 Make a dip in the dry ingredients. Pour in the melted mixture and the beaten egg. Using a fork, stir well to mix then transfer to prepared tin when smooth and evenly combined.
5 Bake in oven centre (any position in fan oven) for 1 hour or until a thin metal skewer, pushed gently into the centre, comes out clean and dry.
6 Cool on a wire rack and store in an airtight tin when completely cold.

Treacle Parkin

serves 10

8oz (225g) plain flour
1 level tsp mixed spice
2 level tsp ground ginger
1 level tsp cinnamon
1 level tsp bicarbonate of soda
8 oz (225g) medium oatmeal
3oz (75g) golden syrup
3oz (75g) black treacle
5oz (150g) butter, margarine or lard
4oz (125g) light-brown soft sugar
¼pt (150ml) milk
1 Grade 3 egg

1 Sift flour, spice, ginger, cinnamon and bicarbonate of soda into a bowl. Toss in oatmeal.

73

2 Melt syrup, treacle, fat and sugar over a low heat.
3 Make a dip in the dry ingredients then gradually stir in the melted ingredients, the milk and egg.
4 Stir briskly until smooth without beating then pour into a 9in (22.5cm) greased and lined square cake tin, or medium-sized greased and lined roasting tin, about 11 x 8in (27.5 x 20cm).
5 Bake 1 hour in centre of oven (any position in fan oven) set to 325°F (160°C), Gas 3. The Parkin is ready when a metal skewer, pushed gently into centre, comes out clean and dry.
6 Leave to stand for 15 minutes then turn out and cool on a wire rack. When cold, store in an airtight container and leave 1 week before cutting into squares or fingers for serving.

Cut-and-Come-Again Fruit Loaf

serves 8-10

Eggless for those who are only allowed a limited amount in the diet, this is an old-fashioned but flavourful cake which improves with keeping.

5oz (150g) golden syrup
4oz (125g) white vegetable fat
10oz (275g) mixed dried fruit, including peel
12 tbsp water
8oz (225g) plain flour
1 level tsp mixed spice
1 level tsp cinnamon
1 level tsp baking powder
2 level tsp bicarbonate of soda

1 Put syrup, fat, fruit and water into a saucepan. Bring to the boil, stirring. Boil for 3 minutes. Set aside to cool.
2 Sift all remaining ingredients into a bowl

and gradually stir into boiled mixture. Beat well then spread smoothly into a greased and lined 2lb (1kg) loaf tin.
3 Bake 50-60 minutes in centre of oven (any position in fan oven) set to 350°F (180°C), Gas 4. Cake is ready when a thin metal skewer, pushed gently into centre, comes out clean and dry.
4 Leave in tin 10 minutes then turn out on to wire cooling rack. Store in an airtight container when cold.

Oil Gingerbread

serves 10
(illustrated on page 90)

6oz (175g) solid vegetable oil
6oz (175g) dark-brown soft sugar
6oz (175g) black treacle
10oz (275g) plain flour
3 level tsp ground ginger
1 level tsp cinnamon
2 Grade 3 eggs, beaten
1 level tsp bicarbonate of soda
½pt (275ml) milk

1 Put the solid vegetable oil, sugar and treacle into a pan and melt over a low heat, stirring occasionally. Do not allow to boil.
2 Sift flour, ginger and cinnamon into a bowl. Stir in the melted ingredients with the eggs and bicarbonate of soda, first dissolved in the milk.
3 When thoroughly mixed, pour into a 7in (17.5cm) greased and lined square cake tin.
4 Bake 1 hour in oven centre (any position in fan oven) set to 325°F (160°C), Gas 3. To test if ready, push a thin metal skewer gently into centre. It should come out clean and dry.
5 Leave to stand 15 minutes, then turn out and cool on a wire rack. Store in an airtight tin when cold and leave 1 day before cutting.

5
Choux Pastry

These two favourites, together with some fancy and rather beautiful gâteaux, are all based on Choux Pastry which bears no resemblance whatever to any other pastry that I can think of. It is cooked in a pan, never rolled out, looks like a thick and golden sauce, and when converted into cream puffs, blows up like miniature cabbages: hence the French name *chou* (shoo) and, for all we know, the endearment for which the French are best known — 'Ma petite chou'. I often wondered at a romantic Frenchman calling his loved one a cabbage, but a cream bun is obviously what was intended — so much more appealing. But before going into the story of Choux Pastry and its versatility, I want to dwell, for a moment or two, on the fillings that go inside such delicacies as Eclairs and Cream Buns. Whipped cream is whipped cream, but below is a lightened adaptation which can also be used for Profiteroles. Then I shall move on to Confectioner's Custard with a basic recipe plus variations.

Chantilly Cream

This amount is sufficient for 10-12 medium-sized Eclairs or Cream Buns.

1 Grade 3 egg white
Pinch of cream of tartar or 2-3 drops of lemon juice
½pt (275ml) double cream
2 level tbsp caster sugar

1 Whisk egg white and cream of tartar or lemon juice together until stiff.
2 Whip cream and sugar together until thick then gently fold in the beaten white. Use straight away.

Flavoured Chantilly Cream

If liked, flavour the cream with any suitable essence or very finely grated lemon, orange, lime or tangerine peel.

Confectioner's Custard

Whatever you call it — Crème Pâtisserie, Crème Pâtissière, Confectioner's Custard, Custard Cream or Pastry Cream — the end result is still the same: a boiled custard-like mixture based on eggs, sugar, flour, milk and flavourings which, when cold, is frequently used in flans, Eclairs and Cream Buns.

It is an excellent filling, not too rich, a bit on the sweet side and beloved in southern climates where fresh cream would perhaps deteriorate too rapidly in the heat to be a viable proposition. And even in North Europe, here at home too, Confectioner's Custard, with its useful stability and keeping properties (it holds well for up to 48 hours) often finds its way into those petite Eclairs and Cream Buns one is given for afternoon tea in expensive restaurants and grand hotels. I find it immensely useful, economical and a boon during a hot summer when whipped cream, on standing, invariably turns yellow and buttery.

This basic recipe will fill 10-12 medium-sized Eclairs or Cream Buns. It is also sufficient to fill and cover the top of an 8in (20cm) sandwich cake, or fill and cover completely a 7in (17.5cm) sandwich cake.

1 Grade 3 egg
1 Grade 3 egg yolk
2oz (50g) caster sugar
1oz (25g) flour (either plain or self-raising)
½pt (275ml) milk
½tsp vanilla essence
½oz (15g) butter or margarine

1 Whisk egg, egg yolk and sugar until very thick and pale in colour.
2 Sift in flour, then gradually add milk and essence.
3 Pour into saucepan. Cook over a medium heat, stirring continuously, until custard comes to the boil and thickens. Stir in butter or margarine.
4 Simmer about 2 minutes still stirring (don't worry; the mixture *won't* curdle) then tip into a basin.
5 Cover top completely with a piece of

77

buttered greaseproof paper, pressing it directly on to custard to prevent a skin from forming.

6 Leave until cold and, unless to be used there and then, refrigerate for up to 48 hours.

7 Remove paper and use as recommended in specific recipes.

Chocolate Custard
Make as Confectioner's Custard but melt 2oz (50g) plain chocolate in the milk over a low heat.

Coffee Custard
Make as Confectioner's Custard but dissolve 2 rounded tsp instant coffee powder in the milk over a low heat.

Mocha Custard
Make as Confectioner's Custard but melt 2oz (50g) plain chocolate and 2 rounded tsp instant coffee powder in the milk over a low heat.

Maple Custard
Make as Confectioner's Custard but reduce sugar by 1oz (25g) and add 1 rounded tbsp maple syrup as soon as custard starts coming to the boil. Omit the vanilla essence.

Lemon Custard
Make as Confectioner's Custard but before starting, very thinly peel 1 large washed and dried lemon. Put peel into the pan with the milk. Bring just up to the boil. Draw aside and cover. Leave to infuse 1 hour then strain before using. Omit vanilla essence.

Orange Custard
Make exactly as Lemon Custard above but use an orange.

Rum Custard
Make as Confectioner's Custard but reduce milk by 2 tbsp and include 2 tbsp dark rum. Omit vanilla essence.

Chocolate Rum Custard
Make as Confectioner's Custard but reduce milk by 2 tbsp. Pour into pan, add 2oz (50g) plain chocolate and melt over a low heat. Draw aside, cool slightly then add 2 tbsp dark rum. Omit vanilla essence.

Orange Blossom Custard
Make as Confectioner's Custard but instead of milk, add 1 tbsp orange-flower water (available from chemists) which smells faintly of eau-de-Cologne. Omit vanilla essence.

Italian-style Frangipane Custard
Make as Confectioner's Custard but after mixture has come to the boil and thickened, stir in 1oz (25g) crushed ratafias or macaroons, 3 tsp dark rum and 1/4 level tsp finely grated lemon peel. Omit vanilla essence.

Now I turn my thoughts back to Choux Pastry which has a knack, when properly made, of puffing up to about three times its original size, leaving one with hollow and breezy-light shapes ready to pack with any filling to taste, from whipped cream to chopped chicken in white sauce.

Ingredients

Flour
This should always be plain — and strong bread flour if possible — as it contains more stretchable gluten and, in consequence, the Choux Pastry will puff up better and also hold its shape.

Salt
This is an optional extra, but I usually add a pinch.

Liquid
Always water unless a particular recipe states otherwise.

Fat

Butter is the prime choice, though good-quality block margarine may be substituted.

Eggs

Either Grade 2 or 3 is satisfactory and they should be at kitchen temperature. They should be very well beaten.

Method

1 Sift flour and salt onto a plate to aerate the mixture and reduce the possibility of lumpiness.
2 Pour the liquid into a fairly roomy pan, preferably *not* a non-stick one. Add the butter or margarine and heat slowly until fat melts. Bring to a galloping boil then add the flour *all in one go*.
3 Stir briskly over a low heat until mixture forms a thick paste in the centre of pan, leaving the sides clean (1-1½ minutes).
4 Draw pan off heat and leave to cool for 5 minutes. Then, using a whisk, beat in the eggs gradually, no more than 2 tsp at a time. This is best done with a metal whisk or fork, which is why I suggested you avoid a non-stick pan.
5 Continue beating until Choux paste is smooth, glossy and forms gentle peaks when whisk is lifted out of bowl. Use straight away for best results; otherwise place a piece of buttered greaseproof paper directly over the top and cover with a lid. Use within 30-60 minutes.

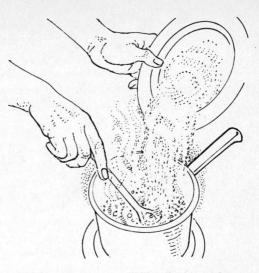

Add flour all at once to boiling liquid and fat

Using a whisk, beat in eggs gradually

Mishaps

Paste too slack with thin-looking consistency

1 Proportions incorrect and insufficient flour used.
2 Water and fat not boiling when flour was added, and/or insufficiently cooked.
3 Mixture underbeaten after eggs were added.

Paste too thick

1 Too much flour or too little water used.
2 Water and fat boiled too long before flour was added and therefore some of the liquid evaporated.

Paste heavy-textured and close with a poor rise

1 Self-raising flour used instead of strong plain.
2 Eggs insufficiently beaten.

79

3 Mixture in pan not cooked for long enough.
4 Oven too cool.

Pastry badly cracked
1 Oven too hot.
2 Pastry baked too near top of oven (this does not apply if using a fan oven).

Pastry pulpy inside
1 Proportions incorrect.
2 Mixture in pan not sufficiently beaten.
3 Oven too cool.

Choux Pastry

2½oz (65g) plain strong flour
Pinch of salt
¼pt (150ml) water
2oz (50g) butter or margarine
2 Grade 3 eggs, kitchen temperature and well-beaten

1 Sift flour and salt onto a plate.
2 Put water and butter into a pan (don't use a non-stick one) and heat slowly until fat melts. Bring quickly to a galloping boil.
3 Tip in flour in one go and stir briskly, over medium heat, until mixture forms a paste in the middle of the pan, leaving sides clean. Allow about 1-1½ minutes — no more as there will be excess evaporation. Leave to cool for 5 minutes.
4 Gradually beat in eggs and continue beating until mixture is smooth, shiny and stands in soft peaks when beaters are lifted out of bowl.

Eclairs

makes 10

Make up Choux Pastry exactly as directed above. Lightly grease one large baking tray. Set oven to 400°F (200°C), Gas 6. Fit a large icing bag with a ½in (1.25cm) plain round tube. Fill bag with Choux mixture then pipe ten 4in (10cm) lengths onto prepared tray. Bake 10 minutes. Reduce temperature to

350°F (180°C), Gas 4. Bake a further 25-30 minutes or until well-puffed and golden-brown. Make a slit in each to allow steam to escape, and return to oven, with heat switched off and door ajar, for 5 minutes to dry through completely. Cool on a wire rack. Halve lengthwise when cold and fill with ¼pt (150ml) double cream, whipped until thick with 1 rounded tbsp caster sugar. Sift a light dusting of icing sugar over each.

Cream Buns
makes 10
Make exactly as Eclairs but spoon or pipe 10 mounds of mixture on to greased tray.

Chocolate Eclairs
makes 10
(illustrated on page 107)
Make as Eclairs then fill with either whipped cream or chocolate-flavoured Confectioner's Custard (page 78). Ice tops with Chocolate Icing or any of its variations (below).

Chocolate Cream Buns
makes 10
Make exactly as the Cream Buns given above then fill with either whipped cream or chocolate-flavoured Confectioner's Custard (page 78). Ice tops with Chocolate Icing or any of its variations (below).

Coffee Eclairs
makes 10
Make up Eclairs as directed then fill with either whipped cream or coffee-flavoured Confectioner's Custard (page 78). Ice top with Coffee Glacé Icing (below).

Coffee Cream Buns
makes 10
Make up Cream Buns as previously directed then fill with either whipped cream or coffee-flavoured Confectioner's Custard (page 78). Ice tops with Coffee Glacé Icing (below).

Mocha Eclairs

makes 10

Fill cold Eclairs with either coffee or chocolate flavoured Confectioner's Custard (page 78), and cover tops with Coffee Glacé Icing (below), or vice-versa.

Mocha Cream Buns

makes 10

Follow directions for Mocha Eclairs.

Chocolate Icing

1oz (25g) plain chocolate
¼oz (1 slightly rounded tsp) butter
1 tbsp warm water
½ tsp vanilla essence
3oz (75g) sifted icing sugar

1 Break up chocolate and put into basin with butter. Melt over pan of hot, but not boiling, water.
2 Stir in water and essence and beat in sugar. When completely smooth, spread over Eclairs or Cream Buns with a round-topped knife. Alternatively, pick up each Eclair or Cream Bun by its base and dip into the icing — that's a professional technique.

Chocolate Rum Icing

Make exactly as Chocolate Icing but use rum instead of water and omit vanilla essence.

Chocolate Orange Icing

Make Chocolate Icing but use 1 tbsp Cointreau or Grand Marnier instead of water. Omit vanilla essence.

Chocolate Peppermint Icing

Make as Chocolate Icing but use 1 tbsp Crème de Menthe instead of water. Omit vanilla essence.

Chocolate Ginger Icing

Make as Chocolate Icing but use 1 tbsp ginger wine instead of water. Omit vanilla essence.

Coffee Glacé Icing

4oz (125g) icing sugar
1 rounded tsp instant-coffee powder or granules
1 tbsp hot water

1 Sift sugar into a bowl.
2 Dissolve coffee in the water then gradually stir into the icing sugar to form a smooth icing.
3 Spread over the Eclairs or Cream Buns.

Profiteroles

makes 8-10
(illustrated on page 108)

The sweet of our times, a pyramid of cream-filled Choux Buns topped with a cascade of chocolate sauce — a wealth of richness and delight for epicures of all ages.

Make up double quantity of Choux Pastry and pipe 40 small mounds on to 2 large, lightly-greased baking trays. Bake one shelf above and one shelf below centre of oven (any position in fan oven) for 25-30 minutes in oven pre-heated to 425°F (220°C), Gas 7. When ready, the puffs should be well-risen and golden. Make a slit in each, then return to oven, with heat switched off and door ajar, for 5 minutes to dry through. Cool on a wire rack. When cold, slit each in half and fill with ½pt (275ml) double cream, whipped until thick with 2 level tbsp caster sugar and 2 tbsp cold milk. Pile into a pyramid shape on a fancy serving-dish. Then coat with Chocolate Icing (above) made up with double quantities of ingredients plus an extra 3 tbsp of water, rum, brandy or whisky. Alternatively, use the following sauce.

Chocolate Sauce

¼pt (150ml) unsweetened evaporated milk
1oz (25g) plain chocolate
2oz (50g) dark-brown soft sugar
1oz (25g) golden syrup
1½oz (40g) cocoa powder, sifted
1 tsp vanilla essence
½oz (15g) butter

1 Put all ingredients into a pan and stir over a low heat until chocolate has melted.
2 Bring slowly to boil then boil briskly, without stirring, for 3-4 minutes.
3 Cool slightly and pour over Profiteroles.

Paris Brest

serves 8-12
(illustrated on page 107)

A French classic, created from rings of piped Choux Pastry. When made in the way of the purists, it is a complicated piece of bakemanship and not, I think, for those of us who want the best without spending an inordinately long time getting there. Therefore, I have on offer a short-cut version which compares favourably with an authentic Paris Brest and looks sumptuous enough anyway.

Make up Choux Pastry (page 80). Leave aside temporarily. Line a large baking tray with non-stick parchment paper. On it, outline an 8in (20cm) circle, using a dinner plate as a guide. With a ¾in (about 2cm) plain pipe and large icing bag, pipe on a ring of Choux Pastry, following the marked line.
Pipe a second ring of Choux Pastry immediately inside the first one, then finally pipe a third ring on top of the other two, completely covering the join where the two rings meet. Brush very lightly with well-beaten egg, then sprinkle with 2 rounded tbsp flaked almonds. Bake for 10 minutes in centre of oven (any position in fan oven) set to 425°F (220°C), Gas 7. Reduce after 10 minutes to 350°F (180°C), Gas 4. Continue to bake a further 25-30 minutes or until rings are well-puffed and golden. Remove from oven and make splits, with the tip of a knife, all the way round to let steam escape. Return to oven, with heat switched off and door ajar, for 10 minutes to dry out thoroughly. Transfer to a wire rack, slit in half horizontally (cutting through the two base rings) and leave until completely cold.
Before serving, have ready some cold Confectioner's Custard (page 77) and stir in 3oz (75g) shop-bought peanut brittle — or any other nut brittle finely crushed. Fill lower half of Paris Brest liberally with the Custard. Stand 'lid' on top (filling should show on the sides) then dust lightly with sifted icing sugar before serving.

Paris Brest with Cream
serves 8-12

Make exactly as previous recipe but fill with ½pt (275ml) double cream whipped until thick with 2 tbsp milk. Before using, fold in 3oz (75g) nut brittle, finely crushed.

Gâteau St Honoré

serves 8-12

Another French special. This *does* need time and patience and I suggest you keep it for a very special occasion.

Make up Pâte Brisée as directed on page 101 and roll out into a neat 8in (20cm) round. Stand on a lightly greased baking tray. Leave aside in the cool. Make up Choux Pastry as directed. Set oven to 425°F (220°C), Gas 7. Prick pastry all over, then dampen rim with a brush dipped in cold water.
Using a plain ½in (1.25cm) tube and large icing bag, pipe a ring of Choux Pastry around the dampened edge of flan pastry. On a separate lightly-greased tray, pipe rest of Choux Pastry into 10 mounds. Place pastry, with its Choux ring, just above centre of oven; Choux rounds in the centre (any position in fan oven). Bake for 15 minutes. Reverse position of trays. Reduce temperature to 375°F (190°C), Gas 5. Continue to bake a further 20 minutes. Remove both trays from oven and carefully transfer pastry round and Choux puffs to wire cooling-racks. Make slits in Choux ring and puffs to allow steam to escape. Leave until completely cold. Whip ¾pt (425ml) double cream until thick with 3 tbsp cold milk and 3 level tbsp caster sugar.
Slice top off the Choux ring. Fill the lower half with cream. Replace top. Halve puffs and also fill with cream. Pile remaining cream in centre, covering the flan pastry

completely. Brush ring thickly with melted and sieved apricot jam, then stand puffs on top. Brush over with jam, then top each puff with ½ glacé cherry. Refrigerate 30 minutes before serving.

Hot Savoury Puffs

makes 8-10

Make up Choux Pastry and convert into Choux Buns. Leave on a wire cooling-rack for 5 minutes, split in half and fill with any freshly made savoury filling, such as chopped mushrooms, diced chicken or flaked smoked haddock, in a hot white sauce. Serve as a starter, allowing 2 per person.

Cold Savoury Puffs

makes 8-10

Make as above but fill with chopped meat or poultry coated with mayonnaise. Alternatively, use either cooked flaked salmon or chopped hard-boiled eggs instead of meat or poultry.

Bouchées

makes 16-20

Small mouthfuls of filled Choux puffs which make perfect cocktail savouries.
Make 16-20 small puffs of Choux Pastry. When cold, split in half and sandwich together with a savoury filling such as given for the Hot Savoury Puffs above. Stand on a baking tray and sprinkle each with a light dusting of grated Parmesan cheese. Re-heat 7 minutes in oven set to 400°F (200°C), Gas 6. Transfer to warm plates and serve while still hot.

6
Meringues

Pure enchantment wrapped in crispness are what meringues are all about and the whole romantic escapade of drifting lightness and whiteness is surely the stuff the best culinary dreams are made of.

My first encounter with meringue-making ended in near disaster and only a patient and kindly chef from Great Yarmouth, who took pity on the then young girl parked in his vast hotel kitchen, saved me from permanent dis-illusionment and failure; I have him to thank, very gratefully, for the instructions and recipes which follow.

Ingredients for Meringue-making

Eggs

Whites only are used for all meringues and very fresh ones do not give such a good volume as those which are a few days old. Also, whites which have been kept in the re-frigerator overnight (covered, as they easily pick up smells from other foods) whip up to a much frothier mass than those at kitchen temperature. Use whites from Grade 2 or 3 eggs.

Acid

A pinch of cream of tartar or a squeeze of lemon, beaten with the whites, gives a grea-ter volume and stiffer consistency.

Sugar

Different cookery writers have an assortment of opinions as to which sugar to add and how much, but I always work with caster and suc-ceed, so I see no reason to change the arrangements. I allow 2½oz (65g) sugar per egg white, unless the meringue is being used to top a pie — as, for example, on Lemon Meringue Pie (see page 95).

Flavourings

Sometimes vanilla essence is added with the last batch of sugar. Obviously other essences may be used, according to taste.

Cornflour and blancmange powder

Either of the above acts as a stabiliser. In other words, a small amount of cornflour pre-vents weeping — and it holds meringues to-gether and encourages crispness and keeping qualities. Blancmange powder acts in the same way but also adds colour and flavour unobtrusively; thus for strawberry merin-gues, I would incorporate strawberry blancmange powder (about 1 level tsp to each egg white) to give a subtle taste and delicate colour.

Method

1 First of all prepare a tray or trays, bearing in mind that as meringues are allergic to all forms of fat and oil (one of the reasons why they stick), *do not apply* any form of grease. Simply line the tray or trays with aluminium foil, greaseproof paper or non-stick parchment paper and leave it at that. You will find the meringue will come away quite easily and will not stick, despite what some cookery books say. Greasing is unnecessary and brings its own troubles.

2 Set oven to cool (unless otherwise stated) 225°F (110°C), Gas ¼.

3 Put egg whites into a large, clean, dry bowl. If a few spots of yolk (which contain fat) have managed to get into the white, re-move the particles with a spoon, making sure you have lifted out every trace. Purists would tip the lot away, but for the most part that is unnecessary and wasteful.

4 Add a pinch of cream of tartar (or 2 drops of lemon juice) to each egg white. Whisk until very stiff and cloud-like in con-sistency, using electric beaters for ease, or a balloon whisk if you have the time and energy.

5 Gradually beat in two-thirds of the sugar, then continue beating until meringue is much stiffer than before and holds up in firm peaks when the beaters or whisk are lifted out of the bowl.

87

6 Using a large metal spoon, gently fold in rest of sugar with essences if used and either cornflour or, for coloured meringues, blancmange powder.
7 Shape and bake as directed in individual recipes.
8 Once cold, the meringues may be stored indefinitely in an airtight tin.

Mishaps

If you go carefully through the method, it is unlikely you will have any problems. *But*, if you grease the foil or paper covering the trays, the meringues will stick; and if you underbeat the whites or use too little sugar, the meringues will weep. Too high a temperature and they will go dark on the outside and remain sticky in the middle. Another point worth noting is that meringues do not work satisfactorily if made during stormy weather. I do not know the reason for this at all but I promise you it is an old wives' tale which holds true.

Meringues

makes 8 pairs

2 egg whites (Grade 2 or 3 eggs)
Pinch of cream of tartar or 4 drops of lemon juice
5oz (150g) caster sugar
2 level tsp cornflour

1 Prepare 1 large or 2 medium baking trays by lining with foil, greaseproof paper or non-stick parchment paper. *Do not grease.* Set oven to 220°F (110°C), Gas ¼.
2 Tip egg whites into large, clean, dry bowl. Add cream of tartar or lemon juice. Whisk until very stiff.
3 Gradually beat in two-thirds of the sugar and continue beating until Meringue is even stiffer than it was before and forms tall, firm peaks (like snow) when beaters are lifted out of the bowl.
4 Using a large metal spoon, fold in rest of sugar and cornflour.
5 Spoon or pipe 16 egg-shaped mounds onto

Spoon or pipe meringue into 16 egg-shaped mounds

prepared tray or trays. Place one shelf below and one shelf above oven centre (any position in fan oven).
6 Bake 45 minutes, then reverse position of trays. Continue to bake a further 45 minutes. Remove from oven. Leave to stand for 10 minutes. Switch off oven heat.
7 Lift Meringues carefully off tray or trays. Turn upside down and return to trays. Place in oven and leave, with door ajar, for about 45-60 minutes to enable them to dry out completely in residual heat.
8 Cool on a wire rack. Store in an airtight tin when cold.

Cream Meringues

makes 8 pairs

Sandwich cold Meringues together with ¼pt (150ml) double cream, whipped until thick with 1 tbsp cold milk. Fill and eat on same day.

Vanilla Cream Meringues

makes 8 pairs

Make as Meringues but fold in ½-1 tsp

(right) Raspberry Cream Gâteau, page 32
(Norway Trade Centre)

88

vanilla essence with the last batch of sugar. Sandwich together with cream as directed in previous recipe. Fill and eat on same day.

Chocolate Surprise Meringues
makes 8 pairs
Make Meringues as directed. Brush flat sides of each thickly with about 3-4oz (75-125g) melted and cooled plain chocolate. Leave to set. Sandwich together with ¼pt (150ml) double cream, whipped until thick with 1 tbsp cold milk. Fill and eat on same day.

Mocha Surprise Meringues
makes 8 pairs
Make as previous recipe but instead of milk, whip cream with 3 level tsp instant-coffee powder dissolved in 1 tbsp hot water, then allowed to cool completely.

Strawberry or Raspberry Meringues
makes 8 pairs
Make as Meringues substituting strawberry or raspberry blancmange powder for cornflour. Sandwich together with ¼pt (150ml) double cream, whipped until thick with a tbsp kirsch or cherry brandy. If liked, top with a whole strawberry or raspberry.

Meringue Tangos
makes 8 pairs
Make Meringues and leave until cold. Whip ¼pt (150ml) double cream until thick with 1 tbsp syrup from can of pineapple rings. Chop up 3 well-drained rings and fold into cream. Sandwich Meringues with pineapple cream then dust lightly with instant-coffee powder.

Meringue Whirls
makes 8 pairs
Make up Meringue mixture. Then, using a large star-shaped tube, pipe 16 whirls onto prepared tray or trays. Bake, cool and fill as directed for any of the other recipes.

(*left*) Vinegar Cake, page 15; Coffee Fudge Cake (iced), page 243; and buttered Oil Gingerbread, page 74 (*Pura Advisory Service*)

Meringue Fingers
makes 16
Very useful for serving with ice cream instead of wafers. Make up Meringue mixture, then pipe with a large star-shaped tube into 16 fingers, directly onto prepared tray or trays. Bake as directed and store in an airtight tin until needed.

Lemon Meringues
makes 8 pairs
Make up Meringue mixture then add 1 level tsp finely grated lemon peel with last batch of sugar. Bake and cool as directed. Sandwich together with ¼pt (150ml) double cream, whipped until thick with 1 rounded tbsp lemon curd and no sugar.

Orange Meringues
makes 8 pairs
Make up Meringue mixture then add 1 level tsp finely grated orange peel with last batch of sugar. Bake and cool as directed. Sandwich together with ¼pt (150ml) double cream, whipped until thick with 1 rounded tbsp orange jelly marmalade. If preferred, use orange curd or chunky marmalade.

Almond Meringues
makes 8 pairs
Make up Meringue mixture then fold in 2oz (50g) very finely chopped, flaked and toasted almonds with the last batch of sugar. Bake and cool as directed. Sandwich together with ¼pt (150ml) double cream, whipped until thick with 1 tbsp of port or sherry instead of milk.

Hazelnut Meringues
makes 8 pairs
Make up Meringue mixture then fold in 2oz (50g) very finely ground hazelnuts (use food processor or coffee grinder) with last batch of sugar. Bake and cool as directed. Sandwich together with ¼pt (150ml) double cream, whipped until thick with 1 tbsp sherry instead of milk.

91

Chocolate Speckle Meringues

makes 8 pairs

Make up Meringue mixture then fold in 2oz (50g) grated plain chocolate with last batch of sugar. Sandwich together with ¼pt (150ml) double cream, whipped until thick with 1 tbsp dark rum.

Coffee Kisses

makes 8 pairs

Make up Meringue mixture then fold in 2oz (50g) ground almonds with last batch of sugar. Sandwich together with half the Coffee Butter Cream recipe as given in Coffee Japonnaise Cakes.

Coffee Japonnaise Cakes

makes 6 pairs

Make up Meringue mixture exactly as given for Hazelnut Meringue above, but use ground almonds instead of hazelnuts. Spread mixture smoothly and evenly into a large Swiss-Roll tin (about 12 x 10in or 30 x 25cm) lined with ungreased foil, greaseproof paper or non-stick parchment paper. Bake 1 hour in oven set to 275°F (140°C) Gas 1. Stamp into 12 rounds with 1½in (4cm) plain biscuit cutter. Leave rounds where they are and return to oven, with heat switched off and door ajar, for 30-45 minutes or until very dry and crisp. Meanwhile, make up Coffee Butter Cream by creaming 3oz (75g) softened butter with 5oz (150g) sifted icing sugar and 2 level tsp instant-coffee powder. Leave in a cool place, covered, to firm up slightly. Remove rounds from tin. Crush trimmings. Sandwich rounds together with butter cream. Spread top and sides with more butter cream, then roll the cakes in trimmings. Top each with a chocolate button.

Chocolate Japonnaise Cakes

makes 6 pairs

Make exactly as previous recipe but use ground hazelnuts or walnuts instead of almonds. Sandwich together with Chocolate Butter Cream made by creaming 3oz (75g) softened butter with 5oz (150g) sifted icing sugar and 2oz (50g) melted and cooled plain chocolate.

Meringue Basket

serves 8-12

An elegant container for any number of delights and always admired whatever the occasion. Line a large, greased baking tray with double thickness of foil, greaseproof paper or non-stick parchment paper. *Do not grease.* Outline a 9in (22.5cm) circle on top of foil or paper. Make up Meringue mixture (page 88), using 3 egg whites, ¼ level tsp cream of tartar, 7½oz (215g) caster sugar and 3 level tsp cornflour. Fill in the circle fairly thickly with meringue mixture, then build up sides by spooning or piping a 1½in (4cm) border all the way round. *Do not try* to make it taller as, unlike commercial Meringues, it might collapse. Place in oven pre-heated to 225°F (110°C) Gas ¼, and bake low down in the oven (any position in fan oven), for about 3 hours or until basket is pale cream in colour and dry. Remove from oven and leave to stand 15 minutes. Lift very carefully and gently away from foil or paper, then turn upside down and put back onto lined tray. Return to oven, with heat switched off, and leave a further hour for Meringue to dry out completely. When completely cold, wrap in tissue paper and store in an airtight container. Fill with whipped cream and fresh or canned fruit before serving.

Strawberry and Cream Basket

serves 8-12

Make as Meringue Basket, but use 3 level tsp strawberry blancmange powder instead of cornflour. When cold, fill with ½pt (275ml) double cream, whipped until thick with 2 tbsp cold milk. Stud top with fresh strawberries. After filling, eat on same day.

Raspberry and Cream Basket

serves 8-12

Make as Strawberry and Cream Basket substituting raspberry blancmange powder for cornflour, and fresh raspberries for strawberries. After filling, eat on same day.

Peaches and Cream Basket
serves 8-12
Make as Strawberry and Cream Basket substituting vanilla blancmange powder for cornflour. After filling with whipped cream, decorate with well-drained peach slices and sprinkle with lightly toasted almond flakes.

Ice Cream Meringue Basket
serves 8-12
A wonderful summer dessert which can be varied to suit the meal: use a rich ice cream filling if the meal has been light, or a sorbet filling if it has been on the rich side.
Make up a Meringue Basket and fill with scoops of any ice cream. Decorate with seasonal fruits and/or a trickle of prettily coloured liqueur — Crème de Menthe (green), cherry brandy (red), Tia Maria (coffee), Chartreuse (yellow) or Mandarin Napoleon (orange).

Sorbet Meringue Basket
serves 8-12
Make up a Meringue Basket and fill with scoops of lemon or orange sorbet. Garnish with mint leaves and slices of orange. Alternatively, stud with berry fruits, to include strawberries, raspberries, loganberries and blackberries. Strings of red and black currants, laid across the top, look very festive indeed — and unusual.

Pavlova

serves 8

Created in honour of the prima ballerina, Anna Pavlova, this froth-like confection seems to be Australia's national cake, now well-known internationally and copied everywhere. It is, basically, a Meringue Basket but softer than the ones previously given, with a crisp exterior and marshmallowy interior. A glorious, stunning-to-look-at whisper of lightness — which the Austra-

lians decorate, appropriately enough, with passion fruit, in addition to other exotics readily available there. My toppings generally are a bit less flamboyant though I do have one or two surprises in store.
In keeping with the jokes made about Australia, Pavlova is an upside down cake, as you will see.

3 egg whites (Grade 2 eggs)
¼ level tsp cream of tartar or lemon juice
7oz (200g) caster sugar
·1 tsp malt vinegar
3 level tsp cornflour

1 Prepare a tray as given for Meringue Basket (page 92). Set oven to 300°F (150°C), Gas 3.
2 In a large, dry bowl, beat egg whites and cream of tartar or lemon juice to a very stiff snow. Gradually add two-thirds of the sugar.
3 Continue to beat until Meringue is heavy and even stiffer than before and forms tall peaks when beaters or whisk are lifted out of bowl. Add rest of sugar, vinegar and cornflour, then gently whisk in. Swirl thickly over circle marked on foil or paper, using a knife dipped in water.
4 Place in oven centre (any position in fan oven) and bake for 1 hour. Remove from oven and leave to stand for 15 minutes.
5 Carefully turn over onto a large, flat plate and peel away paper. The bottom now becomes the top. Leave until cold and a natural hollow forms in the middle.

Cream Pavlova
serves 8
Fill Pavlova with ½pt (275ml) double cream, whisked until thick with 2 tbsp cold milk.

Pavlova in the Old Russian Manner
serves 8
Fill Pavlova with cream as in previous recipe, then stud with small chunks cut from a small peeled pineapple. Coat each portion with sauce made by crushing 8oz (225g) fresh or

frozen strawberries, sweetening to taste with sifted icing sugar and flavouring with 3 or 4 tsp cherry brandy.

Coffee Walnut Pavlova
serves 8
Whip ½pt (275ml) double cream until thick with 2 tbsp very strong, cold coffee. Then fold in 2oz (50g) chopped walnuts. Swirl over Pavlova, and decorate with crystallised violet petals before serving.

Rose Pavlova
serves 8
Whip ½pt (275ml) double cream until thick with 2 tbsp orange-flower water (available from chemists) and ½ tsp rose essence (such as that made by Rayner's or Langdale's). Tint it pale pink with edible food colouring, then swirl it over the Pavlova. Shower with crystallised rose petals before serving.

Fruit and Cream Pavlova
serves 8
Fill Pavlova with ½pt (275ml) double cream whipped until thick with 2 tbsp milk. Stud with seasonal berry fruits.

Opal Pavlova
serves 8
Fill Pavlova with ½pt (275ml) double cream whipped until thick with 4 tbsp Advocaat. Peel 2 kiwi fruit and slice. Wash and dry 2 sharon fruit (persimmons) and cut into slices — as you would slice tomatoes. Arrange fruits attractively over top of cream, then add a few canned and well-drained mandarins.

Baked Alaska

serves 8

Also called Omelette Soufflé Suprême and Norwegian Omelet, this is one of the great classics of all time and every aspiring chef's party trick, especially when he trickles alcohol around the sides and brings the whole thing to the table leaping with flames like an ornate, snow-capped Christmas Pudding.

In fact, it is quite easy to do. Make up Meringue mixture as given for the Meringue Basket (page 92) and leave on one side temporarily. Set oven to hot, 450°F (230°C), Gas 8. Place an 8in (20cm) sponge-flan case (bought or home-made) on a large heatproof plate. Moisten with fruit juice or sherry, or a mixture of the two. Cover base with canned fruit (well-drained) or fresh seasonal fruit, from sliced bananas to stewed blackberries and apple. Top with about 1 litre of ice cream (or a little less), choosing the flavour to complement the fruit. Cover completely with Meringue by swirling it on with a knife. Decorate with about 6 halved glacé cherries. 'Flash' bake for 2-3 minutes near top of oven (any position in fan oven) or until Meringue just begins to turn golden. Remove from oven and serve immediately so that you have warm Meringue and still solid and very cold ice cream underneath.

Baked Alaska Flambé
serves 8
While Alaska is baking, heat 2 tbsp of rum, brandy or whisky to lukewarm. Pour round edge of Baked Alaska as soon as it comes out of the oven. Ignite and take to the table.

Meringue Topping for Pies

Whisk 2 egg whites (Grade 3 eggs) very stiffly. Gradually beat in 3oz (75g) caster sugar and continue beating until Meringue is very firm and forms tall peaks when beaters or whisk are lifted out of bowl.

Hot Meringue Pie
Cover top of pie with Meringue and bake for 30 minutes near top of oven (any position in fan oven) set to 300°F (150°C), Gas 2.

Cold Meringue Pie
Cover top of pie with Meringue and bake in oven centre (any position in fan oven) for 1½-2 hours in oven set to 225°F (110°C), Gas ¼, so that Meringue dries out, turns golden and does not weep on standing.

Lemon Meringue Pie

serves 6-8

Shortcrust Pastry made with 6oz (175g) flour and 3oz (75g) fat (page 99)
2 level tbsp cornflour
2oz (50g) caster sugar
¼pt (150ml) water
Finely grated peel and juice of 2 washed and dried large lemons
2 Grade 3 egg yolks
½oz (15g) butter
¼ tsp vanilla essence
Meringue topping as given above.

1 Roll out pastry fairly thinly and use to line an 8in (20cm) fluted heatproof glass or pottery flan dish. Line with foil to prevent pastry from rising as it cooks. Bake 15 minutes near top of oven (any position in fan oven) set to 425°F (220°C), Gas 7.
2 Carefully lift out the foil. Return pastry to oven and continue to bake until deep gold (15-20 minutes).
3 For filling, mix cornflour and sugar smoothly with half the water. Add rest of water with grated lemon peel and juice.
4 Cook, stirring, until mixture comes to the boil and thickens. Simmer 2 minutes then add egg yolks, butter and vanilla essence. Mix in thoroughly. Pour into flan case.
5 Cover with Meringue topping and bake as directed, depending on whether you are serving the pie hot or cold.

Almond Lemon Meringue Pie

serves 6-8

Make pie exactly as above but sprinkle Meringue with 1oz of lightly toasted, flaked almonds before 'flash' baking.

Lime Meringue Pie

serves 6-8

Make exactly as Lemon Meringue Pie but use 2 fresh limes instead of lemons.

Danish Chocolate Meringue Pie

serves 8
(illustrated on page 133)

Shortcrust Pastry made with 6oz (175g) flour (page 99)
1½oz (40g) cornflour
1oz (25g) cocoa powder
½pt (275ml) cold milk
1oz (25g) Danish butter
2oz (50g) caster sugar
2 Grade 3 egg yolks

Meringue

2 Grade 3 egg whites
4oz (125g) caster sugar

1 Roll out pastry and use to line an 8in (20cm) buttered flan dish. Line the pastry with foil. Bake 20 minutes near top of oven (any position in fan oven), set to 425°F (220°C), Gas 7. Remove foil, press down base gently if it has risen, then return pastry to oven for 10 minutes or until golden brown. Allow to cool.
2 For the filling, combine cornflour and cocoa powder in a saucepan. Gradually mix to a smooth liquid with a little of the milk. Add rest of milk.
3 Cook, stirring constantly, until mixture boils and thickens. Stir in sugar. Cool 5 minutes then beat in egg yolks. Pour into pastry case.
4 Beat egg whites to a stiff snow. Gradually beat in 3oz (75g) sugar and continue to beat until meringue is even stiffer than it was before and stands in tall peaks when beaters are lifted out of bowl. Fold in rest of sugar.
5 Pipe or swirl the Meringue over chocolate mixture then bake 15 minutes near top of oven (any position in fan oven), set to 275°F (140°C), Gas 1.

7
Pastry

Good pastry is the ambition of all keen cooks and, given correct proportions and methods, some pastries are less difficult or daunting to make than many people suppose. The most tricky are Flaky and Puff. Although the latter is readily available frozen, I shall include a recipe all the same, for those of you who want to try to make it yourselves. Strudel Pastry is, I have to admit, very time-consuming, but my eggless version is well-behaved and non-temperamental and, provided one has the energy and a kitchen devoid of teenagers and pets, is both rewarding and fun to produce.

The most popular and widely used pastry, at least in the British Isles, is Shortcrust and its uses are legion. It lends itself admirably to innumerable variations, from sweet to savoury, and is the basis for Pies, Tarts, Flans, Quiches, and assorted Cheese Biscuits and Straws. Here is the basic recipe. As with all the other pastries in this section, no preliminary procedure is given as I have included comprehensive, step-by-step methods, plus a list of the possible mishaps, all the way through (see also Chapter 12 for more tarts and pies as puddings).

Shortcrust Pastry

4oz (125g) plain flour
Pinch of salt
1oz (25g) butter or margarine, at kitchen temperature
1oz (25g) lard or cooking fat, at kitchen temperature
6-8 tsp cold water to mix

1 Sift flour and salt into a bowl through a fine-mesh sieve, metal or nylon. Add fats.

Shortcrust: *a* Cut fat into flour with a round-topped knife

b Rub fat into flour with fingertips

c Add water, then draw mixture together with a fork

Cut into dry ingredients with a round-topped knife until the fat is in pieces no larger than peas.

2 Now rub the fat into the flour with finger-tips, lifting the mixture a little way out of the bowl as you do so for maximum aeration.

3 Continue to rub in until mixture looks like a bowl of fine breadcrumbs then add water by sprinkling it over the top in *one go*. Then, using a fork, draw mixture together to form a paste made up of coarse crumbles.

4 Turn out onto a work surface dusted lightly with flour and knead swiftly until smooth and crack-free. Wrap in foil or cling film and leave to relax for half an hour in the refrigerator before rolling out and using.

Note For Shortcrust Pastry and its variations, plain flour is best unless the recipe states otherwise. Self-raising tends to give a more cakey pastry which often rises when it shouldn't, and being fairly soft rather than crisp and crunchy, breaks easily. It is harder to handle in the raw state than pastry made with plain flour.

Sweet Shortcrust Pastry
For sweet dishes make exactly as directed for Shortcrust Pastry but toss in 1oz (25g) sifted icing sugar before adding the water.

Lemon or Orange Pastry
Use for Fruit Pies made with plums, gooseberries and apples:also Savoury Pies based on lamb and veal.
Make exactly as Shortcrust Pastry but toss in 2 level tsp finely grated lemon or orange peel before mixing to a paste with water. If you want a Sweet Pastry, add 1oz (25g) sugar with the peel.

Herb Pastry
For red Meat and Poultry Pies; also Quiches.
Follow recipe for Shortcrust Pastry but toss in 1 level tsp dried mixed herbs before adding the water.

Parsley and Tarragon Pastry
For Fish Pies and Cheese Flans or Quiches.
Follow recipe for Shortcrust Pastry but toss in 1 tbsp of finely chopped parsley and ½ level tsp dried tarragon before adding the water.

Celery Pastry
For Cheese Flans, Tarts and Pies; also fish dishes.
Make exactly as Shortcrust Pastry but omit ordinary salt and sift flour with ½ level tsp celery salt.

Paprika Pastry
For Chicken and Fish Flans, Tarts, Pies and Quiches; also vegetarian dishes.
Make exactly as Shortcrust Pastry but sift flour with salt and 2 level tsp paprika.

Curry Pastry
For meat, poultry and egg dishes to include Flans, Pies, Quiches and Tarts.
Make exactly as Shortcrust Pastry but sift flour with 2 level tsp mild curry powder.

Walnut Pastry
For Sweet Pies, Flans and Tarts. Also for Quiches and Chicken Pies.
Make exactly as Shortcrust Pastry but toss in 1oz (25g) finely ground walnuts (using food processor or blender for grinding) before adding water. For Sweet Pastry, toss in 1oz (25g) caster or light-brown soft sugar at the same time as the nuts.

Hazelnut Pastry
For Fruit Pies and Jam Tarts; also veal dishes and Quiches.
Make exactly as Walnut Pastry substituting ground hazelnuts for walnuts.

Wheatmeal Pastry
For savoury dishes and Quiches.
Make exactly as Shortcrust Pastry but use brown flour instead of plain.

Flan Pastry
For all special occasion Flans, Tarts, Quiches and pies.
Make exactly as Pâte Brisée (below).

Sweet Flan Pastry
For special occasion Sweet Flans, Tarts and Pies.
Make exactly as Pâte Sucrée (right).

Cheese Pastry
For savoury dishes, Cheese Straws and Biscuits.
Follow recipe for Shortcrust Pastry but sift flour and salt with 1 level tsp powder mustard. Toss in 2oz (50g) very finely grated Cheddar cheese (slightly stale for ease of handling and mature for the best flavour) before adding water.

Enriched Cheese Pastry
For Cheese Biscuits and any baked Cheese Savoury dishes.
Make as Cheese Pastry but use all butter, 1oz (25g) grated Parmesan cheese and mix to a paste with 1 egg yolk and about 4-6 tsp cold water. If preferred, very finely grated Gruyère cheese may be used.

Short-cut Cheese 'Puff' Pastry
For pie toppings and Biscuits.
Make exactly as Shortcrust Pastry but use self-raising flour instead of plain and sift with 1 level tsp powder mustard, 1/4 level tsp cayenne pepper and 1/4 level tsp celery salt. Toss in 3oz (75g) of coarsely grated Cheddar cheese after rubbing in fat. Mix to a fairly stiff dough with 1 1/2-2 tbsp cold milk or single cream. Wrap in cling film and refrigerate for 30 minutes before rolling out and using.

Pâte Brisée
This is French Shortcrust Pastry but made entirely with butter and mixed to a paste with 1 egg yolk and about 4-5 tsp cold water. It should be wrapped and refrigerated for 30 minutes before being used.

Pâte Sucrée
Another version of Shortcrust Pastry but richer, made exactly as Pâte Brisée plus the addition of 1oz (25g) caster sugar tossed in before the egg yolk and water are added. It, too, should be wrapped and refrigerated for 30 minutes before being used. As this pastry is fairly fragile, it is better pressed into position than rolled out. Should it break, patch up the hole with dampened pieces of pastry trimmings.

Tip
To prevent sweet pastries from taking on a speckled appearance, I always use sifted icing sugar instead of caster. This is something you might like to try.

Weight
When a recipe calls for 8oz (225g) Shortcrust Pastry, for example, this *always* refers to the weight of flour. The equivalent shop-bought amount should weigh about 12oz (350g).

Baking blind
This is baking a pastry case unfilled. To do so successfully, which means preventing the pastry from rising as it cooks, line with greaseproof paper and weigh down with dried beans kept especially for the purpose; they should reach almost to the top of the case. Alternatively, try this more modern method which I have found to be very good indeed. Line the uncooked pastry case with a round of foil, pressing it well against base and sides. Remove towards the end of baking time, then return pastry case to the oven until it is a warm golden brown.

Sweet Crumble Topping
For Fruit Crumbles.
Make exactly as Shortcrust Pastry, tossing 1 1/2oz (40g) sugar into the rubbed-in ingredients. Add no liquid.

Savoury Crumbles
For Meat, Poultry and Egg Crumbles.
Make exactly as Shortcrust Pastry, sifting

flour with 1 level tsp powder mustard and ½ level tsp salt, then tossing 1 level tsp dried herbs (type according to dish) into rubbed-in ingredients. Add no liquid.

Mishaps

Pastry tough and leathery

1 Insufficient fat used.
2 Too much liquid used for mixing.
3 Pastry kneaded too heavily and too long on over-floured surface.
4 Oven too cool; most shortcrust pastry should be baked at 425°F (220°C), Gas 7.
5 Pastry cooked too low down in oven.

Pastry refuses to hold together

1 Too much fat used.
2 Fat rubbed in heavily.
3 Insufficient water, or other liquid, used for mixing.
4 Self-raising flour used.

Pastry heavy and damp inside

1 Under cooked and/or oven too cool.
2 Pastry placed directly over very hot filling.
3 No slit made in pastry topping to allow steam to escape.
4 Too much liquid used for mixing the pastry.
5 Pastry topping in direct contact with sugar.

Pastry shrinks

1 Pastry stretched and pulled while it was being rolled out.
2 Not allowed to relax in the refrigerator as directed in the recipe.

Pastry blisters

1 Fat insufficiently rubbed into flour.
2 Liquid mixed in unevenly.
3 Pastry unevenly kneaded and too much surplus flour worked in.

Mince Pies

makes 16

Shortcrust Pastry made with 8oz (225g) flour (page 99)
14oz (400g) mincemeat
1 tbsp whisky or brandy
Beaten egg for brushing
Icing sugar

1 Roll out just over half the pastry fairly thinly and cut into 16 rounds with a 3in (7.5cm) biscuit cutter, re-rolling and re-cutting trimmings to make the correct number. Repeat with rest of pastry, cutting into rounds with 2in (5cm) biscuit cutter for lids.
2 Use larger rounds to line 16 bun tins then fill with equal amounts of mincemeat mixed with whisky or brandy.
3 Top with lids, brush with beaten egg and bake about 20 minutes near top of oven set to 425°F (220°C), Gas 7. Allow to cool, then remove mince pies from tins.
4 Sift icing sugar over tops and serve warm (see also Mince Pies with Walnuts, page 219).

Custard Tarts

makes 12

Shortcrust Pastry made with 6oz (175g) flour (page 99)
12 level tsp fresh white breadcrumbs
1 Grade 3 egg plus 1 extra yolk
¼pt (150ml) single cream or undiluted evaporated milk
2oz (50g) caster sugar
1 level tsp nutmeg

1 Roll out pastry fairly thinly. Cut into 12 rounds with a 2½in (6.25cm) biscuit cutter and line 12 greased bun tins.
2 Sprinkle a teaspoon of crumbs in each (which helps to keep the pastry from getting soggy).
3 Beat egg, yolk, cream (or evaporated milk) and sugar well together then strain into jug. Pour into pastry cases.
4 Sprinkle tops with nutmeg. Place in

centre of oven (any position in fan oven) set to 425°F (220°C), Gas 7. At this stage, reduce temperature immediately as below, to prevent tarts over-cooking.

5 Lower temperature to 375°F (190°C), Gas 5 and bake 30-35 minutes, when pastry should be light golden and custard just set.

6 Leave in tins for 5 minutes then remove carefully and cool on a wire rack. Eat when freshly made if possible.

Fruit Tarts

makes 12

Line 12 bun tins with pastry as directed above. Line in turn with squares of foil to prevent pastry from rising as it cooks. Bake 15 minutes near top of oven (any position in fan oven) set to 425°F (220°C), Gas 7. Remove foil and return cases to oven for a further 5 minutes or until a warm gold. Remove from tins and cool to lukewarm on a cooling rack. Brush insides over with melted apricot jam, fill with fresh or canned (well-drained) strawberries or raspberries (or pie filling) then brush over with more melted jam to glaze. Pie filling does not need the final glaze.

Fruit Tarts with Confectioner's Custard
makes 12
Half-fill tarts with Confectioner's Custard (page 77), then stud with fruit. Glaze by brushing with jam.

Fruit Tarts with Cream
makes 12
Half-fill tarts with sweetened whipped cream, then stud with fruit. Glaze by brushing with jam.

Bakewell Tart

serves 6-8

A much-loved speciality from Derbyshire.

Shortcrust Pastry made with 6oz (175g) flour (page 99)
2 slightly rounded tbsp raspberry or strawberry jam

3 oz (75g) butter or margarine, at room temperature and softened
3oz (75g) caster sugar
½ tsp almond essence
3 Grade 3 eggs, separated
4oz (125g) ground almonds
5oz (150g) cake crumbs (use ready-prepared trifle sponge cakes or Madeira Cake)
Finely grated peel and juice of half a medium lemon

1 Roll out pastry and use to line a 9in (22.5cm) greased flan dish or flan ring standing on a greased baking tray. Spread base with jam.

2 For filling, cream butter or margarine and sugar together with almond essence until light and fluffy. Beat in egg yolks then stir in almonds, cake crumbs and lemon peel with juice.

3 Beat egg whites to a stiff snow then gently fold into filling mixture. When smooth and evenly combined, spread into pastry case.

4 Bake for 45 minutes just above oven centre (any position in fan oven) set to 375°F (190°C), Gas 5.

Treacle Tart

serves 6

Shortcrust Pastry made with 6oz (175g) flour (page 99)
1 rounded tbsp fresh white breadcrumbs
2 level tbsp black treacle
1 level tbsp golden syrup
½ level tsp finely grated lemon rind
2 tsp lemon juice

1 Roll out pastry fairly thinly on floured surface. Use to line an 8in (20cm) well-buttered heatproof plate. Trim off edges and reserve. Mix filling ingredients well together and spread over pastry to within 1in (2.5cm) of edges. Moisten edges with cold water.

3 Roll rest of pastry out thinly and cut into narrow strips. Arrange in trellis design over top of pie, pressing edges of strips firmly on to pastry edges to seal.

4 Bake 30 minutes near top of oven (any position in fan oven) set to 400°F (200°C), Gas 6. Serve warm with cream or custard.

Jam Tart
serves 6
Make as Treacle Tart, omitting crumbs and filling, and spreading base of pastry with 3 level tbsp red jam.

Lemon Curd Tart
serves 6
Make as Treacle Tart, omitting crumbs and filling, and spreading base of pastry with 3 level tbsp lemon curd.

Almond Slices
makes 12
Universal in their appeal, here is a pretty straightforward recipe which always turns out well.
Shortcrust Pastry made with 8oz (225g) flour (page 99)
2 level tbsp red jam
4oz (125g) caster sugar
4oz (125g) icing sugar, sifted
6oz (175g) ground almonds
1 Grade 3 egg, beaten
1 Grade 3 egg white, lightly beaten until just foamy
1 tsp water
1 tsp almond essence
½ tsp vanilla essence
1oz (25g) blanched and split almonds

1 Roll out pastry into a rectangle measuring 10 x 6in (25 x 15cm). Place on greased baking tray and decorate by pinching up edges between finger and thumb. Spread with jam.
2 For almond mixture, put sugars and almonds into a bowl then mix to a thick paste with beaten egg, two-thirds of the beaten white, the water and essences.
3 Spread over pastry with knife dipped in water, then stud with halved almonds, flat sides down.

4 Brush lightly with rest of beaten egg white. Bake 25 minutes just above oven centre (any position in fan oven) set to 400°F (200°C), Gas 6.
5 Transfer carefully to a wire cooling rack, leave until lukewarm, then cut into 12 pieces. Store in an airtight tin when cold.

Chocolate Bakewell Tart
serves 8-9
(illustrated on page 134)
A surprise package of a tart, filled with chocolate flake bars for a touch of luxury.

Shortcrust Pastry made with 8oz (225g) flour (page 99)
2 rounded tbsp red jam
7 flake bars from family pack
3oz (75g) block margarine, at kitchen temperature and soft
3oz (75g) caster sugar
2 Grade 4 eggs, at kitchen temperature
3oz (75g) self-raising flour
1oz (25g) ground almonds
½ tsp almond essence
Icing sugar for topping

1 Roll out pastry fairly thinly and use to line a 9½in (24cm) greased fluted flan dish.
2 Spread base with jam. Arrange flake bars on top like spokes of a wheel. For rest of filling, cream margarine and sugar together until light and fluffy. Beat in eggs, then fold in rest of ingredients with a metal spoon.
3 Spread mixture carefully over flake bars to form an even layer. Bake 15 minutes just above centre of oven (any position in fan oven) set to 400°F (200°C), Gas 6.
4 Reduce temperature to 350°F (180°C), Gas 4 and continue to bake a further 20 minutes. Sift icing sugar over the top and serve warm as a dessert, or cold as a teatime cake.

Top and Bottom Fruit Pie

serves 6

This is a Pie with pastry top and bottom and is sometimes called Double Crust Pie. It is best made on an enamel plate.

Shortcrust Pastry made with 8oz (225g)
  flour (page 99)
1lb (450g) seasonal fruit such as apples,
  apples and blackberries, gooseberries,
  rhubarb, plums, currants, cherries.
5oz (150g) granulated or light-brown soft
  sugar
Beaten egg for brushing

1 Prepare washed fruit according to type, removing stones where possible.
2 Roll out half the pastry and use to line an 8in (20cm) greased enamel plate.
3 Fill with alternate layers of fruit and sugar, ending with fruit to prevent top crust from being soggy. Dampen pastry edges with water.
4 Cover with second portion of pastry, rolled into a lid. Trim edges to neaten, then press well together to seal. Brush with egg.
5 Ridge edges with a fork, make 2 slits in top of pie to allow steam to escape, and stand pie on baking tray to catch any fruit juices. Bake 20 minutes just above centre of oven (any position in fan oven) set to 425°F (220°C), Gas 7.
6 Reduce temperature to 350°F (180°C), Gas 4 and bake a further 30-40 minutes, depending on fruit. Remove from oven, sprinkle with caster sugar and serve hot with cream or custard.

Note If using ready-prepared pie fillings or cold stewed fruit, make as above but allow 30 minutes baking time at the higher temperature.

Covering a Pie

(illustrated on page 135)

To cover a pie with pastry, roll out as directed for Shortcrust, Flaky or frozen puff pastry and cut lid 1in (2.5cm) larger all the way round than top of piedish. Brush dish rim with water then line with strips of pastry to give a firm edge and something for the lid to grip. Brush strips with water then cover with pastry lid. Press edges of lid and lining strips well together to seal, then flake by tapping all the way round with the back of a knife.

Brush with beaten milk or egg (or a mixture of the two) then decorate with pastry leaves cut from trimmings. Brush with more glazing mixture, cut 2 vents in the top to allow steam to escape, then bake as directed in the recipe.

Deep Dish Fruit Pie

serves 6

Follow directions for covering a pie. Fill a 2pt (1.25 litre) dish with 2lb (900g) fruit as suggested for Top and Bottom Fruit Pie (above), alternating layers with 8oz (225g) granulated sugar. Again, end with a layer of fruit. Make 2 slits in pastry lid to allow steam to escape, then brush with beaten egg or milk. Bake 15 minutes just above oven centre (any position in fan oven) set to 425°F (220°C), Gas 7, then reduce temperature to 350°F (180°C), Gas 4 and continue to bake a further 35-45 minutes, according to fruit. To prevent soiling the oven with fruit juice that might seep out of pie, stand dish on a baking tray.

If using cold stewed fruit, bake 25-30 minutes at 425°F (220°C), Gas 7.

Deep Dish Meat Pie

serves 4

Make as Deep Dish Fruit Pie but mix 1½lb (675g) diced stewing steak with 2 level tbsp plain flour, 1 medium peeled and thinly sliced onion, 1-1½ level tsp salt and ¼pt (150ml) stock or water. Bake as directed above but cook pie at the lower temperature for 2 hours. If it browns too much on top, cover with a piece of foil.

If using ready-prepared stew (home cooked) or stewing steak from a can, use cold, cover with pastry and bake 30 minutes just above centre of oven (any position in fan oven) set to 425°F (220°), Gas 7.

Deep Dish Steak and Mushroom Pie

serves 4
Make as Deep Dish Meat Pie, replacing 6oz (175g) meat with sliced mushrooms.

Deep Dish Steak and Kidney Pie

serves 4
Make as Deep Dish Meat Pie, replacing 6oz (175g) meat with diced ox kidney.

Cornish Pasties

serves 4

Cornish Pasties form a complete meal, filled as they are with liver, steak and vegetables. Only the Cornish can produce idyllic Pasties — the rest of us try.

Shortcrust Pastry made with 8oz (225g) flour (page 99)
6oz (175g) ox liver, washed, dried and cut into tiny dice
6oz (175g) frying or rump steak, cut into tiny dice
1 medium onion, peeled and chopped
1 large potato, peeled and cut into tiny dice
Salt and pepper to taste
4 tbsp water or stock
1 Grade 4 egg
2 tsp milk beaten with the egg

1 Divide pastry into 4 equal pieces and roll each out into a 6in (15cm) round.
2 Put liver and steak in mixing bowl and toss in onion, potato, salt and pepper to taste, and the water or stock.
3 Put equal amounts on to centres of pastry rounds then dampen edges with water. Bring edges up to form a centre 'seam', seal well together, and press into flutes.
4 Transfer to a greased baking tray, then brush all over with egg and milk mixture.
5 Bake 15 minutes just above centre of oven (any position in fan oven) set to 425°F (220°C), Gas 7. Reduce temperature to 325°F (160°C), Gas 3.

6 Continue to bake a further 40-50 minutes when ingredients inside Pasties should be cooked. Eat hot or when just cold.

Salmon and Sherry Picnic Pies

makes 12
(illustrated on page 136)

Picnics apart, these could be eaten at any time for a meal or snack.

Shortcrust Pastry made with 12oz (350g) flour (page 99)
1/2oz (15g) butter or margarine
1/2oz (15g) flour
1/4pt (150ml) milk
2 tbsp sherry (not too sweet)
1 can (71/2oz or 213g) pink salmon, drained and flaked
1/4 tsp celery salt
White pepper to taste
Beaten egg for brushing

1 Roll out pastry fairly thinly. Cut into 12 rounds with 3in (7.5cm) cutter and 12 rounds with 21/2in (6cm) cutter. Re-roll and re-cut trimmings to make required number. Put on to plate and refrigerate.
2 To make filling, heat butter or margarine in saucepan. Stir in flour to form a roux. Blend in milk. Cook, stirring, until sauce comes to boil and thickens. Remove from heat.
3 Stir in sherry, salmon, celery salt and pepper. Cover. Leave until cold. Use large rounds of pastry to line 12 bun tins.
4 Spoon equal amounts of filling into each. Top with smaller rounds. Brush with beaten egg. Bake 20-25 minutes near top of oven (any position in fan oven) set to 425°F (220°C), Gas 7.
5 Leave to stand 5 minutes then lift pies on to a wire cooling rack. Eat freshly made, either warm or cold. Store leftovers in a tin or up to 2 days in the refrigerator.

(above right) Chocolate Eclairs, page 81 *(Eggs Information Bureau)*

(below right) Paris Brest, page 82 *(Eggs Information Bureau)*

Quiche Lorraine

serves 6

The classic version with variations to follow. Note that the Quiche from Lorraine contains no cheese and is very similar to our own Egg and Bacon Pie.

Shortcrust Pastry made with 6oz (175g) flour (page 99)
6oz (175g) streaky bacon, unsmoked
1/4pt (150ml) milk
1/4pt (150ml) single cream
3 Grade 3 eggs beaten
1/2 level tsp salt
White pepper to taste
2 pinches nutmeg

1 Line an 8in (20cm) lightly greased flan dish with rolled-out pastry. Leave in the refrigerator temporarily.
2 Coarsely chop bacon and fry gently in its own fat until cooked but still soft. Cool.
3 Beat milk, cream and eggs well together. Season with salt, pepper and nutmeg.
4 Spread bacon over base of pastry then strain in egg mixture.
5 Bake 15 minutes in centre of oven (any position in fan oven) set to 400°F (200°C), Gas 6. Reduce temperature to 325°F (160°C), Gas 3 and continue to bake until custard is set, 35-45 minutes.
6 To test, push a thin metal skewer gently into the Quiche. If it comes out clean and dry, the custard is set. Serve warm or cold, cut into wedges.

Egg and Bacon Pie
serves 6
Make as Quiche Lorraine, but use all milk.

Spinach Quiche
serves 6
Make as Quiche Lorraine, but use 4oz (125g) chopped frozen spinach instead of bacon,

(left) Profiteroles, page 81 *(Stork Margarine)*

and make sure it has completely thawed before spreading over base of pastry. Before baking, sprinkle top with 1 1/2oz (40g) grated Cheddar or Gruyère cheese or 1/2oz (15g) Parmesan cheese.

Tomato Quiche
serves 6
Make as Quiche Lorraine, but use 4oz (125g) blanched, skinned and sliced tomatoes instead of bacon. Before baking, sprinkle top with 1 1/2oz (40g) grated Cheddar cheese.

Mushroom Quiche
serves 6
Make as Quiche Lorraine, but use 4oz (125g) sliced and fried mushrooms instead of bacon. Before baking, sprinkle top with 1 1/2oz (40g) grated Cheddar cheese.

Crab and Onion Quiche
serves 6
Make as Quiche Lorraine, but use 4oz (125g) crabmeat and 4 chopped spring onions instead of bacon. Before baking sprinkle top with 1 1/2oz (40g) grated Cheddar cheese.

Fried Onion Quiche
serves 6
Make as Quiche Lorraine, but use 4oz (125g) sliced and fried onion instead of bacon. Before baking, sprinkle top with 1 1/2-2oz (40-50g) grated mature Cheddar cheese.

Cheese and Chive Quiche

serves 8
(illustrated on page 153)

Shortcrust Pastry made with 6oz (175g) flour (page 99)
4oz (125g) gammon, de-rinded and chopped
1oz (25g) margarine
2 rounded tbsp chopped chives
8oz (225g) Stilton cheese, crumbled finely
2 Grade 3 eggs
1/4pt (150ml) single cream
4 tbsp milk
Shake of Tabasco sauce

109

1 Roll out pastry and use to line a 9in (22.5cm) flan ring standing on a greased baking tray.
2 Fry gammon in margarine until light gold. Cool slightly then sprinkle over base of pastry case. Top with chives and the Stilton cheese.
3 Beat all remaining ingredients well together. Pour into pastry case over cheese mixture.
4 Bake 20 minutes just above centre of oven (any position in fan oven) set to 425°F (220°C), Gas 7.
5 Reduce temperature to 350°F (180°C), Gas 4 and continue to bake a further 20 minutes or until pastry is golden and filling is set. Remove flan ring and serve Quiche hot or cold (*see also* Blue Cheese Flan, Chapter 13).

Southern Cheese and Chive Quiche

serves 8

Decorate edge with halved tomato slices and slices of stuffed olives.

Asparagus Quiche

serves 8

Make as Cheese and Chive Quiche but use 1 can (10oz or 283g) asparagus spears, drained and halved, instead of bacon and 4oz (125g) grated Cheddar cheese instead of Stilton. Decorate with parsley.

Scots Black Bun

serves about 20

A traditional Hogmanay (New Year's Eve) cake in Scotland, Black Bun bears no relation to a bun at all but is composed of a mass of spiced dried fruit encased in pastry. It is best if left to mature for several months before cutting so it can be made during the summer months and stored, wrapped, in an airtight container until required. In Scotland it would undoubtedly be eaten with a glass of whisky but in the South, sherry or ginger wine would make admirable accompaniments, as would a warming glass of mulled wine.

Shortcrust Pastry made with 12oz (350g) flour (page 99)
8oz (225g) plain flour
2 level tsp baking powder
1 level tsp cinnamon
1 level tsp ground ginger
1 level tsp allspice
2lb (900g) mixed dried fruit, including peel
4oz (125g) flaked almonds, coarsely crushed in hands
4oz (125g) dark brown soft sugar
1 Grade 3 egg, beaten
6 tbsp whisky
6 tbsp milk
Extra beaten egg for brushing

1 Roll out pastry thinly and use two-thirds to line a well-greased, deep 8in (20cm) cake tin, letting about 2in (5cm) of pastry hang over the sides of the tin.
2 For filling, sift dry ingredients into a bowl then toss in fruit, nuts and sugar.
3 Add beaten egg, whisky and milk and stir to moisten. Pack into pastry-lined tin then fold over edges of pastry like a hem.
4 Roll out remaining pastry, dampen edges and put on top of Bun to form a lid. Seal edges well together then, using a metal skewer, make 6 holes right through to bottom of cake.
5 Prick lid all over with a fork, brush with egg and bake 2½-3 hours in centre of oven (any position in fan oven) set to 350°F (180°C), Gas 4. If pastry darkens too much, cover with a piece of foil.
6 Leave to stand 30 minutes then turn out and cool on a wire rack. Store in an airtight container, lined with tissue paper, when cold.

Frangipane Flan

serves 8

I quote from Helen Jerome's classic book, *Concerning Cake Baking*, (Pitman, 1932). 'Frangipane is of Italian origin, and may, without undue imagination, be traced farther back, and identified with the making of the pistachio cream tarts of the Arabian Nights.

Frangipane tarts appear to have been introduced into France by Catharine de Medici, and they have become famous as Edinburgh creamed flans through the influence of Mary Stewart.'

This is my adapted version.

Shortcrust Pastry made with 6oz (175g) flour (page 99) or Pâte Brisée (page 101).
2 level tbsp red jam
3oz (75g) butter
3oz (75g) cornflour
¾pt (425ml) milk
2 Grade 3 egg yolks
2oz (50g) caster sugar
3oz (75g) ground almonds
½ tsp almond essence
Decoration
4 tbsp double cream
1 level tbsp caster sugar
1oz (25g) flaked almonds, lightly toasted

1 Roll out pastry and use to line an 8in (20cm) lightly greased flan dish.
2 Line with foil to prevent pastry from rising as it cooks. Bake 15 minutes near top of oven (any position in fan oven) set to 425°F (220°C), Gas 7. Remove foil. Return flan dish to oven for a further 8-10 minutes or until pastry is golden brown. Spread base with jam.
3 For filling, melt butter in saucepan then stir in cornflour. Gradually add milk then cook, stirring, until mixture thickens and forms a ball in centre of pan, leaving sides clean.
4 Gradually beat in egg yolks, sugar, almonds and essence then spread into pastry case over jam.
5 Leave until cold and set. Before serving, beat cream until thick and stir in sugar. Pipe a border of cream round edge of flan then sprinkle with almonds.

Suet Crust Pastry

This is a firm, robust and typically British pastry and one of the few which is dependent on raising agent for its success; either self-raising flour or a combination of strong plain flour with the addition of 3 level tsp baking powder to every 8oz (225g). The latter, I think, results in a firmer and therefore more controllable pastry.

Less popular than it was years ago, because of the animal fat it contains, Suet Crust Pastry can be used for Baked Jam Rolls, Steamed Roly-poly Puddings and Dumplings, and is the traditional pastry for Steak and Kidney Pudding cooked in a basin and another old favourite, Apple Pudding, cooked in a similar way. Whether savoury or sweet, the pudding is spooned out of its basin and rarely inverted onto a plate; purists often tie a white table napkin round the outside, presumably to give it a pristine appearance and catch the drips. Here is the basic recipe with a few variations (see also Chapter 12).

4oz (125g) plain flour
1½ level tsp baking powder
1 level tsp salt
2oz (50g) finely shredded packeted suet
About 4 tbsp cold water to mix

1 Sift flour, baking powder and salt into bowl. Toss in suet either with a fork or fingertips.
2 Add water in one go. Using a round-topped knife, stir mixture to form a soft, but not sticky, dough.

Suet Crust: Toss in suet with a fork or fingertips

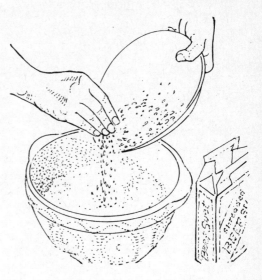

3 Draw pastry together with fingertips. Turn out onto a flour-dusted surface. Knead until smooth and crack-free. Roll out and use as directed in the specific recipe.

Sweet Suet Crust Pastry
for sweet dishes.
Make as Suet Crust Pastry but if liked, sweeten slightly by adding 1oz (25g) caster sugar to every 4oz (125g) flour. Toss in with the suet. Reduce salt to ½ level tsp.

Spicy Suet Crust
for sweet dishes.
Make as Suet Crust Pastry for sweet dishes but sift dry ingredients with an additional level tsp of mixed spice or cinnamon, depending on flavour preferred.

Mustard Suet Crust Pastry
for any kind of Meat Pudding.
Make as Suet Crust Pastry but sift dry ingredients with 1½ level tsp powder mustard.

Sage Suet Crust
for Meat Puddings based on pork and offal.
Make as Suet Crust Pastry but toss in 1 level tsp dried sage with the suet.

Marjoram Suet Crust Pastry
for Meat Puddings based on lamb.
Make as Suet Crust Pastry but toss in 1 level tsp dried marjoram with the suet.

Mishaps

Pastry tough and close-textured
1 Insufficient baking powder used with plain flour.
2 Too much water used for mixing.
3 Pastry handled too much.
4 If baked, as in a Roly Poly, the oven was too hot.
5 If steamed or boiled, water was allowed to go off the boil.

Pastry soggy
1 Water used for steaming or boiling was allowed to go off the boil.
2 Water boiled too vigorously and worked its way under the covering (for boiled puddings in saucepan).
3 Too much water used which went over the top and seeped underneath the covering (for boiled puddings in saucepan).
4 Top of pudding insecurely covered.

Pastry speckled with pieces of unmelted suet
1 Suet bought in the piece from the butcher and then not chopped finely enough.
2 If suet crust was baked, the oven temperature too high.

Steak and Kidney Pudding
serves 4

Suet Crust Pastry (page 111)
1lb (450g) stewing steak, diced
6oz (175g) ox kidney, diced
1 level tbsp flour
1 large onion, peeled and chopped
3 tbsp water, stock or beer

1 Roll out two-thirds of pastry and use to line a 1½pt (1 litre) pudding basin, first well-greased.
2 Mix steak with rest of ingredients and use to fill dish.
3 Dampen edges of pastry with water then cover with lid, rolled from rest of pastry.
4 Press edges well together to seal, then cover securely with a double thickness of greased greaseproof paper or aluminium foil.
5 Steam or boil steadily for 3½ hours, in covered pan, topping up every now and then with extra boiling water to keep up the level. Serve from the basin.

Hot Water Crust Pastry

A pastry specifically used for large and small meat pies, Hot Water Crust dates back to Victorian times, if not earlier, when 'raised' pies, filled with game, poultry, pork or veal, were much in favour; sturdy stuff indeed and very popular as part of the cold collation.

The 'raising' of the pastry referred to the manner in which the crust was moulded by hand into tins (some plain; others ornate and hinged), from the base upwards, leaving a case ready to receive a chosen filling. The technique is very much the same today and Hot Water Crust is still raised or moulded by hand, though it can also be rolled out for ease. It is one of the few pastries I can think of requiring heat (another is Choux) and certainly the only one which, owing to the fact that it is baked for a fairly long time and has to support quite a heavy filling, is rarely moulded or rolled out to less than ¼in (75mm) thick. It is a strong pastry and can well tolerate plenty of kneading; delicacy of handling is not called for.

12oz (350g) plain flour
1 level tsp salt
1 Grade 3 egg yolk
4oz (125g) lard or white cooking fat
¼pt (150ml) water

1 Sift flour and salt into a bowl. Make a hollow in the centre. Drop in yolk.
2 Put lard or cooking fat and water into a pan and heat gently until fat melts. Afterwards increase heat and bring to a brisk boil.
3 Pour liquid round edges of flour mixture then fork all ingredients together to form a dough. Turn out onto a floured surface and knead until smooth and crack-free.
4 Form into a ball and place in a lightly greased basin. Stand the basin over a pan of gently simmering water and cover. Leave the pastry to relax in the warmth for about 30 minutes.
5 Use three-quarters of the pastry for the pie shell. The remainder is for the lid and should be left in the basin over hot water (again covered) until it is ready for use.

Hot Water Crust: pour liquid round edges of flour then fork together

Mishaps

Pastry crumbles and is tricky to mould or roll

1 Not enough fat used.
2 Insufficient water added.
3 Fat and water added when off the boil.
4 Dough was allowed to cool off before being moulded or rolled.
5 Self-raising flour used.

Pastry loses its shape before baking and starts to sag

1 Filling added too soon after pastry was moulded.
2 Not enough filling used.
3 Pastry not thick enough.

Pastry splits before or during baking

1 Pastry moulded or rolled unevenly, resulting in thin patches, unable to take the strain of the filling.

Crust is doughy instead of crisp

1 Self-raising flour used.

Pastry soggy inside pie

1 Filling made over-wet.
2 Oven too hot.
3 Pie or pies underbaked.

Pastry cracks across top and down sides

1 Pastry not kneaded evenly.
2 Pastry too dry through lack of water.
3 Water and fat not boiling when added to flour.

Pastry leathery

1 Pastry too dry.
2 Pastry excessively kneaded and too much excess flour worked in.

Lid separates from pie

1 Lid inadequately sealed to sides of pie.
2 Pie too full.

Game Pie

serves 6-8

Hot Water Crust Pastry (page 113), using quantity and a half
1lb (450g) boned game meat (venison, partridge, pheasant, etc)
12oz (350g) chicken livers
1 small onion, peeled
8oz (225g) pork sausagemeat
2 hard-boiled eggs, shelled and chopped
2 level tsp mixed herbs
6 long rashers streaky bacon
Beaten egg for brushing
2 level tsp gelatine
¼pt (150ml) cold stock or water

1 Roll out two-thirds of pastry and mould over the *outside* of a 7in (17.5cm) round cake tin, first well greased. Keep rest of pastry warm in a bowl over hot water.
2 Turn right way up and tie a wide strip of greaseproof paper round pastry for time being. Very carefully ease out tin, leaving a 'shell' of pastry. Transfer to greased baking tray.
3 Shred raw game meat. Mince raw livers and onion and mix with sausagemeat, eggs and herbs.

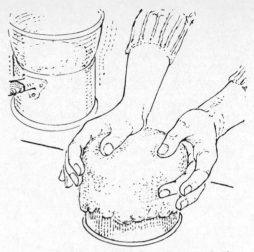

Mould round the outside of a well-greased cake tin

4 Line base and sides of pastry case with bacon then fill with alternate layers of game and liver mixture, leaving a gap at the top.
5 Moisten edges of pastry with water then cover with lid, rolled from rest of pastry. Press edges well together to seal, then trim away surplus. Decorate edges by ridging with a fork. Remove paper from outside.
6 Brush all over with egg, make a hole in centre of lid, then outline with pastry leaves, rolled and cut from trimmings. Brush leaves with more egg.
7 Bake 1 hour in oven centre (any position in fan oven) set to 375°F (190°C), Gas 5. Reduce temperature to 350°F (180°C), Gas 4. Continue to bake a further hour.
8 Soften gelatine in the cold stock or water for 10 minutes. Tip into a saucepan and dissolve over a low heat. Pour into pie through hole in the top.
9 Chill several hours before cutting to give gelatine a chance to set.

Note Instead of gelatine and stock or water, use ¼pt (150ml) liquid aspic jelly.

Chicken Pie
serves 6-8
Make as Game Pie, substituting diced raw chicken for both game and livers.

Pork Pie

serves 6

Make exactly as Game Pie with the following alterations:

1 Use Hot Water Crust Pastry (page 113), without increasing the amount.
2 Mould pastry round outside of 6in (15cm) round, greased cake tin.
3 For filling, mix 1lb (450g) diced stewing pork with 1 small grated onion, 1 level tsp mixed herbs, 4 tbsp water and 1-1½ level tsp salt.

Veal and Ham Pie

serves 6

Make as Pork Pie using 12oz (350g) diced veal and 4oz (125g) uncooked, diced gammon.

Pork and Bacon Plait Pie

serves 8

(illustrated on page 135)

Hot Water Crust Pastry made with 12oz (350g) flour, 4oz (125g) fat, etc (page 113)
1lb (450g) boneless bacon joint (mild), soaked overnight then drained and diced
12oz (350g) stewing pork, diced
2 level tbsp chopped parsley
Finely grated peel and juice of ½ medium lemon
Freshly milled black pepper to taste
Beaten egg for glazing
½pt (275ml) liquid aspic jelly
4 lemon slices, halved
Parsley

1 Cut off one-quarter of the pastry. Put into a bowl, cover, and leave over a pan of hot water to keep warm.
2 Roll out rest of pastry and use to line the inside of a 2lb (1kg) oblong loaf tin. Make sure pastry is even and that there are no thin patches. Allow pastry to hang about ½in (1.25cm) over top edge of tin all the way round.
3 Mix all filling ingredients well together. Spoon into pastry-lined tin.
5 Roll reserved piece of pastry into a strip

measuring 24 x 1in (60 x 2.5cm). Cut this strip, in turn, into 3 narrow strips. Plait. Fold overhanging edges of pastry over meat filling. Brush with beaten egg. Place plait on top (around edges). Brush with more egg.
6 Cover open top with foil. Bake 15 minutes just above centre of oven (any position in fan oven) set to 450°F (230°C), Gas 8. Reduce temperature to 325°F (160°C), Gas 3.
7 Continue to bake a further 2-2½ hours or until meat is tender. Remove from tin with care, when cold, then pour in aspic jelly until it covers the meat.
8 When aspic has half set, top with lemon slices then refrigerate until completely set. Garnish with lemon and parsley. Cut into slices. Serve with salad.

Choux Pastry

See Chapter 5.

Rough Puff Pastry

A kind of compromise pastry which slots in somewhere between a very light Shortcrust and Flaky, or, depending on opinion, between Flaky and Puff. It is less complex to make than the other member of its family and useful if you want a flaky-type pastry without going to too much trouble.

8oz (225g) plain flour
Pinch salt
6oz (175g) mixture of butter or margarine with lard or cooking fat (cold)
¼pt (150ml) well-chilled water
1 tsp lemon juice (which gives pastry greater elasticity and, in consequence, more puff)

1 Sift flour and salt into bowl. Add fats. Using a round-topped knife cut into dry ingredients until they are in squares about half the size of sugar cubes.
2 Mix together water and lemon juice. Stir into flour and fat mixture with knife, taking care not to cut the fat into very small pieces or pastry will not puff.
3 Gather together with fingertips and shape

115

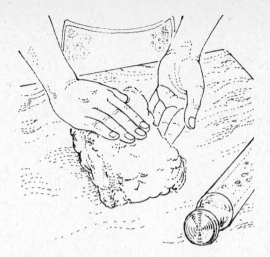

Rough Puff: *a* Stir liquid into flour and fat with a knife

b Shape into a block and roll into an oblong

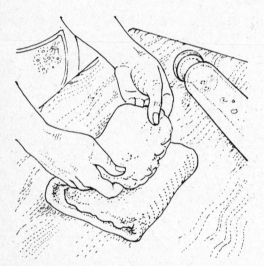

c Fold in three like an envelope

d Seal edges

into a block on a surface coated with flour. Roll out into an oblong measuring about 12 x 6in (30 x 15cm).

4 Fold in 3 like an envelope, seal edges by pressing firmly down with the rolling pin, then turn pastry round (*never over*) so that sealed edges are top and bottom and folds are to the left and right.

5 Re-roll into the same sized oblong as before, then fold in three. Put onto a plate, transfer to the refrigerator, cover loosely and leave to relax 30 minutes.

6 Repeat re-rolling and folding twice more, resting pastry in the refrigerator for 15 minutes each time. Before using, roll out to ½in (1.25cm) in thickness and trim away edges with a sharp knife. Use for covering sweet and savoury Pies, Sausage Rolls, Turnovers and Pasties.

Rough Puff Pastry also makes an unusual Pizza base. *Please note* that Rough Puff Pastry should be baked on a dampened tray.

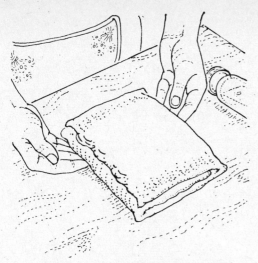

e Turn pastry so that sealed edges are top and bottom, with folds to left and right

Mishaps

See Flaky Pastry (page 119).

Puffy Cheese Straws

makes 20
(illustrated on page 154)

Rough Puff Pastry as made on page 115
1 Grade 3 egg, beaten
4oz (125g) Cheddar cheese, finely grated
1 level tsp powder mustard

1 Roll out pastry on lightly floured work surface to about ½in (1.25cm) in thickness. Turn over.
2 Brush floury side with egg then sprinkle with cheese and mustard, mixed well together.
3 Fold in half and press down all over with a rolling pin. Roll out fairly thinly. Cut into 20 x ¼in (75mm) widths. Twist the straws then put on to dampened baking tray.
4 Bake about 5-7 minutes near top of oven (any position in fan oven) set to 450°F (230°C), Gas 8.
5 Transfer to a wire cooling rack. Store in an airtight tin when cold.

Flaky Pastry

You need patience and a light touch to achieve delicate, flaky pastry but if you follow directions carefully, you should succeed. And if you do, real puff should prove no more problematic.

6oz (175g) mixture butter or margarine and lard or white cooking fat, at kitchen temperature
8oz (225g) plain flour
Pinch salt
¼pt (150ml) well-chilled water combined with 2 tsp lemon juice (for greater elasticity and consequently more flakiness)
Extra flour

1 Mash together both kinds of fat and divide equally into four portions. Put three onto a plate and refrigerate temporarily.
2 Sift flour and salt into a bowl. Add fourth portion of fat. Cut into dry ingredients with round-topped knife then rub in lightly with fingertips.
3 Mix together water and lemon juice. Pour over rubbed-in ingredients in one go. Using the same knife, draw together to form a fairly soft dough.
4 Turn out onto a surface sprinkled with flour and knead lightly until smooth. Roll

Flaky: *a* Put three of the four fat portions on a plate and refrigerate temporarily

117

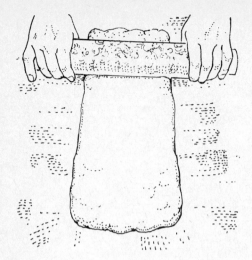

b Roll pastry out into a long strip

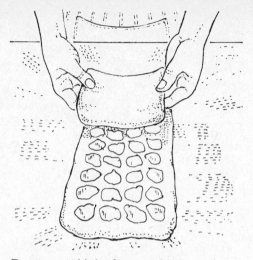

c Dot top two-thirds of pastry with the second portion of fat (from the refrigerator) and sprinkle with flour

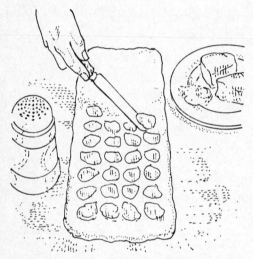

d Place bottom third over centre third

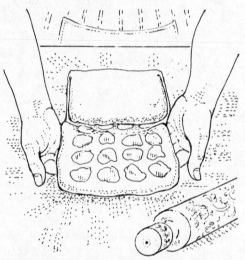

e Bring top third over and seal edges well together

out into a long strip measuring 18 x 6in (45 x 15cm). Keep edges straight.

5 Using a round-topped knife, dot top two-thirds of pastry with small pats of fat, using all of the second portion. Sprinkle lightly with flour. Fold pastry in three, like an envelope, by placing bottom third over centre third and bringing top third over. Press edges well together to seal.

6 Put pastry onto a floured plate inside a polythene bag. Refrigerate 30 minutes.

7 Re-roll into same sized strip as before, then cover the top two-thirds with third portion of fat. Sprinkle with flour. Fold, seal and refrigerate 30 minutes.

8 Roll out again, cover with last portion of fat then re-fold and relax a further 30 minutes. Finally, re-roll and re-fold, and refrigerate 30 minutes. Roll out to 1/4-1/2in (75-125mm) in thickness, trim away edges with a sharp knife and use for Sausage Rolls, covering Pies, Pasties and Turn-

overs. *Please note* that Flaky Pastry should be baked on a dampened tray.

Mishaps

Pastry tough and not as layered or as light as expected

1 Not enough fat in proportion to flour.
2 Pastry over-handled; it needs a light touch after the fat has been added in pats.
3 Pastry made too wet initially.
4 Oven too cool.

Pastry not flaky enough

1 Fats runny and/or lemon juice not included.
2 Pastry rolled too heavily.
3 Pastry not left to relax long enough in the refrigerator between rollings.
4 Baking tray not dampened sufficiently with water.
5 Cut edges stuck together by being brushed with egg or milk, and therefore unable to separate into flakes during baking.
6 Oven too cool.

Pastry dark brown outside and undercooked inside

1 Oven temperature too high.
2 Pastry placed too near top of oven.
3 Pastry undercooked at too high a temperature.

Pastry shrinks whilst baking

1 Pastry rolled too much and stretched.
2 Pastry not left long enough to rest in refrigerator between rollings.
3 Oven temperature not high enough.

Fat seeps out

1 Pastry made too soft initially by the addition of too much water.
2 Fats too soft.
3 Pastry unevenly rolled and folded.
4 Oven too cool.

Pastry rises unevenly and looks lop-sided

1 Pastry rolled and folded unevenly.
2 Fat distributed unevenly.
3 Sides not straight and corners not square when rolling out.
4 Edges not cut away from pastry before using.
5 Pastry not allowed to relax for long enough before being rolled out.
6 Cut sides brushed unevenly with egg and therefore flakes stuck together during baking.

Cream Slices

makes 8

Flaky Pastry, made as directed on page 117.
¼pt (150ml) double cream beaten until thick with 1 tbsp milk
6 level tbsp jam
Icing
8oz (225g) icing sugar, sifted
7-8 tsp warm water
½ tsp vanilla essence

1 Roll out pastry into a 16 x 4in (40 x 10cm) strip and cut into 8 pieces, each 4 x 2in (10 x 5cm).
2 Arrange on wetted baking tray and leave to relax in a cool place for 30 minutes.
3 About 7 minutes before baking, set oven to 450°F (230°C), Gas 8. Bake slices 15-20 minutes towards top of oven (any position in fan oven).
4 Cool on a wire rack. When completely cold, split each into 3 and sandwich together with beaten cream and milk, and jam.
5 Mix sugar with water to a thickish icing, flavour with vanilla essence and spread over tops of Cream Slices.

Chicken Vol-au-Vents

makes 8

Always welcome at parties and for meal starters, these are easily made with homemade

Flaky Pastry or frozen and thawed puff. My directions are for homemade Pastry.

Flaky Pastry made as described on page 117
Beaten egg for brushing

Filling
1oz (25g) butter or margarine
1oz (25g) plain flour
½pt (275ml) milk
12oz (350g) cold cooked chicken, diced
Salt and pepper to taste

1 Roll out pastry to ¼in (75mm) in thickness and cut into 16 rounds with a 3in (7.5cm) plain biscuit cutter.
2 Remove centres of 8 rounds with a 2in (5cm) cutter and reserve for lids.
3 Dampen edges of uncut pastry rounds with water, then top with pastry rings. Tap gently all the way round each with the back of a knife to increase flakiness.
4 Stand the rounds on dampened baking tray with lids beside the vol-au-vents. Brush carefully with beaten egg. Take care not to let it run down sides of cases or the pastry won't rise evenly.
5 Bake until crisp and golden brown, allowing 10-15 minutes near top of oven (any position in fan oven) set to 450°F (230°C), Gas 8.
6 While pastry is cooking, prepare filling. Melt butter or margarine in a saucepan. Stir in flour to form a roux. Cook 1 minute without browning.
7 Gradually blend in milk. Cook, stirring, until sauce comes to boil and thickens. Add chicken. Allow to bubble for 10 minutes. Season.
8 Remove vol-au-vents from oven. Fill with hot chicken mixture. Top with lids and serve, allowing 1 per person as a starter, or 2 as a main course.

Prawn Vol-au-Vents
makes 8
Make exactly as Chicken Vol-au-Vents, but add 8oz (225g) peeled prawns to sauce instead of chicken, and heat through for 2 minutes. Season. If prawns are frozen, defrost before using.

Mushroom Vol-au-Vents
makes 8
Make exactly as Chicken Vol-au-Vents, but omit the chicken, and when making sauce, fry 4oz (125g) sliced mushrooms in the butter or margarine before adding flour.

Smoked Haddock Vol-au-Vents
makes 8
Make exactly as Chicken Vol-au-Vents, but omit the chicken, and add 8oz (225g) cooked and flaked smoked haddock to sauce and heat through for 4 minutes. Season.

Party Vol-au-Vent
serves 4-8
This is a large Vol-au-Vent that can be filled with any one of the fillings previously given and then cut into wedges. Four pieces make a substantial main course; eight are adequate as a meal starter.

Roll out Flaky (page 117) or Puff Pastry to 1in (2.5cm) in thickness and, using a plate as a guide, mark a 7in (17.5cm) circle on top of pastry. Cut out into a round with a sharp knife dipped in warm water. Turn pastry over completely and stand it upside down on a wetted baking tray. Using a 4in (10cm) plate or saucer, outline a ring on the centre of the pastry, then cut halfway down through pastry, so that centre portion — the lid — is later easy to remove. Brush with egg (but *not* sides) and bake 15 minutes just above centre of oven (any position in fan oven) set to 450°F (230°C), Gas 8. Reduce temperature to 375°F (190°C), Gas 5 and bake a further 20 minutes. Remove lid, spoon out soft pastry from inside shell then return both lid and case to oven for a further 10 minutes to dry out. Fill and serve.

Puff Pastry

The trickiest one of the lot and, unless one has a certain amount of expertise and a special way with pastry, it is best bought frozen or ready-made to roll out. However, for those

Puff: Stand block of butter on one half of pastry

Bring over uncovered half of pastry to enclose butter, and press dampened edges to seal

willing to have a try, this is the standard recipe and please do not substitute margarine for butter as the flavour will be spoiled.

8oz (225g) unsalted butter, at kitchen temperature and slightly softened

8oz (225g) strong plain white flour

½ level tsp salt

¼pt (150ml) water mixed with 2 tsp lemon juice and chilled

1 Keep 2oz (50g) butter, cut from whole piece, aside for the moment.

2 Sift flour and salt together into a bowl. Rub in reserved fat with fingertips. Using a round-topped knife, mix to a soft dough with chilled water and lemon juice. Draw together with fingertips.

3 Turn out onto a floured surface and knead until smooth, crack-free and fairly elastic. Roll into an oblong measuring 12 x 6in (30 x 15cm).

4 Press remaining butter between hands into a block of about ¾in (2cm) in thickness. Stand the block on one half of the pastry, leaving ½in (1.25cm) edge of pastry uncovered all the way round the butter.

5 Dampen edges with water then enclose butter by bringing uncovered piece of pastry over covered piece and pressing edges well together to seal.

6 Put onto a plate, cover loosely with foil and refrigerate 30 minutes to give pastry a chance to rest and relax.

7 Place on a floured surface with fold on left or right. Roll into an oblong measuring 18 x 6in (45 x 15cm), keeping edges as straight as possible.

8 Fold in 3 like an envelope. Return to plate. Cover. Refrigerate a further 30 minutes. Repeat 6 more times, resting in between, to give the flaky layers so characteristic of Puff Pastry.

9 After resting for the last time, roll out as specified in the recipe and use for Vol-au-Vents, Cream Horns, Cream Slices, Mille Feuilles ('a thousand leaves') and an assortment of fancy cakes. Bake on a dampened tray.

Notes It is important to roll with slight pressure but not heavily, using forward movements all the time. Do not press down too hard or you will knock all the air out of the pastry.

Mishaps

See Flaky Pastry (page 119).

121

Oil Shortcrust Pastry

Useful for those who need to watch their fat intake, oil pastry is well worth making for savoury dishes, but it does need careful handling.

8oz (225g) plain flour
½ level tsp salt
5 tbsp any salad oil except olive
2 tbsp cold water

1 Sift flour and salt onto a plate.
2 Pour oil and water into a bowl and whisk until well blended.
3 Using a fork, add flour and stir to form a pastry.
4 Draw together with fingertips and shape into a ball. Place between two sheets of non-stick parchment paper or lightly floured foil.
5 Roll out fairly thinly and use as required, but please work with care as pastry is declicate and sometimes breaks.

All-in-One-Pastry

A Blue Band margarine 'special' developed in their test kitchens many years ago, this easy pastry works like a charm with no rubbing-in required!

6oz (175g) plain flour
4oz (125g) easy cream margarine
1 tbsp water

1 Sift flour onto a plate. Put margarine into bowl with two tbsp flour and the water.
2 Using a fork, beat for ½ minute or until well-creamed.
3 Still with a fork, stir in rest of flour to form a fairly firm dough. Foil-wrap and rest in the refrigerator for half an hour before rolling out and using.

Curd Cheese Pastry

A relic, I believe, from the Austro-Hungarian Empire, this is a truly imperial, unusual pastry which melts in the mouth with a light flakiness. Rich, buttery, and quite delicious, it can be used for sweet and savoury dishes and, when curd cheese is unavailable, substitute cottage cheese rubbed through a fine sieve.

4oz (125g) plain flour
Pinch of salt
4oz (125g) butter, taken from the refrigerator
4oz (125g) curd or cottage cheese, the latter rubbed through a fine-mesh sieve of metal or nylon.

1 Sift flour and salt into a bowl. Add butter. Cut into flour until it is in pieces the size of baby peas.
2 Add cheese. Using a fork, stir until pastry forms large crumbles. Draw together with fingertips to form a ball.
3 Wrap in cling film or foil and refrigerate 2-3 hours. Roll out fairly thinly (but just a little thicker than Shortcrust) and use as required for Pies, Turnovers, Sausage Rolls and Biscuits for cheese.

My Own Mock Flaky Pastry

I made this funny combination many years ago and always used it for individual chicken or fish pies. Purists shudder at my use of self-raising flour and cream for mixing, but it was, and still is, a delicious pastry.

8oz (225g) self-raising flour
1 level tsp salt
6oz (175g) butter, margarine, lard or cooking fat (or mixture of fats)
7 tbsp cream for mixing or use Channel Islands milk if preferred.

1 Sift flour and salt into bowl. Add fat. Cut fairly coarsely into dry ingredients with round-topped knife.
2 Add cream (or milk) *in one go* then draw together with knife to form a paste made up of large crumbles.
3 Pat into a ball, wrap in film or foil and chill for 1 hour before rolling out ¼in (75mm) in thickness.
4 Use for Pies, Turnovers, Sausage Rolls

and Pasties. Bake at the same temperature as Shortcrust Pastry.

Strudel Pastry

Although this characteristically paper-thin pastry can be bought ready-made, it is quite a challenge to tackle it for oneself. Use it for Strudels, some of those complicated Greek cakes which call for Phyllo (also Filo) pastry, Ravioli and (patience permitting) Ribbon Noodles. I have been using this versatile egg-less version for a very long time — it gives first-rate results.

8oz (225g) strong plain white flour
Pinch salt
4 tbsp salad oil (I use corn or sunflower)
1 tsp lemon juice
¼pt (150ml) tepid water

1 Sift flour and salt into a bowl. Make a dip in the centre. Pour in all remaining ingredients.
2 Work together with a fork to a soft dough.
3 Turn out onto a floured surface and knead a good 20-30 minutes or until pastry is smooth, elastic in consistency and no longer sticky.
4 If preferred, knead by passing from one floured hand to the other, pulling and stretching, concertina-fashion, as you do so.
5 If pastry remains sticky, work in a little extra flour. Pat into a ball, then transfer to a lightly oiled bowl. Cover. Leave to rest in the warmth of the kitchen for about 30 minutes.
6 Meanwhile, cover a table or work surface with a brightly coloured cloth (I keep an old tablecloth especially for this purpose) then dust it heavily with flour.
7 Put the rested pastry in the middle, and, with a well-floured rolling pin, roll out as thinly as possible until the pattern of the cloth begins to show through the middle of the pastry.
8 At this point, the pastry should be in the

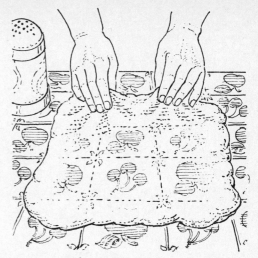

Roll out until the pattern of the cloth shows through the pastry

shape of a rough square with fairly thickish edges. Now begin to pull gently in all directions to stretch the pastry still further and make it literally paper thin and very large.
9 Because this pastry is fairly elastic and pliable, the pulling and stretching is fairly easy to do but does require a certain amount of patience. Tears might occur, and, if they do, simply patch up with scraps of dampened pastry.
10 Cut off any thick edges that remain so that the square is fairly even in shape. Follow by making a 'hem' all the way round by folding in ½in (1.25cm) of pastry. Now you can add filling to taste to make fruit or cream-cheese Strudels.

Apple Strudel

serves 8-12

Belonging both to Hungary (where it is known as Retes) and Austria, this is a splendid cake-cum-pudding which is at its best served warm with whipped cream or ice cream.

Strudel Pastry as made above

Filling

4oz (125g) butter, melted

2 rounded tbsp fresh white or brown
breadcrumbs

2 level tbsp ground almonds

2lb (900g) peeled cooking apples, cored and
very thinly sliced

2 level tsp cinnamon

2oz (50g) sultanas

3oz (75g) light-brown soft sugar

4 level tbsp flaked almonds, lightly toasted

Icing sugar

1 Roll out Strudel Pastry very thinly into a
3ft (1m) square and turn over edges to
make hem number one.

2 Brush thickly with butter then sprinkle
with crumbs and almonds to absorb some
of the juice from the apples.

3 Cover with apple slices then sprinkle with
cinnamon, sultanas, sugar and almonds.
Trickle more butter over the top. Fold
edges over filling to make hem number two
then, with the help of the cloth, roll up
Strudel, tipping it carefully on to a large
greased baking tray.

4 Curve into a horseshoe shape and brush
thickly with more butter. Bake just above
centre of oven (any position in fan oven)
set to 375°F (190°C), Gas 5.

5 Remove from oven and brush with any
butter that is left. Sift icing sugar thickly
over the top, leave until just warm then cut
into slices and serve.

Cherry Strudel

serves 8-12

Use 2lb (900g) halved and stoned Morello
cherries instead of the apples. Increase sugar
by 1oz (25g).

Black Cherry Strudel

serves 8-12

Make as Cherry Strudel, using 2lb (900g)
halved and stoned black cherries.

Cream Cheese Strudel

serves 8-12

This is completely fruitless (apart from some

raisins), and the cheese mixture is spread
over pastry like a filling and then the Strudel
is rolled up. These are the filling ingredients:

1lb (450g) curd cheese or sieved cottage
cheese

3 level tsp cornflour

3oz (75g) caster sugar

2 Grade 3 eggs, beaten

1 carton (5oz or 142ml) soured cream

2oz (50g) butter, melted

1 tsp vanilla essence

½ level tsp finely grated lemon peel

2oz (50g) seedless raisins

1 Beat cheese until smooth then mix in all
remaining ingredients.

2 Spread over the pastry.

Curd Tarts

makes 12

Another version of Maids of Honour, which
were first made in Hampton Court during the
reign of Henry VIII. This is an adaptation of
the so-called original recipe.

1 small packet (about 7oz or 200g) frozen
puff pastry, thawed or homemade (page
120)

4oz (125g) curd cheese

3oz (75g) butter, at kitchen temperature
and softened

2 Grade 3 eggs, beaten

2oz (50g) ground almonds

1 oz (25g) cake crumbs (Madeira or trifle
sponge)

1 tbsp brandy

2oz (50g) caster sugar

1 level tsp finely grated lemon peel

About 1oz (25g) currants

1 Roll out pastry thinly, cut into rounds
with a 2½in (6cm) cutter and use to line
12 bun tins.

2 For filling, put cheese into a bowl then
gradually beat in butter, eggs, almonds,
cake crumbs, brandy, sugar and lemon
peel.

3 Spoon equal amounts into lined bun tins, sprinkle with currants and bake 20-25 minutes in centre of oven (any position in fan oven) set to 425°F (220°C), Gas 7. Remove from tins and cool on a wire rack. Filling will drop slightly but this is in order.

Jalousie

serves 6

The French version of Jam Tart.

1 large packet (13oz or 375g) frozen puff pastry, thawed or homemade (page 120)
4 rounded tbsp jam to taste
Beaten egg for brushing
Caster sugar for sprinkling

1 Cut the pastry into 2 portions and roll each out into a rectangle measuring 8 x 6in (20 x 15cm). Spread jam lengthwise down one piece, leaving edges clear. Dampen edges.
2 Make ½in (1.25cm) slits in second piece of pastry, parallel to the narrow edges and leaving a 1in (2.5cm) margin uncut all the way round.
3 Place pastry with slits on top of pastry with jam and press edges well together to seal. Carefully transfer to wetted baking tray and leave to stand in a cool place for 15 minutes.
4 Brush with egg, sprinkle with sugar then bake about 25 minutes near top of oven (any position in fan oven) set to 425°F (220°C), Gas 7.
5 Leave 5 minutes, carefully transfer to a wire rack and cut into portions when just cold. Eat when freshly made.

Jalousie with Fruit Pie Filling
serves 6
Make as above but use fruit pie filling instead of jam.

Cream Horns

makes 12

1 large packet (13oz or 375g) frozen puff pastry, thawed or homemade Flaky Pastry (page 117)
1 Grade 4 egg, beaten
Caster sugar for sprinkling
12 rounded tsp red jam
½pt (275ml) double cream, whipped with 2 tbsp milk
2 level tbsp caster sugar
1 tsp vanilla essence

1 Roll out pastry and cut into 12 long strips, each about 1in (2.5cm) in width by 12in (30cm) in length.
2 Dampen one side of each strip with water, and wind round cream horn tins, starting from the pointed ends. Overlap pastry as you wind, so that no gaps show. Break off any leftover pastry at the top of the tins.
3 Transfer to a large wetted baking tray, brush with egg and sprinkle with sugar. Leave in the cool for 30 minutes.
4 About 7 minutes before baking, set oven to 425°F (220°C), Gas 7. Put tray of Cream Horns into oven, 1 shelf above centre (any position in fan oven) and bake about 20-25 minutes or until deep gold and puffy.
5 Transfer to a wire cooling rack and leave until almost cold. Remove tins carefully and leave Cream Horns to cool completely.
6 Before serving, drop a teaspoon of jam into the bottom of each then fill with the cream, sweetened with sugar and flavoured with essence.

Savoury Cream Horns
makes 12
Brush Cream Horns with egg but no sugar. While still hot, remove tins carefully and fill the horns with the fillings given for Vol-au-Vents (page 120).

Wensleydale Apple Puffs

makes 6
(illustrated on page 155)

1 small cooking apple, peeled, cored and
   sliced
1 tbsp water
3oz (75g) Wensleydale cheese, grated
1/4 level tsp ground cinnamon or cloves
1 1/2 tsp demerara sugar
1 small packet (7oz or 200g) frozen puff
   pastry, thawed or Curd Cheese Pastry
   (page 122)
2 tbsp lemon curd
Beaten egg for brushing
1/4pt (150ml) fresh double cream, whipped

1 Cook the apple with the water until pulpy.
  Remove from heat. Stir in the cheese,
  cinnamon or cloves and 1 tbsp of the sugar.
2 Roll out the pastry into a rectangle 12 x 8in
  (30 x 20cm). Cut into six 4in (10cm)
  squares. Spread some lemon curd over
  each, then spoon the apple mixture on top
  leaving a border round each edge. Brush
  the edges with egg and fold pastry over
  to form triangles. Press down the edges to
  seal, then knock up with the back of a
  knife. Place on a wetted baking tray, chill
  for half an hour.
3 Brush each puff with egg and sprinkle
  remaining sugar over. Make a small slit in
  the centre of each. Bake in preheated oven
  at 400°F (200°C), Gas 6 for 25-30 minutes
  or until well risen and golden brown.
4 When cold, carefully open puffs along the
  edges and fill with whipped cream. An
  easier alternative is to top the puffs with
  cream, instead of filling them. See also
  Fruit Turnovers, Chapter 12.

Eccles Cakes

makes 8
(illustrated on page 165)

1 small packet (7oz or 200g) frozen puff
   pastry, thawed or homemade Rough Puff,
   Flaky or My Own Flaky Pastry (pages 115,
   117, 122)

1oz (25g) butter
1oz (25g) currants
1oz (25g) mixed chopped peel
2 level tsp light brown soft sugar
1/2 level tsp mixed spice
Milk for brushing
Caster sugar for sprinkling

1 Roll out pastry thinly and cut into 8 rounds
  with a 3in (7.5cm) biscuit cutter. Refrigerate temporarily.
2 Melt butter in a pan and remove from heat.
  Stir in currants, peel, sugar and spice.
3 Lay out pastry rounds and put a heaped
  tsp of filling on to centre of each. Moisten
  edges of pastry with water, then bring
  together at the centre, completely enclosing filling.
4 Pinch edges well together to seal, then roll
  lightly to flatten to 1/2in (1.25cm) in thickness.
5 Transfer to wetted baking tray with joins
  underneath, then make 3 cuts on top of
  each with a sharp knife.
6 Brush with milk, sprinkle with caster
  sugar and bake 20 minutes just above
  centre of oven (any position in fan oven)
  set to 425°F (220°C), Gas 7. Cool on a wire
  rack and eat when freshly made.

Cherry and Chocolate Puff Slice

serves 8-10
(illustrated on page 156)

A sweet, rich pastry confection for high days
and holidays.

1 packet (13oz or 375g) frozen puff pastry,
   thawed
8oz (225g) homemade or shop-bought
   marzipan or almond paste
3oz (75g) desiccated coconut
3oz (75g) glacé cherries, chopped
2 Grade 3 egg whites, lightly beaten until
   just foamy
8 flake bars from family pack
A few tsp caster sugar

1 Roll out pastry into a rectangle measuring 12 x 10in (30 x 25cm). On sugared surface, roll marzipan or almond paste out into a slightly smaller rectangle and place on top of pastry.

2 Mix together the coconut, cherries and enough egg white to bind mixture together. Leave a little white for brushing.

3 Spread over marzipan or almond paste. Arrange flake bars, in pairs, down the centre. Moisten pastry edges with water, then fold the two long sides together and seal well. Also close both ends by pinching together.

4 Place on dampened baking tray. Brush with egg white, sprinkle with sugar, then mark diagonal lines on top with the back of a knife.

5 Bake 15 to 20 minutes just above centre of oven (any position in fan oven) set to 425°F (220°C), Gas 7. The Slice is ready when it is well-puffed and golden brown.

6 Cool on a wire rack and cut into slices when cold.

Sausage Rolls

makes 18
(illustrated on page 165)

9oz (250g) plain flour
Pinch of salt
4½oz (140g) soft lard
A little beaten egg for glazing
1lb (450g) pork or beef sausagemeat

1 Sift flour and salt into a bowl, add the fat straight from the refrigerator and rub in finely.

2 Stir in sufficient cold water to make a fairly soft but not sticky dough, then wrap in greaseproof paper. Leave in a cool place while preparing sausagemeat.

3 Cut the sausagemeat into 3 equal pieces and roll each into a 12in (30cm) length, using plenty of flour to prevent sticking.

4 Roll out pastry into a 14 x 12in (35 x 30cm) rectangle, then cut into 3 pieces, each 12in (20cm) in length.

5 Place a 12in (30cm) roll of sausagemeat on to each piece of pastry, dampen edges with water and fold pastry over.

6 Press edges well together to seal then cut each roll into 6 pieces.

7 Put on to greased baking tray and brush with beaten egg.

8 Bake about 35-40 minutes just above oven centre (any position in fan oven) set to 400°F (200°C), Gas 6.

9 Cool on a wire rack and serve while still warm.

Hasty Pizza

serves 4-6
(illustrated on page 165)

6oz (175g) self-raising flour
Pinch of salt
2oz (50g) soft lard
1 Grade 2 egg
A little milk
2 large tomatoes
1 level tsp dried rosemary
Salt and pepper to taste
4oz (125g) Cheddar cheese, grated
4oz (125g) streaky bacon rashers
Stuffed green olives

1 Sift flour and salt into a bowl. Add the lard straight from the refrigerator and rub in.

2 Mix to a soft but not sticky dough with egg and milk.

3 Turn dough onto a lightly floured surface, knead it quickly until smooth then shape into a 9in (22.5cm) round.

4 Lift onto a baking tray, arrange the tomatoes over the surface and sprinkle with the herbs and some seasoning.

5 Scatter over the cheese, lattice the bacon across the top and arrange half an olive in each space.

6 Bake the Pizza for 25 minutes near top of oven (any position in fan oven) set to 425°F (220°C), Gas 7. Serve straight away.

8
Scones

Scones (also pronounced Skons, depending on which part of the British Isles you come from, and known as biscuits in the United States) are described in Chambers *Twentieth Century Dictionary* as 'a flattish, usually round or quadrant-shaped plain cake or dough without much butter, with or without currants, baked on a girdle or in an oven'. Nothing about their moist, light and soft texture, their longstanding friendship with clotted cream and jam, and the problems these delicious little cakes-cum-bread-cum-biscuits can cause if they are wrongly handled. And here I would take the dictionary to task because two types of scones have been lumped together; baked scones should *not* be flattish. Those cooked on a girdle (also called griddle) are nothing more than pancakes — indeed many of you will know them as Scotch pancakes; these are only about ¼in (75mm) thick. Baked scones are a different matter altogether and the aim of every cook is to get them to double or even treble their ½-1in (1.25-2.5cm) height in the oven; anything else is a total letdown. Yet I know many of you end up with dry, hard, lopsided and brick-like victims and puzzle over the fact that your efforts lack the tall, bronzed and handsome image that is the birthright of every self-respecting scone.

Maybe, as requested by so many of you throughout nearly all my writing life, I can put you on the right track at last and tell you how a ½in (1.25cm) scone can reach the giddy heights of all of 1½in (4cm).

Ingredients

Flour

Use either plain flour plus baking powder (approximately 4 level tsp to every 8oz or 225g) *or* self-raising flour. White or brown flour may be used, depending on preference.

Salt

An optional extra but, if using, add 1 level tsp to every 8oz (225g) flour for sweet scones; 1½ level tsp for savoury scones.

Fats

Here I go along with the dictionary — scones are not rich in fat, and you need no more than 1-2oz (25-50g) to every 8oz (225g) flour. Butter or margarine gives the best flavour.

Sugar

Obviously this is added only to sweet scones; use either caster or light-brown soft sugar.

Liquid

Milk is the most usual and any type may be used. Skimmed milk gives the lightest results.

Method

Speed is of the essence in scone-making, because the faster you work, the lighter the scones will be.

1 Grease and flour the baking tray or whatever ovenware is recommended in the recipe, then pre-heat oven (not necessary for certain types of newer ovens; and in fan oven position of shelf does not matter) to suggested temperature; usually 450°F (230°C), Gas 8.

2 Sift dry ingredients into a bowl. Rub in fat, which should be soft but not runny, with fingertips. Toss in sugar and any other addition suggested in the recipe such as fruit.

3 Now add the cold liquid *all in one go*, working the mixture to a soft, but not sticky, dough with a round-topped knife.

4 Turn out onto a well-floured surface and knead quickly and lightly until smooth. Roll out to thickness given in the recipe, then cut out as directed with a cutter dipped in flour to prevent it snagging the dough. Transfer to baking tray.

5 Brush with milk or egg, place near top of oven (again any position in fan oven), and bake until well-risen and golden; about 10 minutes for small to medium scones, but longer, and at a lower temperature, for a scone round. The recipe will indicate this.

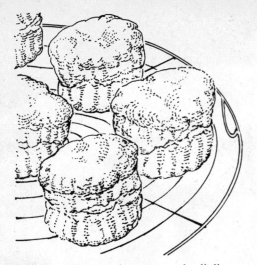

Correctly made scones have a natural split line like a waistband

6 Remove to a wire rack and please notice the natural split line which circles each scone like a waistband. This usually occurs if the scones have been made correctly and is the exact place where each one should be gently prised apart — never cut, as the texture will look doughy and uninviting.

7 Separate scones when just warm, then leave for about 10-20 minutes or until cool. Spread with fillings to taste, and whenever possible, make and eat on the same day.

8 Keep unfilled leftovers in a well-sealed polythene bag or airtight tin for about 24 hours. Re-heat briefly in a warm oven before serving.

Mishaps

Scones unevenly risen (lopsided)

1 Mixture uneven in thickness before being cut out into shapes.
2 Knife or cutter was thrust into mixture at a slight angle so that one side of uncooked scones was deeper than the other.
3 The cutter was twisted as the scones were being cut.

Scones heavy and not well-risen

1 Not enough baking powder used with plain flour.

2 Insufficient milk added; every 1oz (25g) of flour needs about 1 tbsp of liquid.
3 Mixture over-kneaded after the milk was added.
4 Scones were left to stand on their baking tray for too long before being baked. For lightness, they should go into the even straight away.
5 Oven too cool and/or scones were not placed in a high enough position.

Scones looked dry

1 Tops not brushed with egg or milk.
2 Too much flour on the rolling pin.

Scones speckled

1 Flour and baking powder sieved unevenly or not at all.
2 Too much sugar added and/or the sugar was too coarse — for example, granulated sugar could do this.

Scones looked rough

1 Mixture too dry.
2 Mixture insufficiently kneaded.

Scones spread and lost shape

1 Too much milk added so mixture overwet.
2 Baking tray too heavily greased.
3 Again, cutter twisted when scones were being cut.
4 Mixture unevenly kneaded.

(above right) Pear Topsy-turvy Cake, page 67 *(Cadbury Typhoo)*

(below right) Danish Chocolate Meringue Pie, page 95 *(Danish Agricultural Producers)*

(overleaf, above) Chocolate Bakewell Tart, page 104 *(Cadbury Typhoo)*

(overleaf, below) Flaky Festival Gâteau, page 241 *(Cadbury Typhoo)*

132

Sweet Scones

makes 8-9

8oz (225g) self-raising flour
1 level tsp salt (optional)
1-2oz (25-50g) butter or margarine
1-2oz (25-50g) caster sugar
¼pt (150ml) cold milk
Extra milk or beaten egg for brushing

1 Well-grease and lightly flour a flat baking tray. Set oven to 450°F (230°C), Gas 8.
2 Sift flour, and salt if used, into a bowl. Add fat and rub in finely with fingertips.
3 Toss in sugar. Add milk *all at once*, then mix to a soft, but not sticky, dough with a round-topped knife.
4 Put on a floured surface and knead quickly and lightly, also with fingertips, until smooth and crackfree. Pat or roll out (with floured rolling pin) into a round of about ½in (1.25cm) in thickness.
5 Cut into 8 or 9 rounds with a 2½in (6.25cm) plain biscuit cutter, re-shaping and re-cutting trimmings to make required number of scones. Transfer to prepared tray and brush tops with milk or beaten egg. (The latter gives a golden glaze.)
6 Place near top of oven and bake until well-risen and golden brown, allowing about 8-11 minutes.
7 Remove to a wire cooling-rack and leave until almost cold. Prise gently apart along natural split line, then spread with butter or margarine.
8 Either serve as halves or sandwich together again. Accompany with jam, honey, syrup, chocolate spread or lemon or orange curd. Serve, as desired, with whipped or clotted cream.

(*previous page, above*) Pie covered with Flaky or Puff Pastry, page 105 (*McCormick Herbs & Spices*)

(*previous page, below*) Pork and Bacon Plait Pie, page 115 (*Flour Advisory Bureau*)

(*left*) Salmon and Sherry Picnic Pies, page 106 (*Canned Salmon Consumer Bureau*)

Plain Scones
makes 8-9

For sweet or savoury purposes, make exactly as previous recipe but omit sugar.

Fluted Scones
makes 8-9

Make as Sweet Scones but use a fluted biscuit cutter instead of a plain one.

Brown Scones
makes 8-9

Make as Sweet or Plain Scones but use brown flour and baking powder instead of white flour.

Half-and-Half Scones
makes 8-9

Make as Sweet or Plain Scones but use half wholemeal flour and half white flour. Use plain flour and include 4 level tsp of baking powder.

Fruit Scones
makes 8-9

Make as Sweet or Plain Scones but add 1-2oz (25-50g) seedless raisins, sultanas or currants before adding milk.

Spicy Scones
makes 8-9

Make as Sweet or Plain, Brown or Half-and-Half Scones. Sift flour or flours and salt, if used, with 2 level tsp mixed spice.

Date and Nut Scones
make 8-9

Make as Sweet or Plain Scones but toss in 2oz (50g) finely chopped dates and 1oz (25g) chopped toasted almonds before adding milk.

Cherry Lemon Scones
makes 8-9

Make as Sweet Plain Scones but toss in 2oz (50g) Chopped glacé cherries and 1 level tsp finely grated lemon peel before adding milk.

137

Ginger Orange Scones

makes 8-9

Make as Sweet or Plain Scones but sift flour and salt, if used, with 2 level tsp ground ginger. Toss in 1 level tsp finely grated orange peel before adding the milk.

Yogurt Scones

makes 8-9

Make as Sweet or Plain Scones but use 4 slightly rounded tbsp natural yogurt and 5 tbsp cold milk for mixing.

Buttermilk Scones

makes 8-9

Make as Sweet or Plain Scones but use only plain flour and sift with ½ level tsp *each* bicarbonate of soda and cream of tartar. Use buttermilk only for mixing.

Soured-cream Scones

makes 8-9

Make as Sweet or Plain Scones but use 4 slightly rounded tbsp soured cream and 5 tbsp cold milk for mixing.

Cheese Scones

makes 8-9

Make up Plain Scones but sift flour with salt, if used, and 1 level tsp powder mustard. Toss in 2oz (50g) grated Cheddar cheese before adding milk.

Cheese and Peanut Scones

makes 8-9

Make as Cheese Scones above but toss in 1oz (25g) chopped peanuts with the cheese.

Cheese and Parsley Scones

makes 8-9

Make up Plain Scones but sift flour with salt, if used, plus 1 level tsp powder mustard. Toss in 2oz (50g) grated Cheddar cheese and 2 level tbsp chopped parsley before adding milk.

Cheese and Chive Scones

makes 8-9

Make up Plain Scones but sift flour with salt, if used, plus 1 level tsp powder mustard. Toss in 2oz (50g) grated Cheddar cheese and 2 level tbsp chopped chives before adding milk.

Oat Scones

makes 8-9

Make up Plain Scones but toss in 1oz (25g) porridge oats before adding milk.

Ham and Sage Scones

makes 8-9

Make up Plain Scones but toss in 2oz (50g) chopped ham and ½ level tsp dried sage before adding milk.

Brown Cheese Scones

makes 8-9

Make exactly as Cheese Scones but use half plain brown flour, half plain white flour and baking powder.

Scone Round

serves 8

Make up any of the previous scone mixtures and pat into a 1in (2.5cm) thick round. Stand the round on a lightly greased baking tray and mark into 8 segments with the back of a knife, but do not cut right through. Brush with milk or beaten egg. Bake 15-20 minutes near top of oven (any position in fan oven), pre-heated to 425°F (220°C), Gas 7. Remove to cooling-rack and separate into wedges when cold. Split apart and fill as desired.

Sesame Scones

makes 8-9

Make up any of the previous savoury or brown-flour recipes and sprinkle with sesame seeds after brushing with milk or egg. Bake as directed.

Poppy Seed Scones

makes 8-9

Make up any of the previous savoury or brown-flour recipes and sprinkle with poppy seeds after brushing with milk or egg.

Tea Scones

makes 16

Make up any of the previous recipes then cut into about 16 rounds with a 1½in (4cm) fluted cutter, re-shaping and re-cutting trimmings to make required amount.

Scone Triangles

makes 8

Make up any of the previous Scone recipes then cut into 8 triangles instead of rounds.

Cheese Whirls

makes 10-12

Make up any of the previous savoury or brown-flour recipes. Roll out into a rectangle measuring about 8 x 12in (20 x 30cm). Cover, to within 1in (2.5cm) of edges, with 6oz (175g) grated Cheddar cheese mixed with 2 Grade 3 beaten eggs and 1 level tsp powder mustard. Roll up like a Swiss Roll, starting at one of the longer sides. Cut into 10 or 12 slices. Place the slices on a lightly greased baking tray. Bake 20 minutes near top of oven (any position in fan oven) set to 425°F (220°C), Gas 7. Cool on a wire rack but eat while still warm.

Mock Chelsea Buns

makes 10-12

Make up Sweet Scone recipe as directed on page 137. Roll out into a rectangle measuring about 8 x 12in (20 x 30cm). Brush thickly with melted butter (about 1oz or 25g) to within 1in of edges, then sprinkle with 2oz (50g) *each* of light-brown soft sugar and currants. Dust with 1 level tsp mixed spice.

Dampen edges with water. Roll up like a Swiss Roll, starting from one of the longer sides. Cut into 10 to 12 slices. Arrange close together, and in a single layer, in an 8in (20cm) well-greased, deep cake tin. Brush tops with milk or beaten egg and bake about 15-17 minutes near top of oven (any position in fan oven) set to 425°F (220°C), Gas 7. At this stage the 'buns' should be golden-brown, well risen and joined together in the tin. Leave until lukewarm, then carefully turn out onto a wire cooling-rack. Split apart while warm and eat with extra butter.

Iced Mock Chelsea Buns

makes about 10

Make exactly as previous recipe. Before serving, spread tops with a thin coating of Glacé Icing, made by mixing 4oz (125g) sifted icing sugar with a few tsp of warm water. The icing should be of spreadable consistency but not too runny.

American-style Ring Doughnuts

makes about 12

Make up Sweet Scone mixture as previously directed but sift 1 level tsp allspice with the flour and salt (if used). Pat or roll out to ½in (1.25cm) in thickness, and cut into rounds with 2in (5cm) plain biscuit cutter. Remove centres with 1in (2.5cm) cutter, then knead middles together and re-cut to make required number of rings. Fry, a few at a time, in a pan of deep hot oil. Allow 2-3 minutes and turn once with two spoons. Remove from pan and drain on crumpled paper towels. Toss in caster sugar. Serve warm with milky coffee. (In America, this is a favourite breakfast dish.)

American Cinnamon Ring Doughnuts
makes about 12

Make exactly as previous recipe but use 2 level tsp cinnamon instead of allspice.

American Berry Shortcakes

makes 4

A classic US dessert that is both simple to make and a treat to eat. Prepare Sweet Scone mixture as previously directed. Turn on to a lightly floured surface and pat out to 1in (2.5cm) in thickness. Cut into 4 rounds with a 3in (7.5cm) plain biscuit cutter. Bake 15-20 minutes near top of oven (any position in fan oven) set to 425°F (220°C), Gas 7. Cool down for about 10 minutes on a wire rack, then split apart and spread thickly with butter so that it melts into the Shortcake halves. Sandwich together with sliced and sugared strawberries, raspberries or any other soft fruit in season. Put the shortcakes on 4 plates and top each generously with mounds of whipped cream. Serve while still slightly warm.

American Peach Shortcakes

makes 4

Make as American Berry Shortcakes but use canned sliced peaches (well drained) instead of fresh berries.

American Compromise Shortcakes

makes 4

In the winter, when berry fruits are not in season, use a good-quality jam instead of fresh fruit.

Herby Bacon Scone Round

serves 8
(illustrated on page 166)

12oz (350g) self-raising flour
½ level tsp salt
3oz (75g) butter or margarine
4oz (125g) streaky bacon, grilled and finely chopped
1 level tsp mixed herbs
1 rounded tbsp chopped parsley
White pepper to taste
¼pt (150ml) cold milk
Beaten egg for brushing

1 Sift flour and salt into a bowl. Rub in butter or margarine. Toss in bacon, herbs, parsley and pepper to taste.
2 Add milk all at once then, using a fork, mix to a soft dough. Turn out on to a floured surface and knead lightly.
3 Roll or pat out to an 8in (20cm) round and mark through into 8 sections. Brush top with beaten egg.
4 Bake 30-35 minutes just above oven centre any position in fan oven) set to 400°F (200°C), Gas 6. Cool on a wire rack. While still slightly warm, separate the sections then split in half and spread with butter.

Lemony Apple Scones

makes 12
(illustrated on page 166)

8oz (225g) self-raising flour
½ level tsp salt
2oz (50g) butter or margarine
1 level tsp finely grated lemon peel
2oz (50g) caster sugar
1 medium peeled cooking apple, grated
5-6 tbsp cold milk to mix
A little beaten egg for bushing

1 Sift flour and salt into a bowl. Rub in butter or margarine finely.
2 Toss in lemon peel, sugar and apple. Using a fork, mix to a soft dough with the milk.
3 Turn out on to a floured surface and knead lightly until smooth. Pat or roll out into a round of ½in (1.25cm) in thickness.
4 Cut into 12 rounds with a 2in (5cm) biscuit cutter, re-rolling and re-cutting trimmings to make the correct number.
5 Transfer to a greased baking tray, brush tops with beaten egg and bake about 15-18 minutes near top of oven (any position in fan oven) set to 400°F (200°C), Gas 6. Cool on a wire rack then split open and spread with butter. Eat when fresh.

Norfolk Scone Slices

serves 12

(illustrated on page 166)

1lb (450g) self-raising flour
½ level tsp salt
4oz (125g) butter or margarine
2 Grade 3 eggs, beaten
¼pt (150ml) cold milk
Extra milk for brushing
Filling
1oz (25g) butter or margarine
4oz (125g) currants
½ level tsp nutmeg
4oz (125g) demerara sugar

1 Sift flour and salt into a bowl. Rub in butter or margarine finely.
2 Using a fork, mix to a soft dough with eggs and milk. Turn on to a floured surface and knead lightly until smooth.
3 Roll out into a rectangle measuring 12 x 10in (30 x 25cm). Cut in half lengthwise and spread one half with butter or margarine. Mix currants, nutmeg and 3oz (75g) sugar together.
4 Sprinkle over buttered piece of dough, moisten edges with water then cover with second piece of scone dough.
5 Place on greased baking tray, mark into 12 slices then brush with milk. Sprinkle with rest of sugar and bake 25-30 minutes near top of oven (any position in fan oven) set to 400°F (200°C), Gas 6.
6 Cool on a wire rack then cut into 12 slices. Serve when fresh.

Potato Scone Triangles

makes 8

1lb (450g) floury potatoes, peeled and washed
Boiling salted water
2oz (50g) butter or margarine
About 4oz (125g) plain flour
Melted fat for greasing

1 Cut potatoes into chunks and cook in boiling salted water for 15-20 minutes or until tender. Drain but leave in pan.
2 Add butter or margarine and mash very finely then work in the flour to make a stiff dough; a little more than the 4oz (125g) may be needed.
3 Turn out on to a floured surface and knead lightly until smooth. Roll out to ¼in (75mm) in thickness and cut into 8 large triangles.
4 Cook on a heated greased griddle or heavy-based frying pan, frying 2 or 3 at a time. Allow about 4 minutes per side and turn twice. Scones are ready when golden brown and cooked through. Serve hot with butter.

Potato Scone Rounds
makes about 10
If preferred, cut scone mixture into ten 3in (7.5cm) rounds and cook as above.

Singin' Hinnies

makes 12

Named after the noise they make while cooking, Singin' Hinnies are a delicious form of fried scone from Northumberland.

12oz (350g) self-raising flour
2oz (50g) ground rice
½ level tsp salt
2oz (50g) lard, butter or margarine
4oz (125g) currants
2oz (50g) caster sugar
½pt (275ml) rich milk or single cream

1 Sift flour, ground rice and salt into a bowl. Rub in fat finely. Toss in currants and sugar.
2 Using a fork, mix to a softish dough with milk. Roll out to about ¼in (75mm) in thickness and cut into 12 rounds with a 4in (10cm) biscuit cutter. Prick well all over.
3 Fry, a few at a time, on a hot greased griddle or in a greased and heavy-based frying pan. Keep heat moderate and allow about 5 minutes per side until Hinnies are cooked through and golden brown.
4 Split apart, spread with butter and eat warm.

Dropped Scones

makes about 15

4oz (125g) self-raising flour
Pinch salt
½oz (15g) caster sugar
1 Grade 3 egg
½oz (15g) butter or margarine, melted
6-7 tbsp milk to mix

1 Sift flour and salt into a bowl. Toss in sugar.
2 Using a fork, beat to a thick batter with unbeaten egg, the melted fat and the milk.
3 Drop tbsps of mixture on to a hot greased griddle or greased frying pan. Cook about 2 minutes or until bubbles rise to the surface and break. Turn over with a knife and cook second side until golden brown, allowing 2-3 minutes.
4 Wrap in a teatowel as they are cooked to keep warm, then serve straight away with butter or whipped cream and jam, honey, golden syrup or lemon curd.

Note These are also known as Girdle Scones, Griddle Cakes and Scotch Pancakes.

9
Biscuits

Biscuits, the ultimate in crunch, are very much a British institution, copied the world over and baked with gusto by all age groups. The appeal of biscuits (cookies in America) lies in their size and attractive shapes, their 'dunkability' and the wealth of varieties one can produce from just a handful of easy-to-make basic recipes.

Ginger and Walnut Thins

makes about 16

These are interesting in that you will get the same effect by using two different combinations of ingredients. Butter with self-raising flour produces thin, crispy biscuits which flatten as they bake; so does margarine with plain flour. The choice is yours, depending entirely on which flavour you prefer and whether you consider all-butter biscuits are extravagant.

4oz (125g) butter or margarine
2oz (50g) caster sugar
1oz (25g) walnuts, chopped
1oz (25g) crystallised ginger, chopped
½ tsp vanilla essence
4oz (125g) self-raising or plain flour

1 Cream butter or margarine with sugar until light and fluffy. Stir in walnuts and ginger.
2 Using a fork, work in essence and flour. Spoon 16 neat mounds, well apart, onto one or two lightly greased baking trays.
3 Bake about 12-15 minutes, one shelf above and one shelf below oven centre (any position in fan oven), set to 375°F (190°C), Gas 5. Reverse trays at half-time.
4 Leave on trays about 3 minutes then transfer to a wire cooling rack and leave until cold. Store in an airtight tin.

Cherry and Walnut Thins
makes about 16
Make exactly as Ginger and Walnut Thins but substitute 1oz (25g) glacé cherries for ginger.

Chocolate-chip Thins
makes about 16
Make exactly as Ginger and Walnut Thins but substitute 1oz (25g) chocolate dots for the ginger.

Raisin and Peanut Thins
makes about 16
Make exactly as Ginger and Walnut Thins but substitute 1oz (25g) raisins for the ginger and the same amount of coarsely chopped peanuts for walnuts.

Christmas Thins
makes about 16
Make exactly as Ginger and Walnut Thins but substitute 1oz (25g) chopped mixed peel for the ginger and 1oz (25g) coarsely chopped hazelnuts for walnuts.

Coffee Walnut Thins
makes about 16
Make exactly as Ginger and Walnut Thins but cream fat and sugar with 2 level tsp of instant coffee powder and include 2oz (50g) chopped walnuts.

Chocolate Nut Thins
makes about 16
Make exactly as Ginger and Walnut Thins but reduce flour by ½oz (15g) and make up with ½oz (15g) cocoa powder. Include 2oz (50g) any chopped nuts to taste.

Chocolate-speckle Thins
makes about 16
Make exactly as Ginger and Walnut Thins but substitute 1 large crushed chocolate flake bar for ginger and walnuts.

Chocolate Spice Thins
makes about 16
Make exactly as Ginger and Walnut Thins but sift flour with 1 level tsp mixed spice. Substitute 2oz (50g) milk chocolate dots for ginger and nuts.

Assorted Cookies

makes about 16

By following any of the previous recipes but using self-raising flour with margarine *or* butter with plain flour, you will have biscuits which do not flatten too much and look very much like shop-bought cookies.

Brownie Biscuits

makes 24

American in style, these biscuits are oblong in shape and quite different in character from most of the varieties. Also they are very speedy to make.

3oz (75g) plain flour
1½oz (40g) cocoa powder
½ level tsp baking powder
4oz (125g) easy-cream margarine or whipped-up white cooking fat
8oz (225g) dark-brown soft sugar
2 Grade 2 eggs
1 tsp vanilla essence

1 Well grease a large tray measuring 12 x 8in (30 x 20cm).
2 Put all ingredients into bowl. Beat until well-mixed, allowing about 4 minutes.
3 Spread evenly into prepared tin and bake 25 minutes just above oven centre (any position in fan oven) set to 350°F (180°C), Gas 4.
4 Cool 5 minutes then cut into bars. Lift onto a wire cooling rack. Store in an airtight tin when cold.

Walnut Brownie Biscuits

makes 24

Add 2-3oz (50-75g) chopped walnuts to other ingredients.

Brownie Ginger Biscuits

makes 24

Add 2-3oz (50-75g) chopped crystallised ginger to other ingredients.

Currant Oat Cookies

makes 36

4oz (125g) margarine or cooking fat
3oz (75g) light-brown soft sugar
3oz (75g) caster sugar
1 Grade 3 egg
1 tsp vanilla essence
1 tbsp single cream
4oz (125g) currants
4oz (125g) self-raising flour, sifted
3oz (75g) porridge oats

1 Cream margarine or cooking fat with both sugars until light and fluffy.
2 Beat in egg, essence and cream. Fork in currants, flour and oats.
3 Place 36 mounds of mixture, well apart to allow for spreading, onto 2 large greased baking trays.
4 Bake 1 shelf above and 1 shelf below oven centre (any position in fan oven) set to 350°F (180°C), Gas 4. Allow 15-17 minutes or until light brown. Reverse trays at half-time.
5 Cool 5 minutes then lift onto a wire cooling rack. Store in an airtight tin when cold.

Date Oat Cookies

makes 36

Make exactly as Currant Oat Cookies adding 4oz (125g) chopped dates instead of currants.

Figgy Oat Cookies

makes 36

Make exactly as Currant Oat Cookies adding 4oz (125g) chopped dried figs instead of currants.

Fruity Oat Cookies

makes 36

Make exactly as Currant Oat Cookies adding 4oz (125g) dried fruit instead of currants.

Spicy Oat and Nut Cookies

makes 36

Make exactly as Currant Oat Cookies sifting flour with 1½ level tsp cinnamon and adding 2oz (50g) chopped walnuts instead of fruit.

Chocolate Oat Cookies
makes 36
Make exactly as Currant Oat Cookies but add
4oz (125g) chocolate dots instead of currants.

Crispy Mocha Biscuits

makes 30

Marvellous for those who need to bake with
oil instead of any form of solid fat.

4oz (125g) plain flour
1oz (25g) cocoa powder
¾ level tsp baking powder
2 level tsp instant coffee powder
4oz (125g) caster sugar
5 tbsp salad oil
½ tsp vanilla essence
1 Grade 2 egg

1 Sift flour, cocoa, baking powder and instant coffee into a bowl.
2 Beat sugar with oil, essence and egg. Using
   a fork, stir into dry ingredients.
3 Shape into 30 even-sized balls and place on
   to 2 oiled baking trays, leaving room
   between each for spreading.
4 Flatten each with a fork dipped in caster
   sugar, then bake one shelf above and one
   shelf below oven centre (any position in
   fan oven) set to 375°F (190°C), Gas 5.
   Allow about 12-15 minutes, reversing
   position of trays at half-time.
5 Leave for 5 minutes then remove carefully
   to a wire rack. Store in an airtight tin when
   cold.

Crispy Chocolate Biscuits
makes 30
Make exactly as Crispy Mocha Biscuits but
omit coffee.

Crispy Chocolate Orange Biscuits
makes 30
Make exactly as Crispy Mocha Biscuits but
omit coffee. Add 1 level tsp finely grated
orange peel to oil mixture.

Melting Moments

makes 20-24

Oat-wrapped biscuits which flatten out into
meltingly tender rounds.

4oz (125g) butter, softened but not runny
3oz (75g) caster sugar
1 Grade 3 egg yolk
1 tsp vanilla essence
4oz (125g) self-raising flour
1oz (25g) cornflour
Porridge oats

1 Cream butter and sugar together until
   light and fluffy. Beat in egg yolk and
   essence.
2 Using a fork, mix in flour and cornflour.
   Shape into 20-24 marble-shaped pieces.
3 Roll in porridge oats which should be
   spread on a piece of foil or greaseproof
   paper.
4 Stand the biscuits on 2 lightly buttered
   baking trays and bake one shelf above and
   one shelf below oven centre (any position
   in fan oven) set to 375°F (190°C), Gas 5.
5 Allow about 15 minutes, or until pale gold,
   reversing position of trays at half-time.
6 Leave to stand 5 minutes then cool on a
   wire rack. Store in an airtight tin when
   cold.

Chocolate Melting Moments
makes 20-24
Make exactly as Melting Moments but use
½oz (15g) *each* cornflour and cocoa powder
and only 3oz (75g) flour.

Coconut Melting Moments
makes 20-24
Make exactly as Melting Moments but fork
in ½oz (15g) desiccated coconut with flour
and cornflour.

Cherry Melting Moments
makes 20-24
Make exactly as Melting Moments but top
each ball with half a glacé cherry.

147

Currant Melting Moments

makes 20-24

Make exactly as Melting Moments but fork in 1oz (25g) currants with flour and cornflour.

Viennese Whirls

makes 16

Rich, buttery biscuits which are best piped into assorted shapes.

6oz (175g) butter, softened
2oz (50g) icing sugar, sifted
1 tsp vanilla essence
6oz (175g) plain flour

1 Cream butter, sugar and essence together until light and fluffy.
2 Fork in flour. Transfer mixture to icing bag fitted with a large star-shaped tube.
3 Pipe 16 whirls of mixture onto a large buttered baking tray. Bake in oven centre (any position in fan oven) set to 325°F (160°C), Gas 3. Allow about 20 minutes or until very pale gold.
4 Leave 5 minutes then remove to wire cooling rack. Store in an airtight tin when cold.

Viennese Cherry Whirls

makes 16

Make as Viennese Whirls but top centre of each with half a glacé cherry before baking.

Viennese Cherry Snowdrift Whirls

makes 16

Make as Viennese Whirls but sift icing sugar over each after baking, then top centres wth blobs of black cherry jam.

Viennese Cream Sandwiches

makes 8

Make as Viennese Whirls but, after baking, sandwich together in pairs with Vanilla Butter Cream made by creaming 2oz (50g) softened butter with 1oz (25g) sifted icing sugar and ½ tsp vanilla essence. Store in an airtight tin when filling has set.

Viennese Orange Cream Sandwiches

makes 8

Make as Viennese Cream Sandwiches but flavour the butter cream with ½ level tsp finely grated orange peel instead of vanilla essence.

Chocolate Viennese Cream Sandwiches

makes 8

When biscuits have been sandwiched together, apply 2oz (50g) melted chocolate to tops with pastry brush.

Viennese Rings

makes 20

Make as Viennese Whirls but pipe 20 rings onto two trays. For Christmas, these can be tied with ribbon and hung onto branches of the Christmas tree.

Viennese 'S' Shapes

makes 16

Make exactly as Viennese Whirls but pipe 16 'S' shapes onto baking tray. When cold, brush half of each biscuit fairly thickly with 2oz (50g) melted plain dessert chocolate.

Viennese Petits Fours

makes 32

Make exactly as Viennese Whirls but pipe 32 small mounds onto buttered trays and cook for 10-15 minutes. Dust cooked biscuits with icing sugar or drinking chocolate when cold. Transfer to paper sweet-cases for serving.

Chocolate Viennese Whirls

makes 16

Make up any of the above recipes substituting 1oz (25g) cocoa powder for 1oz (25g) flour.

Viennese Raspberry Whirls

makes 8

Make exactly as Viennese Whirls. When cold, sandwich together in pairs with raspberry jam then dust tops with sifted icing sugar.

Viennese Fingers
makes 8

Make exactly as the Viennese Whirls but pipe into 3in (7.5cm) fingers. When cold, sandwich together with apricot jam, then dip ends in about 2oz (50g) melted and cooled plain dessert chocolate. Leave on grease-proof paper until chocolate has set before storing in an airtight tin.

Peanut Cookies

makes 24

2oz (50g) plain flour
¼ level tsp bicarbonate of soda
2oz (50g) butter, softened
2oz (50g) peanut butter
1oz (25g) caster sugar
2oz (50g) light-brown soft sugar
1 Grade 3 egg

1 Sift together flour and bicarbonate of soda.
2 Cream butter, peanut butter and sugar until light and fluffy. Beat in egg.
3 Using a fork, stir in dry ingredients. Spoon 24 mounds of mixture, well apart, onto 2 greased trays.
4 Bake one shelf above and one shelf below oven centre (any position in fan oven) set to 350°F (180°C), Gas 4.
5 Allow 10-12 minutes reversing trays at half-time. Leave to stand for about 3 minutes then cool on a wire rack. Store in an airtight tin when cold.

Digestive Biscuits

makes 12-14

3oz (75g) wholemeal flour
1oz (25g) plain flour
½ level tsp baking powder
2oz (50g) butter or block margarine, at room temperature
1½oz (40g) caster sugar
About 1½-2 tbsp cold milk to mix

1 Tip flours and baking powder into a bowl. Rub in fat finely with fingertips. Toss in sugar.

2 Using a knife, stir in sufficient milk to form a stiff dough.
3 Turn onto a floured surface and knead lightly until smooth.
4 Roll out thinly and cut into 12 or 14 rounds with a 2½in (6cm) plain cutter, re-rolling and re-cutting trimmings to give the required number of biscuits.
5 Transfer to greased baking trays, prick with a fork and place in oven centre (any position in fan oven) set to 375°F (190°C), Gas 5. Bake until pale gold, allowing about 15-20 minutes. Reverse position of trays at half-time.
6 Cool biscuits on a wire rack and store in an airtight tin when cold.

Milk Chocolate Digestive Biscuits
makes 12-14

Spread cold Digestive Biscuits with 2-3oz (50-75g) melted milk chocolate. Leave until set. Store in an airtight tin in a cool place.

Plain Chocolate Digestive Biscuits
makes 12-14

Spread cold Digestive Biscuits with 2-3oz (50-75g) melted plain chocolate. Leave until set. Store in an airtight tin in a cool place.

Traditional Biscuits

makes 30

8oz (225g) self-raising flour
5oz (150g) butter (or block margarine with plain flour)
4oz (125g) caster sugar
1 Grade 3 egg, beaten
2-3 tsp cold milk to mix

1 Sift flour into bowl. Rub in butter or margarine finely.
2 Toss in sugar, then mix to a stiff dough with egg and about 2-3 tsp cold milk.
3 Turn out onto a floured surface and knead lightly until smooth.
4 Foil-wrap and leave 15 minutes in the re-frigerator to relax.
5 Turn again onto floured surface and roll out fairly thinly.

6 Cut into about 30 rounds with a 2in (5cm) plain biscuit cutter. Transfer to 2 lightly greased trays. Prick all over with a fork. Bake one shelf above and one shelf below oven centre (any position in fan oven) set to 350°F (180°C), Gas 4. Allow about 12-15 minutes when biscuits should be pale gold. Reverse position of trays at half-time.

7 Leave to cool 3-4 minutes, then carefully lift off with a knife onto a wire cooling rack. Store in an airtight tin when cold.

Vanilla Biscuits
makes 30
Make exactly as Traditional Biscuits but add 1 tsp vanilla essence with egg.

Almond Biscuits
makes 34-36
Make exactly as Traditional Biscuits but add 2oz (50g) ground almonds with sugar and ½tsp almond essence with egg.

Hazelnut Biscuits
makes 34-36
Make exactly as Traditional Biscuits but grind 2oz (50g) hazelnuts in food processor or blender and add with the sugar. Include ½ tsp vanilla essence and add with the egg.

Almond Flake Biscuits
makes 30
Make exactly as Traditional Biscuits but brush lightly with beaten egg and sprinkle with flaked almonds.

Sugar Biscuits
makes 30
Make exactly as Traditional Biscuits but after arranging biscuits on trays, brush with beaten egg and sprinkle with granulated sugar or fairly finely crushed cube sugar.

Spice Biscuits
makes 30
Make exactly as Traditional Biscuits but sift flour with 2 level tsp mixed spice.

Cinnamon Biscuits
makes 30
Make exactly as Traditional Biscuits but sift flour with 2 level tsp cinnamon.

Seed Biscuits
makes 30
Make exactly as Traditional Biscuits but toss in 2 level tsp caraway seeds with the sugar.

Coconut Biscuits
makes 30
Make exactly as Traditional Biscuits but toss in 2 level tbsp desiccated coconut with the sugar. Add ½ level tsp vanilla essence with the egg.

Currant Biscuits
makes 30
Make exactly as Traditional Biscuits but toss in 1oz (25g) currants with the sugar.

Lemon or Orange Biscuits
makes 30
Make exactly as Traditional Biscuits but toss in either 1 level tsp finely grated lemon or orange peel with the sugar.

Sherry Biscuits
makes 30
Make exactly as Traditional Biscuits but substitute sweet sherry for milk when mixing.

Cherry Biscuits
makes 30
Make exactly as Traditional Biscuits but toss in 2oz (50g) finely chopped glacé cherries with the sugar.

Chocolate Biscuits
makes 30
Make up Traditional Biscuits but substitute 1oz (25g) cocoa powder for 1oz (25g) flour and sift both together. Include 1 tsp vanilla essence with the egg.

Petticoat Tails
makes about 12

Make exactly as Traditional Biscuits then roll into a 10in (25cm) circle, using a dinner plate as a guide. Trim neatly, then remove centre with a 2in (5cm) cutter. Cut remaining ring into wedges to look like skirts. Transfer to baking tray. Ridge wide edges with fork. Prick all over. Dust lightly with caster sugar and bake as directed.

Traffic-light Biscuits
makes 15

Make up Traditional Biscuits and arrange 15 on a greased tray. Using a very small cutter, cut 3 holes out of remaining 15 biscuits. Place biscuits on second tray and bake as directed. When cold, brush first 15 biscuits thinly with apricot jam. Dust tops of biscuits with holes with sifted icing sugar. Stand these carefully on top of jam-covered biscuits. Fill in holes with lemon curd, red jam and green jam to resemble traffic lights.

Fancy-shaped Biscuits
makes 30

Make up any of the recipes previously given and cut into fancy shapes with assorted biscuit cutters. Bake as directed. When cold, either leave plain, brush with melted chocolate or cover with glacé icing made by mixing 4oz (125g) icing sugar to a thickish icing with 2 or 3 tsp fruit juice, liqueur or coffee.

Shortbread Biscuits
makes 20

4oz (125g) butter, softened
2oz (50g) icing sugar, sifted
4oz (125g) plain flour, sifted
1oz (25g) cornflour
Beaten egg for brushing
Caster sugar for sprinkling

1 Cream butter and sugar together until light and fluffy.
2 Fork in flour and cornflour. Draw mixture together then shape into a ball on floured surface.

3 Wrap in film or foil and relax in the refrigerator for 30 minutes. Roll out thinly on floured surface then cut into about 20 rounds with a 1½in (4cm) biscuit cutter, re-rolling and re-cutting trimmings to make the correct number of biscuits.
4 Transfer to 2 lightly greased baking trays. Prick well then brush tops with egg and sprinkle with sugar.
5 Bake 20-25 minutes one shelf above and one shelf below oven centre (any position in fan oven) set to 325°F (160°C), Gas 3.
6 Leave to cool 5 minutes, then carefully lift onto a wire cooling rack. Store in an airtight tin when cold.

Chocolate Shortbread Biscuits
makes 20

Make exactly as Shortbread Biscuits, but substitute ½oz (15g) sifted cocoa powder for the same amount of flour.

Butter Shortbread 1
makes 8-10

4oz (125g) butter
2oz (50g) caster sugar
5oz (150g) plain flour
1oz (25g) semolina
Extra sugar for top

1 Cream butter and sugar together until light and fluffy. Stir in flour and semolina.
2 Spread evenly into 7in (17.5cm) sandwich tin. Prick all over with fork and ridge edges with prongs.
3 Sprinkle with caster sugar then bake in oven centre (any position in fan oven) set to 325°F (160°C), Gas 3.
4 Allow about 30-40 minutes or until shortbread is the colour of pale straw.
5 Leave to cool for about 10 minutes then cut into 8 or 10 wedges. Carefully remove from tin and transfer to a wire cooling rack. Store in an airtight tin when cold.

151

Butter Shortbread 2

makes 8-10

5oz (150g) plain flour
1oz (25g) semolina
4oz (125g) butter
2oz (50g) caster sugar

1 Sift flour into bowl. Add semolina and butter. Cut in butter with a knife, then rub into flour with fingertips.
2 Toss in sugar then draw mixture together with fork. Press into 7in (17.5cm) sandwich tin with the flat of your hand. Prick all over with a fork, then ridge edges to decorate. Sprinkle top with sugar.
3 Bake, cool and store as given for Shortbread 1.

Chocolate Shortbread

makes 8-10
Make Shortbread 1 or 2 but substitute 1oz (25g) cocoa powder for 1oz (25g) flour.

Almond Shortbread

makes 8-10
When Shortbread 1 or 2 is in tin, press 1½oz (40g) flaked almonds, with the flat of your hand, into the top. Bake, cool and store as given for either Shortbread recipe.

Honeyed Ginger Shortbread

makes 18
(illustrated on page 183)

12oz (350g) plain flour
6oz (175g) butter, at kitchen temperature
2oz (50g) caster sugar
4oz (125g) crystallised ginger, finely chopped
3 rounded tbsp thick (or set) honey

1 Sift flour into mixing bowl and rub in butter finely. Toss in sugar and ginger. Preheat oven to 300°F (150°C), Gas 2.
2 Knead in honey with floured hands to form a stiff dough. Divide into 3 portions.
3 Roll each out into a 7in (17.5cm) round, pinch edges between finger and thumb then place on 3 greased and floured baking trays. Mark into sixths with a knife.

4 Bake 30-35 minutes in 3 oven positions, leaving centre tray where it is but reversing top and bottom trays at half-time. This does not apply in a fan oven.
5 Cool on a wire rack then break into triangles when lukewarm. Store in an airtight tin when cold.

Grasmere Shortcake

makes 10

A Lake District speciality which is akin to a spiced shortbread.

8oz (225g) plain flour
¼ level tsp salt
¼ level tsp bicarbonate of soda
1 level tsp ground ginger
4oz (125g) butter or margarine
4oz (125g) light-brown soft sugar

1 Sift flour, salt, bicarbonate of soda and ginger into a bowl.
2 Cut in fat then rub in with fingertips.
3 Toss in sugar. Press loose mixture evenly into an 8in (20cm) round sandwich tin.
4 Press down flat with palm of hand then bake 45 minutes in oven centre (any position in fan oven) set to 300°F (150°C), Gas 2. At this stage it should be golden brown, so remove from oven and leave to stand about 7 minutes.
4 Cut into about 10 pieces, cool on a wire rack and store in an airtight tin when cold.

(right) Cheese and Chive Quiche, page 109 *(St Ivel Stilton Cheese)*

(overleaf) Puffy Cheese Straws, page 117 *(Colman's Mustard)*

Ginger Snaps

makes 20

4oz (125g) self-raising flour
1 level tsp ground ginger
¼ level tsp mixed spice
2oz (50g) butter
2oz (50g) dark-brown soft sugar
About 8 tsp cold tea to mix

1 Sift flour, ginger and spice into bowl. Rub in butter finely. Toss in sugar.
2 Mix to a stiff dough with tea. Turn onto floured surface and knead lightly. Roll out thinly and cut into 20 rounds with 2in (5cm) biscuit cutter, re-rolling and re-cutting trimmings to make the correct number of biscuits.
3 Transfer to 2 lightly greased baking trays, prick all over with a fork and bake one shelf above and one shelf below oven centre (any position in fan oven) set to 350°F (180°C), Gas 4. Allow about 15-20 minutes and reverse trays at half-time.
4 Leave to cool 3-4 minutes, then transfer to a wire cooling rack. Store in an airtight tin when cold.

Ginger Nuts

makes 24

3oz (75g) white cooking fat
2oz (50g) caster sugar
3oz (75g) golden syrup
7oz (200g) plain flour
1 level tsp mixed spice
2 level tsp ground ginger
1 level tsp bicarbonate of soda

1 Put fat, sugar and syrup into a pan and melt over a low heat.
2 Meanwhile, sift dry ingredients into a bowl. Make a dip in the centre and stir in melted mixture to form a stiffish dough. If too stiff, add a few tsp of warm tea.

(previous page) Wensleydale Apple Puffs, page 126 *(National Dairy Council)*

(left) Cherry and Chocolate Puff Slice, page 126 *(Cadbury Typhoo)*

3 Roll into 24 balls and place on 2 greased baking trays, leaving room between each for spreading. Flatten each slightly by pressing with a knife.
4 Bake one shelf above and one shelf below oven centre (any position in fan oven) set to 325°F (160°C), Gas 3. Allow about 15-20 minutes, reversing position of trays at half-time. Leave on tray about 3 minutes then transfer to a wire cooling rack. Store in an airtight tin when cold.

Almond Macaroons

makes 16

A delicious confection for high days and holidays, Macaroons are easy to make at home though still fairly expensive, but at least the results are well worthwhile.

2 egg whites from Grade 2 eggs
4oz (125g) ground almonds
8oz (225g) caster sugar
½oz (15g) ground rice or semolina
½ tsp vanilla essence
1 tsp almond essence
A little extra egg white
8 whole almonds, blanched and halved

1 Line 2 baking trays with non-stick parchment paper. Set oven to 325°F (160°C), Gas 3.
2 Whisk egg whites until just foamy then stir in almonds, sugar, ground rice or semolina and the essences. Mix until evenly combined then pipe or spoon 16 mounds of mixture, well apart as they spread, onto prepared trays.
3 Brush with egg white and top each with half an almond, flat side down. Bake one shelf above and one shelf below oven centre (any position in fan oven) for 20-25 minutes.
4 Leave to cool for a few minutes then carefully remove from paper and cool on a wire rack. Store in an airtight tin when cold.

Coconut Macaroons

makes 24

Less costly than those made with almonds, these are always appreciated by those who like coconut and are easily produced from fairly inexpensive ingredients.

8oz (225g) desiccated coconut (not too coarse)
5oz (150g) caster sugar
1 tsp vanilla essence
2 Grade 3 eggs, lightly beaten

1 Line two baking trays with non-stick parchment paper, non-stick greaseproof paper (fairly new on the market) or aluminium foil.
2 Mix all macaroon ingredients well together. Put 24 mounds onto prepared trays. Bake one shelf above and one shelf below oven centre (any position in fan oven) set to 350°F (180°C), Gas 4.
3 Allow about 15 minutes or until macaroons are pale gold, reversing position of trays at half-time.
4 Leave to stand a few minutes, then carefully lift off on to a wire cooling rack. Store in an airtight tin when cold.

Cherry Coconut Macaroons
makes 24
Make Coconut Macaroons as directed above, but top each with half a glacé cherry before baking.

Coconut Pyramids
makes 24
Make Coconut Macaroons as directed but shape into pyramids with fork before baking. Top each with half a glacé cherry.

Oat Macaroons

makes 36

4oz (125g) self-raising flour
4oz (125g) rolled oats (porridge oats)
4oz (125g) butter or margarine, at kitchen temperature
3oz (75g) light-brown soft sugar

1 rounded tbsp clear honey
1 Grade 3 egg
Finely grated peel of 1 washed and dried small lemon
Flaked almonds for decoration

1 Sift flour into a bowl then toss in oats. In separate bowl, cream butter or margarine and sugar together until light and fluffy. Beat in honey, egg and lemon peel.
2 Using a fork, stir in dry ingredients to form a dough. Roll into walnut-sized pieces and put on to 2 large greased baking trays, leaving room between each piece to allow for spreading.
3 Flatten each with a floured knife then top with a piece of flaked almond. Bake 1 shelf above and 1 shelf below oven centre (any position in fan oven) set to 350°F (180°C), Gas 4.
4 Allow 12-14 minutes, reversing position of trays at half-time. Remove biscuits to a wire rack to cool, then store in an airtight tin when cold.

Flapjack 1

makes 12

4oz (125g) butter
3oz (75g) light-brown soft sugar
5oz (150g) porridge oats

1 Cream butter and sugar together until very light and fluffy in consistency.
2 Stir in oats then spread mixture evenly into an 11 x 7in (27.5 x 17.5cm) Swiss Roll tin.
3 Place in oven centre (any position in fan oven) set to 375°F (190°C), Gas 5. Bake about 20-25 minutes or until top is a warm gold.
4 Leave in tin for about 5 minutes to cool then mark in 12 pieces. Remove from tin when lukewarm. Cool on a wire rack and store in an airtight tin when cold.

Flapjack 2

makes 16

An unusual and old-fashioned version, made with dripping.

3oz (75g) light-brown soft sugar
3oz (75g) dripping, at room temperature
2 level tsp golden syrup
4oz (125g) porridge oats
¼ level tsp salt
1 level tsp ground ginger

1 Cream together sugar, dripping and syrup until very light and fluffy in consistency. Toss oats with salt and ginger. Stir into creamed ingredients.
2 Spread evenly into an 8in (20cm) square tin and bake in oven centre (any position in fan oven) set to 375°F (190°C), Gas 5. Allow about 20-25 minutes. Leave to stand for 3-4 minutes then mark into 16 squares. Cut when lukewarm, remove from tin and cool on a wire rack. Store in an airtight tin when cold.

Flapjack 3

makes 20

4oz (125g) butter or margarine
3oz (75g) golden syrup
3oz (75g) dark-brown soft sugar
8oz (225g) porridge oats
1 tsp mixed spice (optional)

1 Put butter or margarine, syrup and sugar into a pan. Heat slowly until fat melts.
2 Stir in oats and spice if used. Spread into an 8 x 12in (20 x 30cm) Swiss-Roll tin and bake 30 minutes in oven centre (any position in fan oven) set to 350°F (180°C), Gas 4.
3 Leave to stand 5 minutes then cut into about 20 pieces. Cool on a wire rack. Store in an airtight tin when cold.

Muesli Chocolate Bars

makes 10
(illustrated on page 183)

2oz (50g) butter
2 rounded tbsp thick (or set) honey
10oz (275g) muesli
2 bars (each 3½oz or 100g) plain dessert chocolate, melted

1 Melt the butter and honey in a large saucepan. Stir in the muesli. Spread smoothly into a 10 x 8in (25 x 20cm) greased and paper-lined Swiss-Roll tin.
2 Bake 20 minutes in centre of oven (any position in fan oven) set to 350°F (180°C), Gas 4.
3 Spread chocolate thickly over the top and leave to cool to lukewarm. Mark into 10 bars and cut up when completely cold. Store in an airtight container in a cool place.

Refrigerator Biscuits

makes 50-60

Whether these originated in Northern Europe or the US is debatable, but certainly the biscuits are immensely useful. From the roll of wrapped dough you can slice off as many biscuits as required. The rest may be re-wrapped and left in the refrigerator for next time.

8oz (225g) plain flour
1 level tsp baking powder
4oz (125g) butter or margarine, at kitchen temperature
6oz (175g) caster sugar
1 tsp vanilla essence
1 Grade 3 egg, beaten
Milk if necessary

1 Sift flour and baking powder into a bowl. Rub in butter or margarine finely. Toss in sugar. Beat together vanilla essence and egg.
2 Fork into dry ingredients to form a stiffish dough, adding a few tsps of milk if mixture remains crumbly and dry.
3 Knead on a floured surface quickly and

lightly until smooth, then roll into a sausage shape of about 2in (5cm) in diameter. Wrap in foil and twist ends to form a 'cracker'.

4 Refrigerate for at least 3 hours before cutting. To cook, cut off as many biscuits as required, arrange on a greased baking tray and bake 10-12 minutes in oven centre (any position in fan oven) set to 375°F (190°C), Gas 5. Leave on tin 3-4 minutes, then transfer to a wire cooling rack. Store in an airtight tin when cold. Re-wrap rest of dough in foil and return to the refrigerator.

Almond Refrigerator Biscuits
makes 50-60
Make as Refrigerator Biscuits but substitute almond essence for vanilla.

Sherry or Rum Refrigerator Biscuits
makes 50-60
Make as Refrigerator Biscuits but substitute sherry or rum essence for vanilla.

Ginger Refrigerator Biscuits
makes 50-60
Make as Refrigerator Biscuits but sift 3 level tsp ground ginger with flour and use light-brown soft sugar instead of caster.

Cinnamon Refrigerator Biscuits
makes 50-60
Make as Refrigerator Biscuits but sift 3 level tsp cinnamon with flour and use light-brown sugar instead of caster.

Spice Refrigerator Biscuits
makes 50-60
Make as Refrigerator Biscuits but sift 3 level tsp mixed spice with flour and use light-brown soft sugar instead of caster.

Orange or Lemon Refrigerator Biscuits
makes 50-60
Make as Refrigerator Biscuits but omit vanilla and add 3 level tsp finely grated orange or lemon peel with the sugar.

Nut Refrigerator Biscuits
makes 50-60
Make as Refrigerator Biscuits but add 3oz (75g) very finely grated walnuts, hazelnuts or ground almonds with the sugar.

Chocolate Refrigerator Biscuits
makes 50-60
Make as Refrigerator Biscuits but substitute 1oz (25g) cocoa for 1oz (25g) flour.

Chocolate Nut Refrigerator Biscuits
makes 50-60
Make as Refrigerator Biscuits but substitute 1oz (25g) cocoa for 1oz (25g) flour. Add 3oz (75g) finely chopped nuts with the sugar.

Coconut Refrigerator Biscuits
makes 50-60
Make as Refrigerator Biscuits but add 2oz (50g) desiccated coconut with the sugar.

Chocolate Flake Refrigerator Biscuits
makes 50-60
Make as Refrigerator Biscuits but add 2oz (50g) finely grated milk or plain dessert chocolate with the sugar.

Sesame and Honey Cookies
makes 36
(illustrated on page 183)

4oz (125g) sesame seeds
4oz (125g) plain flour
1/4 level tsp bicarbonate of soda
4oz (125g) butter or margarine, at kitchen temperature
4oz (125g) caster sugar
1 rounded tbsp thick (or set) honey
1 Grade 3 egg, beaten

1 Tip sesame seeds into bowl then sift over flour and bicarbonate of soda.
2 Cream butter or margarine and sugar together until light and fluffy. Beat in honey then gradually mix in egg.
3 Stir in dry ingredients to form a stiff dough, turn out on to a floured surface and

shape into a sausage of about 1½in (4cm) in diameter.

4 Wrap in foil or cling film and chill in the refrigerator for about 4-6 hours. Cut off as many Cookies as required and place on greased baking tray, leaving plenty of room round each for spreading.

5 Bake 15 minutes just above centre of oven (any position in fan oven) set to 350°F (180°C), Gas 4. Cool on a wire rack and store in an airtight container when cold.

6 Keep leftover dough in refrigerator and cut and bake more biscuits when required.

Brandy Snaps

makes 16

Although these can now be bought in tins or boxes ready for filling with cream for eating on their own, the home-made variety is still worth trying if you have the time and patience — and at least 2 large baking trays.

2oz (50g) butter or margarine
2oz (50g) dark-brown soft sugar
2½oz (65g) golden syrup
2oz (50g) plain flour
1 level tsp ground ginger
½ level tsp mixed spice
2 tsp lemon juice

1 Well-grease 2 large baking trays. Set oven to 325°F (160°C), Gas 3.

2 Put fat, sugar and syrup into a pan. Leave over low heat until fat and syrup have melted.

3 Sift together dry ingredients then stir into melted ingredients with lemon juice.

4 Put only 4 tsp of mixture onto each tray. Bake for 8 minutes one shelf above and one shelf below oven centre (any position in fan oven), reversing position of trays at half-time.

5 Leave for a few seconds to firm up slightly then lift off trays and roll quickly and loosely round thickish handle of wooden spoon. If the Snaps suddenly harden too much to wrap round the spoon handle, return these to the oven for about 1 minute to soften.

6 Repeat, using all the mixture to make total of 16 brandy snaps. Store in an airtight tin when cold.

Chocolate Brandy Snaps
makes 16
To serve with coffee at the end of a meal instead of Petits Fours, dip ends of Brandy Snaps in about 2oz (50g) melted plain dessert chocolate. Leave on a sheet of greaseproof paper or aluminium foil until set.

Palmiers

makes about 10

Made from trimmings of Puff Pastry, Palmiers are named after palm leaves which they are said to resemble in appearance. It is difficult to estimate an exact quantity because so much depends on the amount of Puff Pastry one happens to have spare. On the other hand, Palmiers are so good that you may feel inclined to keep some Puff Pastry on hand just for making these unusual and not over-sweet biscuits.

Gather trimmings of pastry into a ball and knead very gently and quickly on surface dusted thickly with caster sugar. Roll out into an 8in (20cm) square. Make two folds from each side towards the centre (the second fold should reach the exact centre), then fold one piece on top of the other, leaving you with one long strip comprised of folds. Cut into ½in (1.25cm) slices, arrange on 2 baking trays and bake, one at a time, near top of oven (any position in fan oven) for about 5-6 minutes at 400°F (200°C), Gas 6. Turn over and bake another 5 minutes so that both sides caramelize and turn golden brown. Cool on a wire rack and store in an airtight tin when cold.

Cream-filled Palmiers
makes 5 pairs
Sandwich together in pairs with whipped cream

Cream and Jam Palmiers

makes 5 pairs

If preferred, sandwich together with jam and whipped cream.

Florentines

makes 12

Elegant and acceptable anywhere and at any time, Florentines are well worth making since they are fairly easy and far less costly than if shop bought.

3oz (75g) unsalted butter
2 tbsp single cream
2 tbsp milk
4oz (125g) icing sugar, sifted
1½oz (40g) plain flour
3oz (75g) chopped mixed peel
2oz (50g) glacé cherries, finely chopped
3oz (75g) flaked almonds
1tsp lemon juice
¼oz (8g) extra butter, melted
4oz (125g) plain dessert chocolate, melted

1 Cover 2 large baking trays with non-stick parchment paper.
2 Put butter, cream, milk and sugar into a saucepan. Stand the pan over a low heat until the butter melts.
3 Remove from heat. Stir in all remaining ingredients except chocolate and extra butter. Leave until cold.
4 Spoon equal amounts of mixture (well apart, as they spread), onto prepared trays. Bake one shelf above and one shelf below oven centre (any position in fan oven) for 10 minutes in oven set to 375°F (190°C), Gas 5. Reverse position of trays at half-time.
5 Leave until lukewarm. Carefully remove from paper and cool on a wire rack.
6 When completely cold, stir melted butter into chocolate and spread over undersides of Florentines.
7 Leave until the chocolate is almost set, then mark with wavy lines, using a fork. Store in an airtight tin when completely cold and keep in a cool place.

Oatcakes

makes 16
(illustrated on page 184)

8oz (225g) medium or fine oatmeal
½ level tsp salt
¼ level tsp bicarbonate of soda
2oz (50g) lard, bacon dripping or margarine, melted
Boiling water

1 Tip oatmeal into a mixing bowl. Toss in salt and bicarbonate of soda.
2 Add melted fat and sufficient boiling water to make a very stiff dough. Turn out on to surface dusted thickly with oatmeal and knead until smooth.
3 Divide equally in two. Roll each out into a round of ¼in (75mm) in thickness. Cut each into 8 triangles.
4 In Scotland, where they are well practised in the art of making Oatcakes, these would be cooked on a girdle or griddle. For the rest of us, arrange on a lightly greased baking tray and dry out in centre of oven (any position in fan oven) set to 300°F (150°C), Gas 2. Allow about 1 hour.
5 Cool on a wire rack and store in an airtight tin when cold.

Cheese Biscuits for Elevenses

makes 12

I have always been a devotee of home-made Cheese Biscuits and below is a selection which I hope will please everyone.

4oz (125g) plain flour
Large pinch of salt
½ level tsp powder mustard
2oz (50g) butter or margarine
2oz (50g) Cheddar cheese, very finely grated
1 Grade 3 egg yolk
Cold milk to mix if necessary

1 Sift flour, salt and mustard into bowl. Rub in fat finely. Toss in cheese.
2 Using a fork, mix to a stiff dough with egg yolk and cold milk if necessary.
3 Turn out on to a floured surface and knead lightly until smooth.

4 Roll out thinly and cut into 12 rounds with 2in (5cm) plain biscuit cutter, re-rolling and re-cutting trimmings to make the correct number of biscuits.
5 Transfer to a large greased tray and bake about 7-10 minutes just above oven centre (any position in fan oven), set to 425°F (220°C), Gas 7.
6 Cool on a wire rack. Store in an airtight tin when cold.

Poppy Seed Cheese Biscuits
makes 12
Make as Cheese Biscuits for Elevenses but brush tops with lightly beaten egg white, then sprinkle thinly with poppy seeds.

Caraway Cheese Biscuits
makes 12
Make as Poppy Seed Cheese Biscuits substituting caraway seeds for poppy.

Celery Cheese Biscuits
makes 12
Make as Poppy Seed Cheese Biscuits but sprinkle lightly with celery salt instead of seeds.

Paprika Cheese Biscuits
makes 12
Make as Poppy Seed Cheese Biscuits but sprinkle lightly with paprika instead of seeds.

Sesame-Seed Cheese Biscuits
makes 12
Make as Poppy Seed Cheese Biscuits but sprinkle lightly with sesame seeds instead of poppy.

Bran Cheese Biscuits
makes 12
Make as Cheese Biscuits for Elevenses but add 2 rounded tbsp bran with the cheese.

Walnut Cheese Biscuits
makes 12
Make as Cheese Biscuits for Elevenses but add 1oz (25g) finely chopped walnuts with the cheese.

Peanut Cheese Biscuits
makes 12
Make as Cheese Biscuits for Elevenses, but omit salt. Add 1oz (25g) finely chopped salted peanuts with the cheese.

Chilli Cheese Biscuits
makes 12
Make as Cheese Biscuits for Elevenses but sift 1 level tsp mild chilli seasoning (a dark, almost purple powder used for Chilli Con Carne) with the flour and salt.

Oaty Cheese Biscuits
makes 12
Make as Cheese Biscuits for Elevenses but brush with lightly beaten egg white then sprinkle thinly with porridge oats.

Fiery Cheese Biscuits
makes 12
Make as Cheese Biscuits for Elevenses but sift 1 level tsp cayenne pepper with the flour and salt.

Cheese Straws
makes 36
Make up Cheese Biscuits for Elevenses then cut into about 36 x ¾in (2cm) strips. Place carefully on baking trays. To give impression of bales, make 2in (5cm) rings, cut from pastry trimmings. Put onto trays with the straws. Bake as biscuits. Cool on a wire rack. When cold, thread straws through rings (See also Chapter 7).

Cheese Sandwich Biscuits
makes 12
Make up Cheese Biscuits for Elevenses then cut into 24 rounds with 1in (2.5cm) biscuit cutter. Put onto 2 lightly greased baking trays. Bake as directed but place one shelf above and one shelf below oven centre (any position in fan oven). When cold, sandwich together with cheese spread or cream cheese.

163

Serve with mid-morning coffee or as an after-dinner savoury.

Cheese Butterflies

makes 12

Make as Cheese Sandwich Biscuits but cut 12 biscuits in half for wings before baking. Bake altogether as previously directed. When cold, pipe or spoon a line of cheese spread (useful if it is in tube form) or cream cheese down centre of biscuit, then add 2 wings to each at an angle to look like a butterfly in flight. Dust lightly with paprika or very finely chopped parsley.

Cheese Fingers

makes 12

Make up as Cheese Biscuits for Elevenses, but cut into fingers instead of rounds. Brush lightly with egg white before baking.

Cheese Squares

makes 12

Make up Cheese Biscuits for Elevenses then cut into squares instead of rounds. Brush lightly with egg white before baking.

Biscuits for Cheese

makes about 24
(illustrated on page 183)

1oz (25g) plain flour
8oz (225g) oatmeal
2oz (50g) butter
1 rounded tbsp thick (or set) honey
1-2 tsps milk if required

1 Sift flour into a bowl. Toss in oatmeal. Rub in butter. Mix to a stiffish paste with honey adding 1-2 tsp of milk if mixture fails to hold together.
2 Place on large sheet of floured greaseproof paper. Cover with a second piece of floured greaseproof paper and roll out very thinly.
3 Remove top sheet of paper and cut rolled dough into 2in (5cm) rounds with plain biscuit cutter.
4 Gather up trimmings and re-roll between paper as before. Cut into more rounds to make required number.
5 Place on greased baking trays and bake for 10 minutes 1 shelf above and 1 shelf below oven centre (any position in fan oven) set to 350°F (180°C), Gas 4. Reverse position of trays at half-time.
6 Remove from trays and cool on a wire cooling rack. Store in an airtight tin when cold.

(right) Hasty Pizza, page 127; Sausage Rolls, page 127; and Eccles Cakes, page 126 (*Pura Advisory Service*)

(overleaf) Herby Bacon Scone Round, page 140; Lemony Apple Scones, page 140; and Norfolk Scone Slices, page 141 (*Flour Advisory Bureau*)

10
Cheesecakes

Once considered Middle European and Jewish specialities, Cheesecakes are sweeping across Britain just as they once did over the USA and enjoying unrivalled popularity as a teatime or coffee-morning treat and after-dinner sweet — but they are a far cry from Ye Olde English Curd Cakes!

Ingredients

Base

I always use crushed digestive biscuits. Crush them in a polythene bag, rolling firmly with a rolling pin. Other types of crusts can be used, including Flan Pastry (page 101).

Cheese

If you are near a delicatessen or supermarket chain with a delicatessen counter, ask for curd cheese (lowish fat) which makes the best cheesecakes of all. If unavailable, use either German Quark which is almost identical to curd cheese, or French soft cheese, often sold in tubs, which is low fat and very white. In this group, you may also use cottage cheese but it must be rubbed through a very fine-mesh sieve until smooth, or blended in blender goblet or food processor. For a richer cake altogether, use a cream cheese such as Philadelphia.

Eggs

I use Grade 2 and allow 1 to every 8oz (225g) cheese.

Sugar

The best is caster and 2oz (50g) to every 8oz cheese is adequate.

Flavourings

The basic is vanilla and/or lemon but be guided by the recipe as sometimes both are recommended. Cheesecakes take well to the addition of fruit and fruit-based liqueurs — you will find a selection which make excellent party fare.

Extras

Either melted butter or cream but this will depend on the recipe.

Cornflour

About 1½ level tsp to every 8oz (225g) cheese helps to stabilize the mixture and keep it firm.

Gelatine

This is used only in chilled cheesecakes.

Toppings and decorations

See individual recipes.

Cheesecake 1

serves 10

4 oz (125g) digestive biscuits finely crushed
1½lb (675g) curd cheese, German Quark, French cheese, sieved or blended cottage cheese, or cream cheese (kitchen temperature)
6oz (175g) caster sugar
4oz (125g) unsalted butter, melted
3 Grade 2 eggs (kitchen temperature)
1 tsp vanilla essence
4½ level tsp cornflour

1 Well grease an 8in (20cm) spring-clip tin (with hinged sides and loose base) or an 8in (20cm) loose-bottomed cake tin. For a flatter cake (better for parties) use a 10in (25cm) spring-clip tin or cake tin. Sprinkle crushed biscuits over base in an even layer.
2 Put all ingredients for cake into a bowl and beat thoroughly until very smooth and creamy. Alternatively, put into large-capacity blender or food processor and run machine until mixture is absolutely smooth. Pour into tin over crumbs.
3 Bake in oven centre (any position in fan oven) set to 300°F (150°C), Gas 2. Allow about 1 hour for the 10in (25cm) cake and 1¼ hours for the smaller one. At this point, filling should have set like a Baked Egg Custard or Quiche.

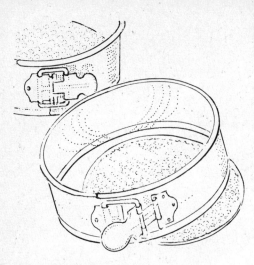

Spring clip tin

4 Switch off heat, open oven door and leave cake to settle for a further 15 minutes. Remove from oven and cool completely.
5 Remove ring from around cake (either from spring-clip tin or the cake tin) but leave Cheesecake on its metal base as it is difficult to remove and may break if you try. Stand on a doily-lined plate and cut into wedges for serving.

Notes

1 It is essential to keep the oven heat low, otherwise — like a Baked Egg Custard — the cake will puff up, collapse and possibly weep as it cools. It might also brown too much.
2 As soon as Cheesecake is cold, chill for several hours before cutting.
3 The larger-sized cake takes less time to cook than the smaller one because it is shallower.

Cheesecake 2
serves 10
Make exactly as previous recipe but substitute ¼pt (150ml) double cream for the melted butter. Increase cornflour to 2 level tbsp.

170

Vanilla Cheesecake
serves 10
Make exactly as Cheesecake 1 or 2 adding 1 tsp vanilla essence with rest of cake ingredients.

Lemon Cheesecake
serves 10
Make exactly as Cheesecake 1 or 2 adding the grated peel and juice of one medium washed and dried lemon. Include also the vanilla essence.

Orange Cheesecake
serves 10
Make exactly as Cheesecake 1 or 2 adding the grated peel and juice of one medium washed and dried orange. Include also the vanilla essence.

Jewish-style Cheesecake
serves 10
Make exactly as Cheesecake 1 or 2 adding the grated peel and juice of one medium washed and dried lemon, vanilla essence and 2-3oz (50-75g) seedless raisins.

Golden Cheesecake
serves 10
Make exactly as Cheesecake 1 or 2 adding vanilla essence and/or finely grated peel and juice of 1 medium washed lemon, plus 6 tsp or 2 level tbsp custard powder instead of cornflour.

Spicy Cheesecake
serves 10
Make exactly as Cheesecake 1 or 2 but mix crushed biscuits with 1½ level tsp mixed spice or cinnamon before sprinkling over base of tin.

Ginger Cheesecake
serves 10
Make exactly as Cheesecake 1 or 2 but use crushed ginger snaps instead of digestive biscuits.

Chocolate Crust Cheesecake

serves 10

Make exactly as Cheesecake 1 or 2 but use crushed plain chocolate digestive biscuits instead of ordinary ones.

Soured-cream Cheesecake

serves 10-12

A luxury version which is very rich.

Make exactly as Cheesecake 1 or 2. As soon as cake is cooked, cover top with one carton (5oz or 142ml) soured cream. The heat coming from the cake will set the cream. Leave undisturbed until cold, then refrigerate for several hours before cutting into wedges for serving.

Pineapple Peppermint Cheesecake

serves 10-12

Make up exactly as Cheesecake 1 or 2. Cover biscuit base with six rings of well-drained, canned pineapple (large size). Flavour cheese mixture with 2 tbsp Crème de Menthe.

Orange Blossom Cheesecake

serves 10-12

Make up exactly as Cheesecake 1 or 2. Cover biscuit base with one can of well-drained mandarins. Flavour cheese mixture with 1 tbsp Cointreau or Grand Marnier and 1 tbsp orange-flower water (obtainable from some chemists or oriental shops).

Whisky Peach Cheesecake

serves 10-12

Make up exactly as Cheesecake 1 or 2. Cover biscuit base with one can (about 1lb or 450g) drained peach slices. Flavour cheese mixture with 2 tbsp whisky.

Strawberry Kirsch Cheesecake

serves 10-12

Make up exactly as Cheesecake 1 or 2. Cover biscuit base with 8oz (225g) sliced fresh strawberries. Flavour cheese mixture with 2 tbsp kirsch.

William Pear Cheesecake

serves 10-12

Make up exactly as Cheesecake 1 or 2. Cover biscuit base with one can (about 1lb or 450g) drained pear halves cut into thin slices. Flavour cheese mixture with 2 tbsp Poires Williams (a strong fruit brandy which is colourless and made from William pears).

American-style Eggnog Cheesecake

serves 12-14

Based on a recipe passed onto me by the chefs at the Vista International Hotel in New York, this is a luxury cheesecake that needs to be made in a 10in (25cm) spring-clip tin. It is based on Cheesecake 2. Crush 6oz (175g) digestive biscuits and mix with 2oz (50g) melted butter, 2oz (50g) light-brown soft sugar and 1 level tsp cinnamon. Sprinkle over base of well-buttered tin. Keep cheese mixture the same, but increase eggs to 4, add an extra 2oz (50g) caster sugar and use 3 level tbsp cornflour. Include also 4 slightly rounded tbsp Advocaat. Cook for 1¼-1½ hours at 300°F (150°C), Gas 2. The cake is ready when it feels firm to the touch and the top is just lightly golden brown.

Novelty Cheesecakes

Fruit-topped Cheesecake

serves 10-12

Make exactly as Cheesecake 1 or 2. Cover top with one can (about 1lb or 450g) fruit pie filling to include cherry, blackcurrant or any other variety to suit personal taste.

Cream-topped Pistachio Cheesecake

serves 10-12

Make exactly as Cheesecake 1 or 2. Whip ¼pt (150ml) double cream until thick with 1 level tbsp caster sugar. Swirl over cold Cheesecake, then sprinkle with ½oz (15g) blanched and finely chopped bright green pistachio nuts (unfortunately very expensive).

Coffee Walnut Cheesecake

serves 10-12

Make exactly as Cheesecake 1 or 2. Whip
¼pt (150ml) double cream until thick with 2
level tsp instant coffee powder and 1 level
tbsp caster sugar. Swirl over top of cake then
shower with 2oz (50g) finely chopped walnuts.

The Incredible Chocolate Cheesecake

serves 12

Rich, velvety, smooth and somewhat akin to
a superlative chocolate mousse.

6oz (175g) plain chocolate digestive biscuits,
   crushed
4oz (125g) unsalted butter
4oz (125g) plain chocolate (Suchard or
   Bournville), broken into squares
1½lb (675g) cream cheese (*not* curd in this
   case)
5oz (150g) caster sugar
3 Grade 2 eggs
1 tsp vanilla essence
1 level tbsp cornflour

1 Brush a 10in (25cm) spring-clip tin (with
   hinged side and loose base) with melted
   butter. Cover base evenly with crushed
   biscuits.
2 Melt butter then pour into basin. Add
   squares of chocolate. Stand the basin over
   pan of hot, not boiling, water until melted,
   stirring occasionally.
3 Meanwhile, beat cheese smoothly with
   rest of ingredients. Stir in butter/chocolate
   mixture and beat until absolutely smooth
   and creamy.
4 Pour into tin over biscuits. Bake about 1
   hour in oven centre (any position in fan
   oven) set to 300°F (150°C), Gas 2. Remove
   from oven. Leave until cold.
5 Refrigerate overnight, unclip sides then
   stand cake (still on its metal base) onto a
   large plate. Cut into wedges for serving.

Black Forest Cheesecake

serves 12

Make up the Incredible Chocolate Cheesecake, adding 2 tbsp cherry brandy to choco-
late/cheese mixture. When cold, spread a
can (1lb or 450g) cherry pie filling over the
top, leaving a 1in (2.5cm) margin uncovered
all the way round. Decorate with ¼pt
(150ml) whipped cream, either by piping
round edge or spooning.

Mocha Cheesecake

serves 12

Make up the Incredible Chocolate Cheesecake but add 2 rounded tsp instant coffee
powder, dissolved in 1 tbsp hot water, to
the basin of butter and chocolate while
melting.

Dairy Cheesecake

serves 8-10

Quite different from all the other Cheesecakes, this one originates from the Milk
Marketing Board.

Flan Pastry made with 6oz (175g) flour
   (page 101).
2 level tbsp cornflour
2 tbsp single cream (you can use Channel
   Islands milk instead)
2oz (50g) butter, softened but not runny
2 Grade 3 eggs, at kitchen temperature and
   separated
8oz (225g) cream cheese
8oz (225g) cottage cheese, rubbed through a
   fine-mesh sieve
2oz (50g) caster sugar
½ tsp vanilla essence

1 Brush an 8in (20cm) spring-clip tin (with
   hinged sides and loose base) with melted
   butter then line base and sides with rolled
   out pastry. Line completely with foil to
   stop pastry from rising as it cooks.
2 Bake for 20 minutes in oven set to 375°F
   (190°C), Gas 5. Take out of oven and remove foil.
3 For filling, mix cornflour smoothly with

cream in mixing bowl. Add butter, egg yolks, both cheeses, sugar and essence.

4 Whisk until completely smooth, either by hand or in a blender or food processor. Beat egg whites to a stiff snow, then beat one-third into cheese mixture. Fold in remaining whites, then pour mixture into pastry-lined tin.

5 Return to oven (at same temperature) and bake about 30-35 minutes or until slightly risen and golden. Remove from oven, cool, unclip sides and refrigerate 1-2 hours when cheesecake is completely cold.

Dairy Cheesecake with Raspberries
serves 8-10

Make up Dairy Cheesecake and leave until cold. Before serving, cover top with 4 tbsp double cream and 8oz (225g) raspberries. Dust thickly with sifted icing sugar.

Chilled Orange Honey Cheesecake

serves 8-10

This recipe is hardly 'baking' as it is 'cooked' in the refrigerator; but the following cheesecakes are, nevertheless, worth including.

4oz (125g) chocolate digestive biscuits, crushed

2oz (50g) butter, melted

2oz (50g) caster sugar

Filling

1 large packet (8oz or 225g) Philadelphia cream cheese

2 Grade 2 eggs, separated

1 carton (5oz or 150g) natural yoghurt

2 level tsp clear honey

3 level tsp gelatine

4 tbsp cold water

2oz (50g) caster sugar

Finely grated peel and juice of 1 medium washed and dried orange

1 Brush an 8in (20cm) spring-clip tin (with hinged sides and loose base) with melted butter. Mix together biscuits, butter and sugar. Sprinkle thickly over base of tin.

2 Beat together cheese, egg yolks, yoghurt and honey. Leave aside temporarily.

3 Soften gelatine by mixing with cold water and leaving to stand 10 minutes. Afterwards melt, without boiling, in small pan over minimal heat.

4 Work into cheese mixture. Beat egg whites to a stiff snow. Gradually add sugar and continue to beat until meringue is very thick and shiny.

5 Whisk one-third into cheese then, using a large metal spoon, fold in remainder. When smooth and evenly combined, pour into prepared tin.

6 Refrigerate until set. To loosen sides, dip tin (with cake still in it) up to its rim into hot water. Count up to six (the heat melts the gelatine slightly), then remove from water and wipe dry. Run a knife round cake, then unclip sides. If obstinate, dip again in water and count up to six. Leave cake on its base to serve.

Chilled Lemon Cheesecake
serves 8-10

Make as Orange Honey Cheesecake but omit orange peel. Instead, add the finely grated peel of 1 small washed and dried lemon, 2 tsp lemon juice and 1/4 tsp vanilla essence.

Lime Cheesecake
serves 8-10

Make as Orange Honey Cheesecake but omit orange peel. Instead, add the finely grated peel of 1 washed and dried lime, 2 tsp lime juice and 1/4 tsp vanilla essence.

Cool Green Chilled Cheesecake
serves 8-10

Perfect as a summer sweet. Decorate the tops of any of the Chilled Cheesecakes with peeled, halved and de-seeded grapes, cut sides downwards. Tuck mint leaves here and there for decoration.

Chilled Party Cheesecake

serves 10-14

2oz (50g) butter, melted
2oz (50g) caster sugar
4oz (125g) digestive biscuits crushed
Filling
4 level tsp gelatine
4 tbsp cold water
1lb (450g) curd cheese
¼pt (150ml) double cream
2 Grade 3 eggs, separated
4oz (125g) caster sugar
Finely grated peel and juice of 1 washed and
  dried lemon
1 tsp vanilla essence

1 Brush an 8in (20cm) spring-clip tin (with
  hinged sides and loose base) with melted
  butter. For base, mix butter and sugar
  with biscuits and sprinkle thickly over
  bottom of tin.
2 To make filling, soften gelatine for 10
  minutes in water then melt, without boiling, in a small pan over minimal heat.
3 Beat cheese with cream, egg yolks, sugar,
  lemon juice and peel, and vanilla essence.
  Stir in the melted gelatine. Leave aside
  in the cool for a few minutes.
4 Whisk egg white to a stiff snow. Beat about
  one-third into cheese mixture. Fold in remainder with a large metal spoon.
5 When smooth and evenly combined, pour
  into prepared tin. Refrigerate until set,
  then unmould as directed in recipe for
  Chilled Orange Honey Cheesecake.

'Fruit Flan' Chilled Party Cheesecake
serves 10-14

Cover top of cake with ¼pt (150ml) soured
cream, then add rings of seasonal fresh fruits,
working from the outside edge inwards.
Choose halved grapes, pieces of pineapple,
halved cherries, halved slices of peeled kiwi
fruit, etc. Brush with melted and sieved apricot jam before serving.

Spiced Chilled Party Cheesecake
serves 10-14

Cover top of cake with ¼pt (150ml) double
cream, whipped until stiff with 1 level tbsp
caster sugar and 1 level tsp cinnamon.

Chilled Party Cheesecake Exotica
serves 10-14

Cover top of cake with ¼pt (150ml) double
cream, whipped until stiff with 1 level tbsp
caster sugar. Stud with halved canned
lychees and slices of canned mangoes, well-
drained.

Chilled Party Cheesecake with Persimmons and Kiwi
serves 10-14

Cover top of cheesecake with alternate slices
of sharon fruit (persimmons from Israel
which look like tomatoes) and peeled kiwis.
This is an ideal combination for December/
January when both fruits are in the shops.

11
Baking with Yeast

Baking with yeast is presently creating enormous interest among those who appreciate the taste and texture of a home-baked loaf and value the sheer economy of this DIY form of cooking. The many kinds of popular white and brown breads — which actually taste like bread and not plastic — the fancy rolls, buns, cakes and special recipes from overseas have all been included in this comprehensive section. I hope those of you who warm to the comforting aroma of a cottage loaf or Hot Cross Buns will take to the kitchen, follow the directions and, whether experienced or not, thoroughly enjoy the mixing, kneading, shaping and all the pleasurable involvement which is part and parcel of yeast cookery.

Ingredients

Flour

There are three kinds of flour used for bread making.

Plain strong white is one of the best choices as it contains a high quality, elastic-type substance called gluten which enables dough to stretch or expand as it bakes, yielding a good rise, characteristic of a successful loaf or cake. As the bran and wheatgerm have been removed from white flour, it is relatively low in fibre. If you are worried about the lack of fibre in your diet, you would probably be better to use the next two types of flour.

Wholemeal and wholewheat flour are what I term complete flours, in that nothing is added or taken away. An excellent source of fibre, doughs made from either of these flours have a mildly nutty flavour and fairly dense texture. For a lighter result, half wholemeal or brown flour and half white may be used.

Brown flour has had 10-15% of the bran and wheatgerm removed. The flours are still healthy and yield a slightly lighter dough than wholemeal and wholewheat flours.

Flours made from other grains such as rye and barley are low in gluten and should always be mixed with half white flour.

It is essential that flour should be kept dry and preferably in a cool place. It is advisable to tip contents of packets into well-stoppered jars.

Salt

Use only the amount stated in the recipe as too much salt kills off yeast and prevents it acting successfully as a raising agent. Conversely, too little makes the dough sticky and difficult to manage. A general proportion is about 1-2 level tsp salt to every 1lb (450g) flour.

Sugar

Although the yeast converts starch in the flour to sugar of its own accord, a little sugar is added to a yeast mixture to give it a boost and speed up its initial action.

Yeast

There are two types available — fresh and dried. Fresh can be found at some health-food shops and local bakeries, and should look putty-like in colour and break easily and cleanly (if brown in colour, it is stale). It freezes well but it is advisable to do so in amounts suitable for use, such as ½oz (15g) or 1oz (25g). Wrap in cling film and freeze for up to six weeks. To use, either thaw 20 minutes or add directly to warm liquid. If left in a small plastic container with airtight lid, or in a polythene bag tied at the top, yeast should stay fresh for up to two weeks in the refrigerator. To use, either blend with warm liquid or, depending on the recipe, rub into the flour.

Dried yeast is available in tins or sachets and once opened, should be stored in an airtight container where it will remain active for a maximum of four months. Because it is concentrated, ½oz (15g) dried yeast (or 1 level tbsp) is equivalent to 1oz (25g) of fresh yeast. Dried yeast has to be reconstituted before

When ready, reconstituted dried yeast is foamy, like a glass of beer

use, so stir the required amount, with a little sugar, into the warm liquid (see individual recipes) and leave to stand for 10-15 minutes in water and 20-25 minutes in milk. When ready, the yeast mixture will have foamed up and look like a glass of beer. If nothing happens, this indicates that the yeast is stale and you need to start again with a fresh batch. Dried yeast is available from health-food shops, chemists and many supermarket chains.

Fat

Butter or margarine and lard or white cooking fat are added for enrichment and to make the texture of the dough softer and more attractively-coloured. Oil may be substituted, in the proportion of 1 tbsp to every $\frac{1}{2}$oz (15g) of fat. Fat or oil added to a yeast mixture helps the loaf to stay fresh longer.

Liquid

Water is the most widely used, followed by milk, in the proportion of $\frac{1}{2}$pt (275ml) to every 1lb (450g) flour. The temperature of the liquid should be at blood heat, easily achieved by mixing 1 part of boiling milk with 2 parts of cold. Milk adds nutritional value to any dough and improves its keeping qualities. It also produces baked goods with a softer, browner crust. Unless the recipe gives an alternative instruction, the liquid should be added *in one go* to the dry ingredients.

Eggs

These are added for richness, nutritional value and colour. Also doughs containing eggs go stale less quickly than those without. It is important to note that if eggs are added, the amount of liquid should be reduced accordingly.

Note Any dough enriched with fat, milk, sugar and eggs will take longer to rise than a plain dough.

Method

Directions will be given in each group of recipes but below are a few general points worth observing.

1 After drawing the dough together and unless otherwise stated, turn out onto a floured surface and knead thoroughly until smooth, elastic and no longer sticky. This could take up to half an hour, depending on quantity, how you knead, and the type of flour used. If the dough remains obstinately sticky, work in a little extra flour. For speed, you can use the dough hook attachment of an electric mixer but even so, knead by hand for 2-3 minutes at the very end.

2 Rising times may be varied to suit individual requirements, but however it is done, the dough *must double in size*. This is called *proving* the dough. For a quick rise, put dough into a clean, oiled bowl and cover with an oiled plate. Put into a warm airing cupboard or sink half-filled with hot water. Leave about 1-1½ hours. For a medium-quick rise, leave dough in a clean oiled bowl, covered with an oiled plate, at kitchen temperature for 2-2½ hours. For a slow rise, leave in a cool pantry or larder, also covered, for about 4 hours. For an overnight rise, halve the amount of yeast

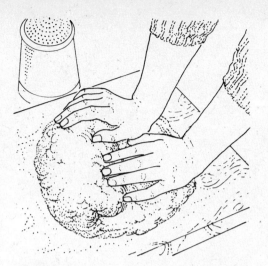

Knead thoroughly, until smooth, elastic and no longer sticky

given in the recipe and leave the dough, covered in an oiled bowl, overnight in the refrigerator.

3 To freeze uncooked dough, divide into 1lb (450g) amounts *before* allowing to rise. Put into oiled and roomy polythene bags. Tie each loosely at the top. Freeze plain doughs up to a 1 month and the richer doughs up to 3 months. Thaw completely then knead thoroughly and leave to rise as previously described.

4 To freeze cooked yeasted loaves and buns, wrap well then seal, label and store up to six months. If freezing French-type bread or rolls with a crisp crust, store up to 1 week only as the crusts will start peeling off.

Mishaps

Top crust broke away from loaf

1 Dough under-risen and/or dried out while rising.

2 Oven too hot.

Crust split along one side of loaf

1 Bread, etc baked too high up in oven.

Rising times may be varied, but the dough must double in size

Loaf, etc, had flat instead of domed top

1 Soft flour used (ie not marked 'strong')

2 Insufficient salt added.

3 Too much liquid used and dough became over-wet.

Crust cracked after loaf was removed from oven

1 Dough left to rise for too long and was over-proved.

2 Oven too hot.

3 Loaf, etc allowed to cool in a draught.

Dough fell in on itself while baking

1 As Point 1 above.

Texture close and loaf poorly risen

1 Flour too soft.
2 Too much salt added.
3 Dough insufficiently kneaded and not proved for long enough.
4 Dough allowed to rise in atmosphere that was too hot.

Texture open, coarse and crumbly

1 Dough made too wet.
2 Dough over-proved.
3 Oven temperature not hot enough.

Texture peppered with large holes and also uneven

1 Dough left uncovered while rising.
2 Dough insufficiently kneaded after first rising.

Strong yeast taste and/or smell

1 Yeast creamed with sugar.
2 Yeast was stale (especially if fresh).
3 Too much yeast used.
4 Dough over-risen.

Bread goes stale quickly and crumbles

1 Too much yeast used.
2 Flour too soft.
3 Dough rose too quickly in too warm an atmosphere.
4 Dough under or over-risen.

Plain White Bread

makes 3 loaves

½oz (15g or 1 level tbsp) dried yeast *plus*
   2 level tsp caster sugar *or*
   1oz (25g) fresh yeast
1½pt (850ml) warm water (see page 178)
1oz (25g) caster sugar
1 bag (3lb or 1.2kg) strong plain white flour
3-4½ level tsp salt

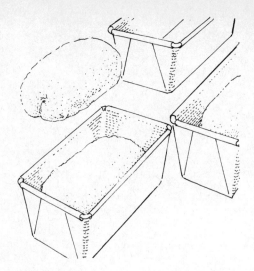

Divide into three portions and shape each to fit a 2lb (1kg) loaf tin

2oz (50g) butter, margarine, lard or cooking fat
Beaten egg for brushing

1 Mix dried yeast and sugar with warm water and leave 10-15 minutes or until frothy. Alternatively, mix fresh yeast with water and blend in 1oz (25g) sugar.
2 Sift dry ingredients into bowl and rub in chosen fat. Add yeast liquid to form a soft dough, stirring with fingertips or knife.
3 Turn out onto floured surface. Knead up to half hour or until dough is smooth and elastic and no longer sticky. If it remains tacky, work in a little extra flour.
4 Put into oiled bowl, cover with an oiled plate and leave to rise as directed on page 178.
5 Turn dough out again on floured surface and knead briefly (called 'punching down' or 'knocking back') to break down air bubbles produced by the yeast. Otherwise the air bubbles would produce large holes throughout the texture. This is a quick process and should take no longer than 5 minutes when the dough will once again be smooth and elastic.
6 Divide into three portions and shape each to fit a 2lb (1kg) well-greased loaf tin. Cover with oiled polythene and leave to

When risen to top of tins, brush gently with egg, and bake

rise about 45 minutes in a warm place or until dough reaches tops of tins and looks light and puffy.

7 Brush gently with egg (or milk or salted water) and bake 45-50 minutes just above centre of hot oven (any position in fan oven) set to 450°F (230°C), Gas 8. When ready, loaves should be golden brown and nicely domed.

8 Turn out and cool on a wire rack.

Cottage Loaves
makes 3
Make up Plain White Bread then, after dividing dough into three portions, take about one-third off each. Shape large pieces of dough into rounds and then repeat with smaller pieces. Brush large pieces with egg, milk or salted water. Top with small pieces and hold in position by pushing down, through centre of each loaf, with the floured handle of a wooden spoon. Dust top of loaves lightly with flour. Bake as directed for Plain White Bread.

Farmhouse Loaves
makes 3
Make up Plain White Bread. When loaves are in their tins, dust lightly with flour and leave in a warm place to rise. Just before baking, make slits along length of loaves with a sharp knife. As the loaves bake, the splits will open out and widen.

Bloomer Loaves
makes 3
Make up Plain White Bread. Shape loaves into 9in (22.5cm) 'sausages'. Put onto a large baking tray then make 6 diagonal slashes, 1in (2.5cm) apart, on top of each. Brush with beaten egg then leave to rise. Bake as directed.

Assorted Breads
Using one batch of dough, you can make three assorted-shaped loaves as previously described.

Hotel Rolls
makes 36
Make up Plain White Bread dough then roll into 36 balls. Place on two greased baking trays. Cut a cross on top of each with scissors. Bake one shelf above and one shelf below oven centre (any position in fan oven) for 25-30 minutes at the same temperature as bread. Reverse position of trays at half-time. Remove from oven and brush with water which, when dry, gives a light glaze to the rolls.

Sesame Rolls
makes 36
Make as above but brush with egg immediately before baking then sprinkle lightly with sesame seeds.

Knots
makes 36
Roll dough into 36 x 6in (15cm) lengths and tie loosely into knots. Bake as directed for Hotel Rolls.

Poppy Seed Knots
makes 36
Make as Knots. Brush lightly with beaten egg before baking then dust lightly with poppy seeds.

181

Cottage Rolls

makes 36

Roll dough into 36 balls, a little smaller than those for Hotel Rolls. Top with remainder of dough, rolled into 36 smaller balls. Push a floured finger through each. Brush with milk then leave to rise.

Plaits

makes 36

Divide dough into 36 pieces then divide each piece into three. Roll the 3 pieces into 4in (10cm) strands and plait together. Put onto baking tray. Leave to rise. Brush with egg immediately before baking.

Sesame Plaits

makes 36

Make Plaits then sprinkle with sesame seeds after brushing with egg.

Caraway Plaits

makes 36

Make Plaits then sprinkle with caraway seeds after brushing with egg.

Poppy Seed Plaits

makes 36

Make Plaits then sprinkle with poppy seeds after brushing with egg.

Onion Plaits

makes 36

Make Plaits then sprinkle with dried onions after brushing with egg.

Cloverleaves

makes 36

Divide dough into 36 pieces then divide each into three pieces and roll into small balls. Drop three balls into greased bun tins. Repeat with rest of balls. Leave to rise in a warm place. Brush with egg immediately before baking.

Hamburger Buns

makes 36

Divide dough into 36 pieces and flatten into a 1½in (4cm) thick round. Leave to rise. Brush with beaten egg immediately before baking.

Large Hamburger Buns

makes 24

Divide dough into 24 pieces and make as above.

Sesame Hamburger Buns

makes 36

Make as Hamburger Buns then sprinkle with sesame seeds after brushing with egg.

Crescents

makes 36

Divide dough into 36 pieces and roll each into a triangle. Roll up, starting from the edge opposite the point. Curve into crescents. Leave to rise. Brush with egg immediately before baking.

Salted Crescents

makes 36

Make as Crescents but sprinkle with coarse sea salt after brushing with egg.

Soft-sided Rolls

makes 36

Shape dough into 36 balls. Stand them fairly close together on two greased baking trays (18 rolls on each). Leave to rise until they join together. Brush tops with milk immediately before baking. Ease apart before serving.

Assorted Rolls

makes 36

Make different-shaped rolls for variety and offer a selection, rather than one kind.

(above right) Biscuits for Cheese (left), page 164; Muesli Chocolate Bars, page 159; and Sesame and Honey Cookies, page 160 *(Gale's Honey)*

(below right) Honeyed Ginger Shortbread, page 152 *(Gale's Honey)*

Muffins

makes 9

These are nostalgic and delicious — one of my most novel souvenirs of the past is an individual, silver-plated muffin warmer which I use when entertaining visitors from abroad. They always find it most intriguing!

Take one-third of Plain White risen bread dough. Roll out to ½in (1.25cm) in thickness. Cut into 9 rounds with a 3½in (9cm) plain biscuit cutter. Place on well-floured baking tray or board and leave in a warm place to rise for about 45 minutes or until double in size. Bake near top of hot oven (any position in fan oven) set to 450°F (230°C), Gas 8 for 8-10 minutes or until golden brown, turning over with a palette knife at half time. To serve, pull apart edges to make an opening, then toast on both sides (outsides only should be toasted). Split in half and put a slice of butter inside each. Keep warm until ready to eat for afternoon tea.

'Griddle' Muffins

makes 9

If preferred, cook muffins on a floured griddle over a fire or other source of heat, allowing 5 minutes per side. A large, floured frying pan (manual or electric) may be used instead.

Pizza

The full quantity of Plain White Bread dough makes 6 large pizzas, so either make the full quantity and freeze spares, or halve the quantity of flour (keeping amount of yeast the same) and make 3 pizzas for about 6 people. I shall base the recipe on one large pizza with assorted toppings for variety (see Chapter 7 for Hasty Pizza).

Roll out one portion of dough (one-sixth) and press into a 13 x 9in (32.5 x 22.5cm) greased Swiss Roll tin, covering base completely. Alternatively, press over base of two 9in (22.5cm) greased sandwich tins. Brush to within ½in (1.25cm) of edges with olive oil then cover with one can (about 14oz or 400g) drained and chopped tomatoes. (Keep liquid for soup or stews.)

Pizza Neapolitan

serves 2

Top tomatoes with 8oz (225g) sliced Mozzarella cheese and 8 chopped canned anchovy fillets (in oil). Sprinkle with 1 rounded tsp dried oregano. Leave 30 minutes in a cool place, then bake 30 minutes near top of oven (any position in fan oven) set to 425°F (220°C), Gas 7. Pizza is best if *not* left to rise before baking. The period of rest in a cool place improves the quality of the finished product.

Pizza Margherita

serves 2

Popular all over Italy, I first tasted this version in the south of the country and found it very tasty indeed. Make exactly as Pizza Neapolitan but omit achovies and use dried basil instead of oregano.

(*above left*) Christmas Eve Cake, page 238 (*Danish Agricultural Producers*)

(*below left*) Croissants, page 197; Bap rolls, page 190; Wholemeal Plait, page 188; and Oatcakes, page 162 (*Rank Hovis McDougall*)

Pizza Sicilian
serves 2
Make as Pizza Neapolitan but add 12-18 black olives with other ingredients.

Pizza with Mushrooms
serves 2
Top tomatoes with 4oz (125g) sliced mushrooms before adding the cheese and herbs. If liked, sprinkle the mushrooms with 2 crushed cloves of garlic.

Pizza with Ham
serves 2
Sprinkle tomatoes with 4oz (125g) chopped ham before adding cheese and herbs.

Pizza with Prawns
serves 2
To save over-cooking, make up the Pizza Margherita and, as soon as it comes out of the oven, stud with cooked seafood to taste, eg peeled prawns, mussels, clams.

Cheese Bread

makes 3 loaves

This is very useful for savoury sandwiches and toast. Make up Plain White Bread dough but after rubbing in the fat, toss in 12oz (350g) grated Cheddar cheese and 6oz (175g) grated and lightly fried onion (or same amount of chopped and fried celery). Add yeast liquid and continue as directed.

Herb Bread
makes 3 loaves
Also useful for savoury eating, make as Cheese Bread but toss in 1 level tbsp dried mixed herbs after rubbing in fat. Add yeast liquid and continue as directed. Omit cheese.

Cheese and Herb Bread
makes 3 loaves
Make up Plain White Bread Dough but after rubbing in fat, toss in 12oz (350g) grated Cheddar cheese and 1 level tbsp mixed herbs. Add yeast liquid and continue as directed.

Fast White Bread

makes 2 loaves

Experiments carried out by the Flour Advisory Bureau in London have proved that the inclusion of a small amount of ascorbic acid (Vitamin C, readily available from chemists) makes the first rising of dough unnecessary. The whole process is therefore speeded up to about 1¾ hours from start to finish. Fresh yeast is recommended — and more than the usual proportion.

1oz (25g) fresh yeast
¾pt (425ml) warm water (page 178)
25mg tablet of ascorbic acid (Vitamin C), crushed
1½lb (675g) strong plain white flour .
2 level tsp salt
1 level tbsp caster sugar
1 oz (25g) butter, margarine, lard or white cooking fat
Beaten egg for brushing

1 Blend yeast with warm water. Add the Vitamin C tablet. Sift flour and salt into a bowl. Toss in caster sugar. Rub in the fat.
2 Using a fork, stir in yeast liquid to form a soft dough. Turn out onto a floured surface. Knead up to half an hour or until smooth, elastic and no longer sticky. If dough remains tacky, work in a little extra flour. You can use the dough hook attachment of an electric mixer if preferred.
3 Divide in half and shape to fit two 1lb (450g) greased loaf tins. Cover with greased polythene or greased greaseproof paper and leave to rise in a warm place until dough doubles in size and reaches tops of tins; about 50 minutes.
4 Brush lightly with beaten egg and bake just above oven centre (any position in fan oven) set to 450°F (230°C), Gas 8. Allow about 45-50 minutes. Cool on wire rack.

Fast White Cobs
makes 2
Make as above but divide dough in half and shape each piece into a round loaf. Place on a greased baking tray. Rise and bake as above.

Assorted Shaped Loaves

For other shaped loaves, follow directions given under Plain White Bread (page 180).

Fast White Rolls

makes 18

Divide dough into 18 pieces and shape as directed under Plain White Bread. Leave to rise about 15 minutes in warm place. Brush with egg, milk or salted water. Bake at same temperature as Fast White Bread for 10-15 minutes. Cool on a wire rack.

Seeded Rolls

makes 18

If liked, sprinkle rolls of whatever shape with poppy, caraway or sesame seeds after brushing with egg.

Shortcut Brown Bread

makes 1 loaf

Another fast-to-make loaf, based on brown flour; a lovely moist and nutty-tasting bread which I have been making for years with never a failure.

2 level tsp dried yeast *plus*
    1 level tsp caster sugar *or*
    1/2oz (15g) fresh yeast
1/2pt (275ml) warm water
1lb (450g) brown flour
1 level tsp salt
1oz (15g) butter, margarine, lard or white
    cooking fat *or* 2 tsp salad oil
Plain white flour for sprinkling.

Make dough exactly as given for Plain White Bread excluding the addition of the 1oz (25g) extra sugar. If using oil, mix with the water and blend into dry ingredients. Knead dough thoroughly. Shape to fit a 1lb (450g) well-greased loaf tin (lard is best for this). Cover with greased polythene or greased grease-proof paper and leave to rise in a warm place for 45 minutes, or at kitchen temperature 1 1/4-1 1/2 hours, or in a cool place 2-2 1/2 hours. Dust lightly with flour. Bake as Plain White Bread, allowing 45-50 minutes.

Brown Cob

makes 1 loaf

Shape dough into large ball and place on greased tray. Flatten slightly then cut a criss-cross pattern on top. Glaze by brushing with salted water. Leave to rise then bake as directed for Shortcut Brown Loaf.

Brown Rolls

makes 12

Divide dough into 12 pieces and shape as directed for rolls in recipe for Plain White Bread. Leave to rise about 30 minutes. Bake 12-15 minutes.

Irish Brown Soda Bread

makes 1 loaf

This recipe comes from a marvellous book of Irish recipes put out by the National Dairy Council. It is called *Irish Recipes — Traditional and Modern* and here is the recipe as published (without metrication).

'3/4lb wholemeal flour
1/4lb white flour
1/2 tsp salt
3/4 tsp bread soda (bicarbonate of soda)
1/2 pt buttermilk (a little extra if required)
2oz margarine

Mix all the dry ingredients together, rubbing in the margarine. Mix to a very wet dough with buttermilk or well-soured milk. Knead lightly. Put into a 7in greased cake tin. Make a cross on top with a floured knife. Cover with lid and bake in a hot oven for about 45 minutes.'

Irish White Soda Bread

makes 1 loaf

From the same book comes the white version of the Brown Loaf.

'1lb flour
1/2 teaspoonful bread soda
1/2 teaspoonful salt
1/2pt buttermilk or soured milk

Sift flour, salt and finely powdered bread soda into a bowl. Mix to a loose dough with well-soured milk. Turn out onto a floured board and knead lightly until the underside is smooth. Turn the smooth side up. Place in a well-heated, greased 8in cast iron pot. Make a cross on top with a knife. Cover with lid. Bake in hot oven for about 40 minutes. Alternatively, a baking tin may be used instead of an iron pot.'

Wholemeal Bread (Traditional)

makes 3 loaves

Make exactly as Plain White Bread (page 180) but use wholemeal flour and increase dried yeast to ¾oz (23g or 4 level tsp) and fresh yeast to 1½oz (40g).

Crunchy Topped Bread

makes 3 loaves

Brush tops of loaves with salted water or milk before proving the second time, then sprinkle with kibbled wheat (available from health food shops).

Wholemeal Coburgs

makes 3

Divide dough equally into three portions and shape into round balls. Place on one large baking tray. Using a sharp knife, make a cross cut on top of each. Brush with salted water or milk. Prove and bake.

Wholemeal Plaits

makes 3

(illustrated on page 184)

Divide dough into 9 equal pieces and roll each into a 15in (37.5cm) long sausage. Plait together in threes. Place on greased baking tray. Brush with salted water or milk to glaze. Prove and bake.

Fancy Wholemeal Rolls

makes 36

Make as given in recipe under Plain White Bread.

Brown Pizza

Almost preferable to White Bread Dough for pizza, use the Wholemeal Dough given above, following instructions for Pizzas made with Plain White Bread dough.

Light Brown Bread

makes 3 loaves

Follow recipe for Wholemeal Bread (Traditional) but use half wholemeal flour and half white.

Rye Bread

makes 3 loaves

Follow recipe for Wholemeal Bread (Traditional), but use half rye flour and half white flour.

Granary Bread

makes 3 loaves

Follow recipe for Wholemeal Bread (Traditional), but use half granary flour and half white flour.

Apricot and Walnut Bread

makes 3 loaves

More favoured all over the world than in Britain, sweet yeasted breads take a lot of beating if sliced and buttered and served for tea or supper. This one is delicious, nutritious and colourful. Make up Wholemeal Bread as directed. Knead in 1lb (450g) apricots (soaked until soft then wiped dry and chopped) and 6oz (175g) walnuts, coarsely chopped.

Divide into three and shape each piece to fit a 2lb (1kg) loaf tin. Cover with greased polythene or greased greaseproof paper and leave to rise until doubled in size (about 45 minutes). Bake about 45-50 minutes just above oven centre (any position in fan oven) set to 425°F (220°C), Gas 7. Turn out and cool on a wire rack.

Prune and Peanut Bread

makes 3 loaves

Make as above substituting 1lb (450g) chopped stoned dates for apricots, and 6oz (175g) chopped unsalted peanuts for walnuts.

Fig and Almond Bread
makes 3 loaves

Make as above substituting 1lb (450g) chopped dried figs for apricots and 6oz (175g) toasted and chopped almonds for walnuts.

Cheese and Cashew Bread
makes 3 loaves

Make as above substituting 12oz (350g) grated Edam cheese for fruit and 6oz (175g) toasted and chopped cashews for walnuts.

Family Sausage Rolls
makes 20

Take one-quarter of the Wholemeal Dough and roll into a rectangle measuring 20 x 9in (50 x 22.5cm). Cut dough in half lengthwise, giving two pieces of 20 x 4½in (50 x 11.25cm). Roll 1lb (450g) pork or beef sausagemeat into 20in (50cm) long rolls. Put onto strips of dough. Brush edges with water. Press well together to seal. Place on greased baking tray. Brush with egg. Prick diagonally all the way along rolls to allow steam to escape. Cover with greased polythene or aluminium foil and leave to rise in a warm place 30 minutes. Bake 25 minutes just above oven centre (any position in fan oven) set to 425°F (220°C), Gas 7. Cut into 2in (5cm) lengths and serve warm.

Cocktail Sausage Rolls
makes 40

Make as previous recipe but cut Sausage Rolls into 1in (2.5cm) pieces.

Picnic Sausage Rolls
makes 14

Make as previous recipe but cut into 14 rolls, each just under 3in (7.5cm) long. Cool completely before packing and do not re-heat.

Enriched White Bread or Milk Bread

This is a richer version of Plain White Bread and the warm liquid used (1½pt or 850ml) should be half milk and half water. Increase the fat from 2oz (50g) to 6oz (175g). The method is exactly the same but the dough may take a little longer to rise the first and second times. This bread has a silky, moist texture but it must be stored in dry and cool conditions.

Milk Loaves
makes 3

Make Enriched White Bread and shape to fit three 2lb (1kg) well-greased loaf tins. Brush tops with beaten egg or milk before baking. Bake just above centre of oven (any position in fan oven), set to 400°F (200°C), Gas 6. Allow 50-60 minutes or until golden brown. Turn out and cool on a wire rack.

Milk Plait
makes 3

Make Enriched White Bread and divide risen dough into 3 equal pieces. Divide each piece into a further 3 equal pieces and roll into 16in (40cm) strands. Plait together, in threes, to make 3 loaves. Place on baking tray. Brush with beaten egg or milk before baking. Bake as directed for Milk Loaves.

Seeded Plait
makes 3

Make Plaits as above. After brushing with egg or milk, sprinkle with poppy, sesame or caraway seeds before baking.

New Yorker Plaits
makes 3

Make Plaits as given above. When cold, eat with butter, cream cheese and smoked salmon.

Bap Loaves

makes 3

Make Enriched White Bread and divide risen dough into 3 equal pieces. Shape into balls. Put onto 3 greased baking trays. Press down to ½in (1.25cm) in thickness. Leave to rise, covered with greased greaseproof paper or polythene, for about 40 minutes in a warm place. Gently press down centre of each Bap with the back of a wooden spoon to prevent it from blistering. Dredge with flour, then bake on 3 shelves in oven for about 25-30 minutes or until light gold. Leave the middle loaf where it is, but reverse position of top and bottom Baps at half-time (not in a fan oven). Transfer to wire racks and at once cover with tea-towels to ensure soft crusts.

Bap Rolls or Morning Rolls

makes 36

(illustrated on page 184)

Make Enriched White Bread and divide risen dough into 36 pieces. Shape each into a ball and flatten into a ½in (1.25cm) thick round. Put onto 3 large greased baking trays, cover and leave to rise in a warm place for 30-35 minutes. Dredge with flour and bake on 3 shelves of oven for 15 minutes at 400°F (200°C), Gas 6. Leave centre tray of rolls on middle shelf but reverse position of top and bottom trays of Baps at half time. Transfer rolls to a wire rack and cover as above.

Bridge Rolls

makes 36

Make Enriched White Bread and divide risen dough into 36 pieces. Shape each into a 'cigar' shape the length of an index finger. Stand reasonably close together, on 3 large greased baking trays, so that the rolls join together while proving; this should take about 25-30 minutes when rolls should be light, puffy and double in size. Keep covered with greased greaseproof paper or polythene and brush with egg before baking. Bake exactly as Bap Rolls. Gently break rolls apart and cool on a wire rack.

Cocktail Bridge Rolls

makes 72

Make as Bridge Rolls, but shape into 'cigars' of only 2in (5cm) in length, put onto trays and bake as Bap Rolls in two or three batches.

Grissini or Italian Bread Sticks

makes 30

The Enriched White Bread recipe makes a large number of sticks which store well in an airtight container. However, to make only 30 Grissini, make up Enriched White Bread then divide risen dough into 3 equal portions. Shape 2 portions into any of the loaves given above then divide third portion into pieces the size of walnuts. Roll into thin strands measuring 12in (30cm) in length. Arrange on greased baking tray. Brush with milk or lightly beaten egg white. Cover. Leave to rise in a warm place for 15 minutes. Bake just above oven centre (any position in fan oven) set to 425°F (220°C) Gas 7, until golden brown and crisp. Allow about 15-17 minutes. Cool on a wire rack.

Grissini Salt Sticks

makes 30

Sprinkle Grissini with coarse sea salt before baking.

Grissini Sesame Sticks

makes 30

Sprinkle Grissini with sesame seeds before baking.

Grissini Poppy Seed Sticks

makes 30

Sprinkle Grissini with poppy seeds before baking.

Grissini Parmesan Sticks

makes 30

Sprinkle Grissini with Parmesan cheese before baking.

Grissini Celery Sticks
makes 30
Sprinkle Grissini with celery salt before baking.

Grissini Paprika Sticks
makes 30
Sprinkle Grissini with paprika before baking.

Currant Loaf

Make up Enriched White Bread dough and take off one-third of risen dough. Into it knead 4-6oz (125-175g) currants. Shape to fit a 2lb (1kg) greased loaf tin. Leave to rise, covered, for about 1 hour in a warm place. Brush top with beaten egg then bake 50 minutes just above centre of oven (any position in fan oven) set to 400°F (200°C), Gas 6. Turn out and cool on a wire rack.

Mixed Fruit Loaf
Make as Currant Loaf but instead of currants, knead in the same amount of mixed dried fruit.

Sultana and Lemon Loaf
Make as Currant Loaf but instead of currants, knead in the same amount of sultanas and grated peel of one small washed and dried lemon.

Fruit Horseshoe
Make as Currant Loaf but instead of currants, knead in the same amount of mixed dried fruit, 1oz (25g) chopped glacé cherries, 1 level tsp ground cardamom and 1 level tsp grated orange peel. Shape into a horseshoe on a greased baking tray and brush with egg.

Selkirk Bannocks

makes 2

This is a Scottish speciality, eaten at Hogmany and first made in a Selkirk bakery in 1859.

Make up Enriched White Bread dough and take off one-third of risen dough. Into it knead 4oz (125g) mixed dried fruit and 2oz (50g) caster sugar. Divide into 2 equal pieces and shape each into an 8in (20cm) round. Transfer to large greased baking tray, cover with greased greaseproof paper or polythene and leave to rise for about 40 minutes in a warm place. Brush with milk. Bake 25-30 minutes just above oven centre (any position in fan oven) set to 375°F (190°C), Gas 5. When ready, the cakes should be golden brown. Cool on a wire rack. When cold, slice and eat spread with butter.

Lardy Cake

(illustrated on page 210)

Once upon a time when housewives baked daily this was made with leftover dough, but it is now made with a specially prepared dough as follows. Make Enriched White Bread dough and take off about one-third. Roll risen dough into an oblong of ½in (1.25cm) thickness. Divide 4oz (125g) lard into 3 portions. Cover top two-thirds of dough with 1 portion of lard, applied in small pats. Sprinkle with 1½oz (40g) caster sugar, 1 oz (25g) sultanas and ½ level tsp mixed spice. Fold in three by bringing bottom (uncovered) third to centre and folding top third over. Seal edges, turn and roll out like Flaky Pastry (see page 117) twice more, using up all the lard plus another 3 oz (75g) caster sugar, 2oz (50g) sultanas and 1 level tsp mixed spice. Finally roll out to fit a greased roasting tin measuring 10 x 8in (25 x 20cm). Cover. Leave to rise in a warm place until light and puffy, about 50-60 minutes. Bake for 40 minutes just above centre of oven (any position in fan oven) set to 425°F (220°C), Gas 7. Allow to cool in tin until all the melted fat has been absorbed by the cake. Turn out onto a wire cooling rack. Serve the cake upside down while still slightly warm. Accompany with extra butter.

Cornish-style Saffron Cake

Make up Enriched White Bread dough and take off one-third of risen dough. Into it knead 6oz (175g) mixed dried fruit including peel, 2oz caster sugar and the liquid from ½ level tsp saffron stamens soaked in 3 tsp hot water. Shape to fit a well-greased 8in (20cm) round cake tin. Cover. Leave to rise in a warm place up to 1 hour or until double in size. Bake about 50 minutes just above centre of oven (any position in fan oven) set to 400°F (200°C), Gas 6. The cake is ready when it is well-domed and golden brown. Cool on a wire rack. When cold, slice and serve plain or buttered.

Fruit Buns

makes 12

Make Enriched White Bread dough and take off one-third. Work in 4oz (125g) mixed dried fruit then divide mixture into 12 pieces. Shape into round buns. Put onto greased baking tray. Cover with greased greaseproof paper or polythene and leave to rise in a warm place until double in size, about 30-40 minutes. Brush with beaten egg or milk and bake 20 minutes just above centre of oven (any position in fan oven) set to 425°F (220°C), Gas 7. Cool on a wire rack.

Sticky Fruit Buns
makes 12
As soon as the buns have come out of the oven, brush with melted golden syrup, clear honey or warm, sieved apricot jam.

Date and Walnut Buns
makes 12
Make as Fruit Buns but instead of mixed dried fruit, use 2oz (50g) *each*, chopped dates and walnuts.

Cherry and Almond Buns
makes 12
Make as Fruit Buns but instead of mixed dried fruit, use 1oz (25g) chopped glacé cherries and 1oz (25g) toasted almond flakes.

Swiss Buns

makes 12

Use one-third of Enriched White Bread dough and divide into 12 pieces. Shape each into a 4in (10cm) 'cigar'. Place on a large greased baking tray. Leave to rise, covered, for about 30 minutes in a warm place. Bake 15 minutes just above centre of oven (any position in fan oven) set to 425°F (220°C), Gas 7. Cool on a wire rack. When completely cold, spread tops with glacé icing made by mixing 6oz (175g) sifted icing sugar to a spreadable icing with about 7 tsp water and ½ tsp vanilla essence. If liked, tint pale pink.

Cornish Splits
makes 12
Make as Swiss Buns but shape into 12 round buns and bake as directed. When cold, split in half and fill thickly with clotted cream and red jam. Sift icing sugar over tops.

Devon Chudleighs
makes 12
Make as Cornish Splits but while the buns are still warm, split in half and fill with clotted cream and jam.

'Thunder and Lightning'
makes 12
Make as Cornish Splits, but fill the cold and halved buns with clotted cream and black treacle.

Danish Teacakes

makes 8
(illustrated on page 209)

2 level tsp dried yeast
1 tsp caster sugar
¼pt (125ml) milk
¼pt (125ml) water
2oz (50g) slightly salted butter
1lb (450g) plain white flour
1oz (25g) caster sugar
1 tsp salt
2oz (50g) mixed dried fruit

Glaze

2 tbsp milk

1 tbsp caster sugar

1 Sprinkle the yeast and 1 tsp sugar into the warmed milk and water and stir. Leave until frothy — about 5 minutes.
2 Rub the butter into the flour and mix in the 1oz sugar, salt and fruit. When the yeast is frothy add to the mixture. Knead until smooth and no longer sticky. Place the dough in a lightly oiled plastic bag and leave in a warm place until doubled in size — about 1½ hours.
3 Knead again and cut dough into eight pieces.
4 Roll out into 4in (10cm) circles. Place well apart on baking sheet. Cover and leave in a warm place to double in size.
5 Brush with the milk and sugar and bake for 15 minutes at 425°F (220°C), Gas 7.

To serve, split and spread with butter.

Danish Teabread

makes 2 loaves

(illustrated on page 209)

Divide the dough into two, knead and put in two 1lb (450g) greased loaf tins. Then prove and glaze as for Teacakes. Bake 30-35 minutes at same temperature as Teacakes.

Bun Loaf

Made from an egg-enriched dough, this mixture also lends itself admirably to variations as you can see from the selection which follows.

½oz (15g) or 1 level tbsp dried yeast *or* 1oz (25g) fresh yeast

1 level tsp syrup or honey

8fl oz (225ml) warm milk

1lb (450g) strong plain white flour

1 level tsp salt

2oz (50g) butter or margarine

2oz (50g) caster sugar

6oz (175g) mixed dried fruit, including peel

1 Grade 3 egg, beaten

Extra beaten egg for brushing

1 Mix dried yeast and syrup or honey with warm milk and leave for 15-20 minutes in a warm place until frothy. Alternatively, blend syrup or honey and fresh yeast into the milk.
2 Sift flour and salt into bowl. Rub in fat. Toss in sugar and dried fruit. Mix to a dough with yeast liquid and egg.
3 Knead about 20-30 minutes or until smooth, elastic and no longer sticky. Place in a greased bowl, cover, then leave to rise in a warm place until doubled in size; about 1¼-1½ hours.
4 Knead quickly until smooth, then shape to fit a 2lb (1kg) loaf tin. Cover. Leave to rise again in the warm until light, puffy and double in size; again about 1-1¼ hours.
5 Bake until golden brown, allowing about 50 minutes just above centre of oven (any position in fan oven) set to 400°F (200°C), Gas 6. Turn out and cool on a wire rack.

Chelsea Buns

makes 12

Popular with King George III and his wife Queen Charlotte, these buns date back to the eighteenth century when they were eaten for tea on Sundays. Make Bun Loaf mixture but omit fruit. Roll out risen dough into a 12 x 9in (30 x 22.5cm) oblong. Brush with 1oz (25g) melted butter or margarine then sprinkle with 4oz (125g) mixed dried fruit including peel, 2oz (50g) caster sugar and 1 level tsp mixed spice or the same amount of finely grated lemon peel. Roll up, starting from one of the longer sides, then cut into 12 slices. Place on a large greased baking tray. Cover. Leave to rise in a warm place until buns have doubled in size and joined together, about 40 minutes. Bake 20-25 minutes just above centre of the oven (any position in fan oven) set to 425°F (220°C), Gas 7. Cool on a wire rack and separate when cold.

Glazed Chelsea Buns

makes 12

Make as above, then glaze by melting 1½oz (40g) caster sugar in 2 tbsp *each* of milk and water. Bring to the boil then boil steadily until syrupy (about 5 minutes).

Iced Chelsea Buns

makes 12

Make as above then ice by brushing with a stiffish glacé icing made by mixing 3oz (75g) sifted icing sugar with a few tsps of cold water or fresh strained lemon juice. Leave until icing has set then separate the buns.

Yorkshire Tea Cakes

makes 6

Make Bun Loaf mixture but omit mixed dried fruit and add 3oz (75g) currants instead. Divide risen dough into 6 equal pieces and shape each into a round of ½in (1.25cm) in thickness. Place on two well-greased baking trays. Cover. Leave to rise 50 minutes in a warm place. Brush with milk. Bake one shelf above and one shelf below oven centre (any position in fan oven) set to 425°F (220°C), Gas 7. Reverse position of trays at half-time and allow a total of 18-20 minutes baking time or until Tea Cakes are golden brown. To serve, split, toast and butter.

Plain Yorkshire Tea Cakes

makes 6

Make as above but omit fruit.

Doughnuts

makes 12

Make Bun Loaf mixture but omit fruit and reduce sugar to 1oz (25g). Shape risen dough into 12 balls. Leave to rise, covered, until twice their original size, allowing about 30-40 minutes. Fry in deep hot oil (temperature 180°C or 350°F) until well browned, turning frequently with a spoon and allowing about 7-10 minutes. Drain on crumpled kitchen paper and toss in caster sugar.

Note If oil is too hot, Doughnuts will turn brown on the outside and be uncooked in the middle. If the oil is too cool, Doughnuts will be soggy. If oil begins to smoke, this is a clear indication that it has overheated and should be left to cool down a little before the Doughnuts are added.

Jam Doughnuts

makes 12

Make Doughnuts as above then, using a star-shaped tube and icing syringe, push into centre of each Doughnut and 'inject' some melted, sieved plum jam.

Finger Doughnuts

makes 12

Instead of balls, shape dough into 5in (12.5cm) lengths and fry as above. Drain. Toss in sugar.

Fresh Cream Doughnuts

makes 12

Split round or finger Doughnuts in half and fill with sweetened whipped cream.

Fresh Cream and Jam Doughnuts

makes 12

Split round or finger Doughnuts in half and fill with sweetened whipped cream and jam.

Fresh Cream and Chocolate Doughnuts

makes 12

Split round or finger Doughnuts in half and fill with chocolate spread and sweetened whipped cream.

Ring Doughnuts

makes 12

Roll out risen dough to ½in (1.25cm) in thickness and cut into 3in (7.5cm) rings, re-rolling, and re-cutting middles to give the correct number. Fry as given for Doughnuts, allowing about 5 minutes. Drain on crumpled kitchen paper, then toss in caster sugar flavoured with powdered cinnamon to taste.

Hot Cross Buns 1

makes 12
(illustrated on page 210)

Make up a Bun Loaf mixture but sift flour with 4 level tsp allspice or mixed spice. Shape into 12 buns. Top each with a cross of Shortcrust Pastry. Transfer to 2 well-greased baking trays. Cover. Leave to rise 45 minutes in a warm place. Bake one shelf above and one shelf below centre of oven (any position in fan oven), set to 425°F (220°C), Gas 7. Allow 15-20 minutes or until golden brown. While still hot, brush with honey, melted golden syrup or with the glaze given for Chelsea Buns (opposite). Cool on a wire rack.

Hot Cross Buns 2

makes 12

Make as previous recipe but instead of topping buns with pastry, cut a cross on top of each with a knife dipped in flour.

Hot Cross Buns 3

makes 12

Make buns as previously directed but instead of topping with pastry, pipe a cross on top of each with Royal Icing (page 40). Buns must be cold before icing is applied.

Bath Buns

makes 24

Here is an amusing historical note from the Flour Advisory Bureau. Bath Buns, it seems, were invented by a Dr Oliver in the eighteenth century for patients who visited Bath to take the waters. In order to counteract the Bun's fattening effects, he also invented the famous Bath Oliver biscuits — very plain and dry — which were meant to be both slimming and nourishing!

Make Bun Loaf mixture but use 6oz (175g) sultanas and 2oz (50g) chopped mixed peel instead of the other dried fruit combinations. Beat risen dough for about 1 minute then spoon 24 equal amounts, well apart, on to two large greased baking trays. Cover. Leave to rise until well-puffed and doubled in size, about 35 minutes. Brush with egg, sprinkle with crushed cube sugar and bake one shelf above and one shelf below oven centre (any position in fan oven) set to 425°F (220°C), Gas 7. Allow 15-20 minutes or until well-browned. Reverse position of trays at half-time. Cool buns on a wire rack.

Scandinavian Tea Rings

makes 2

Make up Bun Loaf mixture and divide risen dough into 2 equal-sized pieces. Roll each out into a rectangle measuring 15 x 9in (37.5 x 22.5cm). Brush each with 1oz (25g) melted butter then sprinkle with 2oz (50g) light-brown soft sugar and 1 level tsp cinnamon. Roll up from one of the long sides, place on to two greased baking trays, then form into rings by pinching ends together with dampened fingers.

Holding scissors at an angle of 45 degrees, cut almost completely through the dough at 1in (2.5cm) intervals. Turn the cut pieces on their sides to give a pinwheel effect. Cover. Leave to rise about 45 minutes in a warm place or until Tea Rings double in size. Bake for 25-30 minutes one shelf above and one shelf below oven centre (any position in fan oven) set to 400°F (200°C), Gas 6. Cool on wire racks.

Scandinavian Tea Rings with Cardamom

makes 2

Make as the recipe above but sprinkle each piece of dough with 1 level tsp ground cardamom instead of cinnamon.

Glazed Scandinavian Tea Rings

makes 2

When rings are removed from the oven, brush with glaze as given for Chelsea Buns (opposite).

Iced Scandinavian Tea Rings
makes 2

Coat each with glacé icing made from 8oz (225g) sifted icing sugar mixed to a thickish icing with fresh strained orange juice.

Christmas Tea Rings
makes 2

Ice as above, then decorate with halved red, green and yellow glacé cherries. Add walnut halves or hazelnuts.

Stollen
makes 2

A German fruit bread speciality eaten at Christmas. Use all butter in the dough if possible. Make up Bun Loaf mixture and divide risen dough into 2 pieces. Knead the following into each piece.

1oz (25g) blanched almonds, chopped
½ level tsp finely grated lemon peel
5oz (150g) dried fruit including peel
½oz (15g) butter, softened

Roll each piece of dough out into a 10in (25cm) diameter round then fold in 3 like an omelet. Press lightly together with fingers (join on top) and transfer to one large greased baking tray. Cover. Leave to rise in a warm place for about 45 minutes or until double in size. Brush lavishly with about 3oz (75g) of melted butter. Bake 35-40 minutes just above oven centre (any position in fan oven) set to 425°F (220°C), Gas 7. Cool on a wire rack then sift icing sugar thickly over each. Store in airtight tins when cold.

Marzipan Stollen
makes 2

Before folding up like omelets, place a 4oz (125g) 'sausage' of almond paste along the centre of each.

Cherry Stollen
makes 2

Substitute 3oz (75g) glacé cherries for the almond paste.

Pitta
makes 6
(illustrated on page 211)

A typical oval Middle Eastern bread, which is hollow in the middle. It is filled with Kebabs (off their sticks) and mixed salad, or used to scoop up Taramasalata and Hummous.

Take one-third of risen Plain White Bread dough (page 180) and divide it equally into 6 pieces. Roll out into thin ovals of about 10 x 5in (25 x 12.5cm). Transfer to 2 well-greased baking trays. Leave to stand, *uncovered*, for 5 minutes only.

Bake 6-8 minutes, one shelf above and one shelf below oven centre (any position in fan oven) set to 475°F (240°C), Gas 9, reversing position of trays at half-time. Watch carefully to ensure Pittas do not overbrown. Remove from oven, then slit each to enable steam to escape and also to make the pockets or hollows for the filling. Wrap up together while still hot in a clean tea-towel to keep the crusts soft. Unwrap when cold, then before serving, warm quickly on both sides under a hot grill.

Baigels or Bagels
makes 24

Very much delicatessen rolls, eaten worldwide by the Jewish community and part of the breakfast scene in New York and Israel — served with cream cheese and smoked salmon (and sometimes scrambled eggs as well).

¼oz or 8g (2 level tsp) dried yeast *or*
   ½oz (15g) fresh yeast
1 level tsp caster sugar
8fl oz (225ml) warm water
1lb (450g) plain strong white flour
1 level tsp salt
2 tbsp corn or sunflower oil
2 level tsp clear honey or golden syrup
1 Grade 3 egg, beaten

1 Mix together yeast (dried or fresh), sugar and warm water. If using fresh yeast, mash

against sides of jug so that it blends in smoothly. Leave in a warm place until the mixture froths up to at least double its original volume, about 30 minutes.

2 Sift flour and salt into bowl. Mix to a dough with yeast liquid, oil, honey or syrup and egg. Turn out onto a floured surface. Knead until smooth, elastic and no longer sticky, 20-30 minutes.

3 Place in oiled bowl then cover with an oiled plate. Leave to rise in the warm for about 1-1¼ hours. Turn onto floured surface. Knead quickly and lightly until smooth.

4 Divide into 24 pieces. Roll each between hands into 6in (15cm) lengths (coming to a point at both ends). Join ends together to form rings.

5 Place on a floured board, cover with greased greaseproof paper or foil and leave to rise in the warm until double in size and also light and puffy, about 20-25 minutes.

6 Poach, singly, in a large pan of gently boiling water for 15-20 seconds or until the Baigel floats to the surface. Lift out with a slatted fish slice and transfer to large greased baking trays (you will need about 3 trays).

7 Bake until deep gold for 10-15 minutes in three positions of oven set to 400°F (200°C), Gas 6. Reverse position of top and bottom trays at half-time. Cool Baigels on a wire rack. Before serving (and they should be served fresh) split, then spread with butter.

Toasted Baigels Day-old Baigels may be split, toasted and buttered before serving.

Croissants — easy style

makes 12
(illustrated on page 184)

Make up Baigel dough but do not leave to rise. Instead, roll out into a piece measuring 12 x 8in (30 x 20cm) and treat exactly as Flaky Pastry (page 117), using a total of 6oz (175g) butter or firm margarine (block margarine, not the whipped-up or easy-cream varieties). Do not leave to rest between roll-ings but when the three folds have been made and all the fat incorporated, cover and refrigerate for 20 minutes. Roll out on floured surface into an oblong of 18 x 12in (45 x 30cm) and, with a sharp knife dipped in flour, cut off uneven edges. Cut pastry into 6 squares, then cut each square into 2 triangles. Brush each with beaten egg then loosely roll up towards the pointed end.

With points underneath, curve into crescents on two large, well-greased baking trays. Cover. Leave to rise in a warm place for 30-40 minutes or until puffy and double in size. Brush with well-beaten egg then bake one shelf above and one shelf below centre of oven (any position in fan oven) set to 400°F (200°C), Gas 6. Allow 20 minutes — when Croissants should be golden brown — reversing position of trays at half-time. Cool on wire rack. Serve warm, Continental-style, with butter and marmalade or jam.

Danish Pastries

makes 24

Make dough as for Baigels but use ordinary plain flour instead of strong, and mix with warm milk (see page 178) instead of water. Using 6oz (175g) butter, treat dough exactly as Flaky Pastry (page 117), distributing fat in thirds. After resting for the last time, divide dough into 4 equal-sized pieces and leave aside temporarily. The dough can be filled with a variety of fillings and formed into Windmills, Turnovers etc, as shown below.

Place the completed Danish Pastries on to 2 large, greased baking trays. Cover. Leave to rise in a warm place for about 30-40 minutes or until light, puffy and double in size. Brush with beaten egg. Bake 15 minutes one shelf above and one shelf below centre of oven (any position in fan oven) set to 425°F (220°C), Gas 7. Cool on a wire rack. If liked, glaze as for Chelsea Buns (page 194).

Spice filling
Cream together 1½oz (40g) *each* butter and caster sugar with 1 level tsp cinnamon.

Almond filling

Mix together 1½oz (40g) *each* ground almonds and caster sugar. Add ¼ tsp almond essence and a little beaten egg to form a *stiff* paste.

Apple filling

Peel, core and slice 1 large cooking apple. Cook until very soft with minimal water (about 2 tsp) in covered pan. Beat until smooth with 1 level tbsp caster sugar and ¼ level tsp mixed spice. Cool completely.

Windmills
makes 6

Take one portion of pastry and roll into an oblong measuring 6 x 4in (15 x 10cm) and cut into 6 pieces, each 2in (5cm) square. Make 1in (2.5cm) cuts from each corner towards centre. Take alternate corners to middle, overlapping a little in the centre and pinching well together with damp fingers to seal.

Turnovers
makes 6

Take one portion of pastry and roll into an oblong measuring 6 x 4in (15 x 10cm) and cut into 6 pieces, each 2in (5cm) square. Put a little apple filling on to the centre of each, dampen edges of dough with water then fold over to form triangles. Pinch edges well together to seal.

Envelopes
makes 6

Take one portion of pastry and divide into six pieces. Roll each out into 4in (10cm) squares. Put a little almond paste onto centres then dampen edges with water and bring the corners to the middle, completely enclosing almond paste. Press down well to seal.

Pinwheels
makes 6

Take one portion of pastry and roll out to a rectangle measuring 8 x 4in (20 x 10cm). Spread with spice filling then sprinkle with 2 rounded tbsp mixed dried fruit. Roll up

tightly, starting from one of the shorter sides, then cut into 6 slices.

Iced Danish Pastries

Brush cold pastries with a thinnish glacé icing flavoured with a little lemon or vanilla essence. Decorate middle of windmills with half glacé cherries.

Nut Danish Pastries

Make as Iced Danish Pastries but before icing sets, sprinkle with chopped walnuts or flaked and toasted almonds, coarsely crushed.

Apricot Turnovers

Instead of apple mixture, use chunky apricot jam.

Cherry Turnovers

Instead of apple, use black cherry jam.

Curd Cheese Turnovers

Instead of apple, fill turnovers with 1½oz (40g) curd cheese mixed with 1 egg yolk, 2 rounded tsp caster sugar and ¼ level tsp grated lemon peel.

French Brioche

makes 12

¼oz or 8g (2 level tsp) dried yeast *or*
   ½oz (15g) fresh yeast
½ level tsp caster sugar
3 tbsp warm milk
8oz (225g) strong plain white flour
½ level tsp salt
3 extra level tsp caster sugar
2oz (50g) unsalted butter, melted
2 Grade 3 eggs, well-beaten
A little extra egg for brushing

1 Mix dried or fresh yeast with sugar and warm milk. Leave to stand in a warm place for about 20 minutes or until frothy and at least double in volume.
2 Sift flour and salt into a bowl. Toss in caster sugar. Mix to a soft dough with yeast liquid, butter and eggs.

3 Knead until dough is smooth, elastic, and no longer sticky, about 15 minutes.
4 Return to oiled bowl. Cover. Leave to rise in a warm place for about 1¼-1½ hours or until dough doubles in size and is light and puffy.
5 Turn out on to a floured surface and knead quickly and lightly until smooth. Divide two-thirds of the dough into 12 pieces of equal size. Roll into balls and drop into buttered plain bun or fluted bun tins (the latter are traditional). Roll rest of pastry into 12 equal-sized miniature balls.
6 Brush tops of rolls in tin with beaten egg then top with smaller balls to make what look like miniature cottage loaves. Cover. Leave to rise in a warm place for about 45-60 minutes or until Brioches have doubled in size and are light and puffy.
7 Brush again with egg then bake 12-15 minutes near top of oven (any position fan oven) set to 450°F (230°C), Gas 8. Cool on a wire rack. Serve freshly baked and accompany with butter and jam. Alternatively, serve with butter and a mild cheese.

Mousseline Brioche
makes 2
Take the risen dough and into it knead 6oz (175g) mixed dried fruit, 2oz (50g) chopped glacé cherries and 2 level tsp finely grated lemon peel. Divide in half. Shape into balls. Drop into two 7in (17.5cm) fluted deep tins, first brushed with unsalted, melted butter. Cover. Leave to rise in a warm place for 40-50 minutes. Brush with milk. Bake until golden brown, allowing 30-35 minutes just above centre of oven (any position in fan oven) set to 400°F (200°C), Gas 6. Turn out and cool on a wire rack. Before serving, decorate with thin glacé icing made from sifted icing sugar and dark rum; allow about 2oz (50g) icing sugar and a few tsp rum.

Cheese Brioche
makes 1
Take the risen dough and knead into it 3oz (75g) of grated Gruyère cheese. Place into an 8in (20cm) round cake tin, first well-greased with unsalted, melted butter. Cover. Leave to rise 1 hour in a warm place. Brush with beaten egg and sprinkle with 1oz (25g) extra grated Gruyère cheese. Bake as Mousseline Brioche.

Sally Lunn
makes 2
Sally Lunns were first eaten in the streets of Bath during the eighteenth century and one theory is that they were named after the girl who sold them. Others attribute the name to her cry of 'Sol et lune', the French translation meaning 'sun and moon' which aptly describes the appearance of the cakes.

Make up Brioche mixture but increase flour to 1lb (450g) and liquid to 13fl oz (375ml) warm milk. Beat the resultant batter until smooth then pour equal amounts into two 6in (15cm) well-greased round cake tins. Cover. Leave to rise in a warm place for about 1½ hours or until double in size. Bake 20 minutes just above centre of oven (any position in fan oven) set to 425°F (220°C), Gas 7. Remove from oven and brush with glaze made by dissolving 2 level tsp granulated sugar in 2 tbsp water then boiling fast for 2 minutes until thick. Turn cakes out of tins, cool to lukewarm. Slice each into 3 layers and fill with clotted cream or softened butter. Cut into wedges and eat warm.

Rum Babas
makes 12
¼oz or 8g (2 level tsp) dried yeast *or*
    ½oz (15g) fresh yeast
5 tbsp warm milk
6oz (175g) strong plain white flour
1 level tbsp caster sugar
Large pinch salt
3 oz (75g) butter
3 Grade 3 eggs, beaten
1 Stir yeast into warm milk. If using dried yeast, leave to stand for 5 minutes. Blend

in 1oz (25g) flour and 1 tsp sugar. Leave in a warm place for about 20-30 minutes or until mixture froths up to almost twice its original volume.

2 Sift remaining flour and salt into a bowl. Toss in remaining sugar. Rub in butter finely with fingertips. Beating continuously, add yeast liquid and eggs. Continue to beat hard for a further 3 minutes.

3 Well-grease twelve 3½in (9cm) Baba moulds, or 3in (7.5cm) individual flan tins or castle pudding tins, also known as dariole moulds. Half-fill with Baba mixture.

4 Cover. Leave to rise in a warm place until tins are two-thirds full, about 30 minutes.

5 Bake near top of oven (any position in fan oven) set to 400°F (200°C), Gas 6. Allow 10-15 minutes or until golden brown. Turn out onto a large wire rack with one or two plates underneath.

6 Prick Babas all over with a fork then coat with rum syrup. Decorate with whipped cream then stud with pieces of glacé cherry and angelica.

Rum Syrup

3oz (75g) golden syrup
3oz (75g) caster sugar
6 tbsp water
2 tbsp rum

1 Put syrup, sugar and water into a pan. Stir over low heat until sugar dissolves. Bring just up to the boil. Take off heat. Stir in rum. Spoon over Babas. The surplus will collect on the plates underneath the rack and may be kept for fruit salads or drinks.

Glazed Babas

For a golden glaze, brush Babas, after soaking, with sieved apricot jam, first warmed and melted. Decorate with cream and jam on top of the glaze.

Fruited Babas

Make as basic Baba recipe but add 2oz (50g)

currants to the rubbed-in ingredients before mixing to a dough.

Savarin

serves 8

Make exactly as Rum Baba mixture then spoon into an 8in (20cm) well-greased ring tin with a hole in the middle. Cover. Leave to rise in a warm place until mixture reaches top of tin, about 30-40 minutes. Bake in centre of oven (any position in fan oven) set to 400°F (200°C), Gas 6. Allow 20-25 minutes when Savarin should be golden brown. Turn out onto a wire cooling rack.

Rum Savarin

serves 8

Soak with syrup as given for Rum Babas.

Kirsch Savarin

serves 8

Soak with syrup as given for the Rum Babas, replacing the rum with kirsch.

Fruit Syrup Savarin

serves 8

Soak with syrup from a can of fruit to which 2 tbsp of rum, sherry, port or Cointreau (my favourite) have been added.

Glazed Savarin

serves 8

Brush Savarin all over with warmed apricot jam, melted and sieved, after soaking with syrup.

Fruit Savarin

serves 8
(illustrated on page 00)

Put Savarin onto serving dish then fill centre with mixed fruit.

Fruit and Cream Savarin

serves 8

Put Savarin onto a serving dish then fill centre with sweetened whipped cream and canned or fresh fruits.

Glacé Fruit and Cream Savarin
serves 8

Flavour syrup with 2 tbsp of brandy instead of rum or kirsch. Also add 1 or 2 tbsp brandy to sweetened whipped cream. Stand Savarin on serving dish then pile whipped cream into centre. Stud with pieces of glacé fruits.

Kiwi Fruit Savarin
serves 8

Stand Savarin on serving dish. Pile centre with sweetened whipped cream to which 1 level tsp finely grated orange peel has been added. Cover with slices of peeled kiwi fruit.

Mocha Rum Savarin
serves 8

Soak Savarin in syrup flavoured with 1 tbsp coffee liqueur and 1 tbsp rum. Stand on serving dish. Fill centre with sweetened whipped cream to which 1 tbsp coffee liqueur has been added. Scatter grated plain chocolate over the top. Stud with peeled green grapes.

Streusel Cake
serves 10-12

Very Middle European in character, this is a yeast cake with a crumble topping, unusual and splendid served fresh with butter and jam or honey.

½oz or 15g (1 level tbsp) dried yeast *or*
   1oz (25g) fresh yeast
2 level tsp caster sugar
6 tbsp warm milk
10oz (275g) plain strong white flour
½ level tsp salt
4oz (125g) butter or block margarine
2oz (50g) caster sugar
6oz (175g) mixed dried fruit
Finely grated peel and juice of 1 medium
   orange
2 Grade 3 eggs, beaten
Crumble Topping
1oz (25g) plain flour
½oz (15g) butter or margarine
½oz (15g) caster sugar
½ level tsp cinnamon
2 slightly rounded tbsp plum jam, melted

1 Stir dried yeast and sugar into milk and leave to stand in a warm place for 15-20 minutes or until frothy. Alternatively, blend sugar and fresh yeast into milk until smooth.
2 Sift flour and salt into a bowl. Rub in butter or margarine then toss in caster sugar and fruit.
3 Mix to a dough with orange peel and juice, yeast liquid and eggs. Beat well with a wooden spoon for 2 minutes.
4 Spread evenly into a well-greased 2lb (1kg) loaf tin or into an 8in (20cm) well-greased square cake tin. Brush top with jam.
5 For crumble, sift flour into a bowl. Rub in fat then toss in sugar and cinnamon. Sprinkle over jam. Cover. Leave to rise in a warm place for 1 hour.
6 Bake in centre of oven (any position in fan oven) set to 400°F (200°C), Gas 6. Allow 50-55 minutes or until thin metal skewer, pushed gently into centre, comes out clean and dry. Leave for 5 minutes then turn out onto a wire cooling rack. Cut when just cold and serve with butter.

Streusel Cake with Apricots
serves 10-12

Make as previous recipe but instead of mixed fruit, add 6oz (175g) well-washed dried apricots, scissor-snipped into small pieces.

Plain Streusel Cake
serves 10-12

Omit orange and use 2 Grade 1 or 2 eggs

Streusel Cake with Honey
serves 10-12

Instead of brushing cake with jam, brush with clear honey.

Streusel Cake with Lemon
serves 10-12

Make as Plain Streusel Cake, tossing in 1 level tsp finely grated lemon peel with the sugar.

Pumpernickel Loaf

A richly flavoured, dark bread, eaten all over Central Europe.

2 level tsp dried yeast *plus*
   1 level tsp caster sugar *or*
½oz (15g) fresh yeast
½pt (275ml) water (see page 178)
2 tbsp black treacle
1 tbsp gravy browning
6oz (175g) rye flour (available from Health Food shops)
1oz (25g) maize meal
14oz (400g) wholemeal flour
1 level tsp salt
½oz (15g) margarine or cooking fat
5oz (150g) freshly cooked potatoes, mashed then pressed through a nylon sieve
1oz (25g) bran
1 level tsp caraway seeds

1 Mix dried yeast and sugar with water. Leave in a warm place until it froths up, about 20-30 minutes. Alternatively, blend fresh yeast smoothly with water.
2 Add treacle and gravy browning to yeast mixture. Tip rye flour and maize meal into a bowl. Add half the wholemeal flour and salt.
3 Rub in fat finely then mix in yeast liquid to form a thick batter. Using a wooden spoon, work in rest of wholemeal flour, the boiled potatoes, bran and caraway seeds.
4 Knead on floured surface for a good 10-15 minutes or until smooth. Shape into a ball and put into an oiled bowl. Cover. Leave to rise in a warm place for 1½-1¾ hours.
5 Again knead on a floured surface until smooth then form into a 'sausage' shape to fit a 2lb (1kg) well-greased loaf tin. Prick surface all over with a fork. Cover with a piece of oiled greaseproof paper or polythene. Leave to rise in a warm place for about 50 minutes or until double in size, then bake for 1¼ hours in centre of oven (any position in fan oven) set to 350°F (180°C), Gas 4. Remove from oven and leave to stand for 20 minutes. Turn out onto a wire cooling rack and store in a bread tin for 2 days before cutting.

Pumpernickel Cobs
makes 2

Make Pumpernickel as directed in previous recipe then divide risen dough into two equal pieces. Shape each into a round loaf, rather like a cob. Prick all over, place on a large greased baking tray and cover. Leave to rise in a warm place for about 50 minutes. Bake as for the Pumpernickel Loaf, allowing only 15 minutes.

Rye Loaves

makes 2

Widely eaten in Scandinavia, these are pleasantly appetizing loaves and perfect for open sandwiches.

¼oz or 8g (2 level tsp) dried yeast *or*
   ½oz (15g) fresh yeast
1 level tsp sugar
½pt (275ml) warm water (see page 178)
2oz (50g) rye flour
15oz (425g) strong plain white flour
1½ level tsp salt
½oz (15g) lard or white cooking fat

1 Mix dried yeast with sugar and water. Leave in a warm place for about 20 minutes or until frothy. Alternatively, blend fresh yeast with sugar and water until smooth.
2 Tip rye flour into a bowl then sift in white flour and salt. Rub in fat finely then mix to a soft dough with yeast liquid. Turn out on to a floured surface and knead about 10 minutes until smooth.
3 Place in oiled bowl, cover and leave to rise about 1¼ hours in a warm place. Knead briefly until smooth, divide in half and shape into two 'cigars' measuring about 6in (15cm) in length.
4 Place loaves on large greased baking tray and make 5 diagonal cuts on top of each. Cover. Leave in a warm place to rise for 45 minutes or until double in size.
5 Bake 50 minutes just above oven centre

(any position in fan oven) set to 400°F (200°C), Gas 6. Cool on a wire rack.

Caraway Rye Loaves
makes 2
Make as previous recipe but toss in 1 level tsp caraway seeds with the salt.

Chapati

makes 8

This is a West Pakistan and Indian-style unleavened bread, used in place of cutlery to scoop up curries. It should be made from 'Atta', a specific type of Indian wholemeal flour, but our own wholemeal flour makes an acceptable compromise.

8oz (225g) wholemeal flour
1 level tsp salt
6fl oz (175ml) water

1 Sift flour and salt into a bowl. Mix to a soft dough with water. Turn out onto a floured surface and knead until smooth, elastic and no longer sticky, about 8-10 minutes.
2 Place inside an oiled bowl, cover and leave at kitchen temperature for 1 hour.
3 Divide the dough equally into 8 pieces. Roll out each piece as thinly as possible to give an 8in (20cm) diameter round.
4 Sprinkle 1 rounded tsp of flour over base of large frying pan (9-10in or 22.5-25cm) and heat until it turns golden brown.
5 Carefully tip out, add a knob of vegetable fat to pan and brush over base with a twist of kitchen paper.
6 Toss Chapati from one hand to the other to shake off surplus flour then place in the hot pan. Cook ½ minute or until upper surface has darkened. Turn Chapati over and cook second side for 1½-2 minutes or until pale golden brown. Turn again and cook first side for a further minute.
7 While Chapati is frying, press it round the edges with the back of a wooden spoon to help the dough puff up. Repeat the greasing and frying until all the Chapatis are cooked.

8 Pile one on top of another as they are cooked and then wrap in a clean tea-towel to keep warm. Fold each in four. Serve while still fresh and warm.

Naan Bread

makes 6

The traditional puffy bread eaten with Tandoori chicken, Naan Bread is cooked under the grill and is best when fresh. It is also ideally suited to barbecue foods and may be reheated on the barbecue grill itself to that it becomes impregnated with the characteristic smoky flavour.

¼oz or 8g (2 level tsp) dried yeast *or*
    ½oz (15g) fresh yeast
1 level tsp caster sugar
7fl oz (200ml) warm milk
1lb (450g) plain white flour
1 level tsp salt
1 level tsp baking powder
2 level tsp extra caster sugar
1 Grade 3 egg, beaten
2 level tbsp salad oil
4 level tbsp natural yogurt

1 Mix dried yeast and sugar with milk and leave in a warm place for 20-30 minutes or until frothy. Alternatively, blend fresh yeast smoothly with sugar and milk.
2 Sift flour, salt and baking powder into a bowl. Toss in extra caster sugar. Add egg, oil, yogurt and yeast mixture. Mix to a soft dough with fingertips or wooden spoon.
3 Turn out onto floured surface and knead until smooth, elastic and no longer sticky, about 10-15 minutes. Place in a lightly oiled bowl, cover and leave to rise 45-60 minutes in a warm place.
4 Knead quickly until smooth, divide equally into 6 pieces and roll each piece into a 10 x 4in (25 x 10cm) oval.
5 Pre-heat grill pan until hot and brush each Naan Bread with water. Put into grill pan, 2 at a time. Grill 2-3 minutes when Naan should be golden brown and puffy. Turn over and grill second side until golden.

Serve warm with Tandoori or Barbecue dishes.

Herb Naan Bread
makes 6
Squeeze 2 level tsp fresh chopped coriander into each piece of Naan dough before grilling.

Onion Naan Bread
makes 6
Make as Herb Naan Bread, using 1 level tsp finely grated onion instead of coriander.

Sesame Naan Bread
makes 6
Make as Herb Naan Bread, using ½ level tsp sesame seeds instead of herbs.

12
Puddings

While in Europe cheese and fruit will often suffice, in Britain no meal is complete without a pudding, which invariably means something cooked and served with cream, custard, ice cream or sauce. Puddings are a subject by themselves and could fill a book with complete ease, so I have picked a selection which I believe to be popular with everyone and include such old favourites as steamed puddings, milk puddings, fruit crumbles and pies, turnovers and tarts, Charlotte and pancakes. Good sound stuff, one and all, and the sort of traditional afters that are envied worldwide.

Baked Egg Custard

serves 4

3 Grade 2 eggs plus 1 egg yolk
1pt (575ml) creamy milk (Long Life gives the smoothest result), warmed to blood heat
1oz (25g) caster sugar
Grated nutmeg

1 Well grease a 2pt (1·25 litre) heatproof dish.
2 Beat eggs, milk and sugar well together. Strain into prepared dish.
3 Sprinkle top with nutmeg. Stand in roasting tin containing enough hot water to come halfway up the sides of the dish.
4 Bake 1 hour in centre of oven (any position in fan oven) set to 325°F (160°C), Gas 3. Serve warm or cold.

Crème Caramel

serves 4

3oz (75g) granulated sugar
2 tbsp hot water
2 tsp cold water
3 Grade 2 eggs
½pt (150ml) single cream
1oz (25g) caster sugar
½ tsp vanilla essence

1 Melt granulated sugar in a saucepan in the 2 tbsp hot water. Bring to the boil. Boil without stirring until syrup turns the warm golden colour of clear honey. Stir in cold water.
2 Pour carefully into a 1½pt (1 litre) greased round dish or oblong pie dish, making sure it covers the base.
3 Beat all remaining ingredients well together and strain into dish over caramel. Bake as Egg Custard.
4 Cool to lukewarm then refrigerate overnight. Before serving, turn out on to a dish and accompany with single cream.

Individual Crème Caramel
serves 4
Make as above but pour hot caramel mixture into 4 individual greased moulds. Fill with custard mixture and bake as directed above, allowing 35 minutes.

Rice Pudding

serves 4

2oz (50g) round-grain pudding rice
1pt (575ml) milk
1½oz (40g) caster sugar
2in (5cm) length of lemon peel
Grated nutmeg
½oz (15g) butter or margarine

1 Wash rice and drain. Put into a 2pt (1·25 litre) greased pie dish.
2 Stir in milk, sugar and lemon peel.
3 Leave to stand 30 minutes as this partially softens the rice. Stir round. Sprinkle with nutmeg, then add flakes of butter or margarine.
4 Bake 2½ hours in centre of oven (any position in fan oven) set to 300°F (150°C), Gas 2. Stir three times during the first hour as this makes pudding more creamy. Serve hot.

Mince Tart

serves 6-8

Shortcrust Pastry made with 8oz (225g) flour (page 99)

1lb (450g) mincemeat

1 level tsp finely grated orange peel

1 tbsp whisky or brandy

Beaten egg for brushing

Icing sugar

1 Divide pastry equally into 2 portions then roll out one piece and use to line an 8in (20cm) flat heatproof plate, lightly greased.
2 Mix mincemeat with orange peel and alcohol then spread over pastry to within 1in (2.5cm) of edges. Dampen pastry edges with water.
3 Cover with lid, rolled from rest of pastry. Trim edges to neaten then press well together to seal.
4 Brush with egg, make 2 slits in the top then bake 15 minutes just above oven centre (any position in fan oven) set to 425°F (220°C), Gas 7.
5 Reduce temperature to 400°F (200°C), Gas 6 and continue to bake for a further 30-35 minutes or until golden brown.
6 Remove from oven and sift icing sugar over the top. Serve hot, in wedges.

Plum and Apple Pie

serves 6
(illustrated on page 221)

Pastry

8oz (225g) plain flour

Pinch of salt

4oz (125g) soft lard

2-3 tbsp cold water to mix

Filling

1lb (450g) cooking apples, peeled and sliced

12oz (350g) dessert plums, halved and stoned

3oz (75g) demerara sugar

1 level tbsp plain flour

1 level tbsp extra demerara sugar

1 Sift flour and salt into bowl, add the lard straight from the refrigerator and rub it in quickly and lightly with the finger tips.
2 Stir in sufficient cold water to make a fairly stiff dough then wrap in greaseproof paper and chill for 15 minutes.
3 Meanwhile put the fruit into a bowl and mix it with the demerara sugar and flour.
4 Cut the pastry into 2 pieces, one a little larger than the other, and use the smaller piece to line an 8in (20cm) pie plate.
5 Place the filling on top, dampen pastry edges then cover the pie with lid, rolled from rest of pastry.
6 Press edges well together to seal, trim off excess pastry then scallop the edges.
7 Brush with water, sprinkle with the demerara sugar, then bake the Pie for 40-50 minutes just above oven centre (any position in fan oven) set to 375°F (190°C), Gas 5. Serve warm with custard.

Fruit Turnovers

makes 6

Flaky Pastry (page 117) or 1 large packet (13oz or 375g) frozen puff pastry, thawed

8oz (225g) cooking apples, rhubarb, gooseberries, blackberries, plums, currants, damsons or a mixture of fruit, washed and prepared according to type

2oz (50g) caster sugar

1 Grade 3 egg white

Extra caster sugar

1 Roll out Flaky Pastry to ¼in (75mm) in thickness or use bought pastry as directed on the packet.
2 Cut into 6 squares, each measuring 4in (10cm).
3 Put equal amounts of fruit on to centre of each square. Sprinkle with sugar.
4 Dampen pastry edges with water then fold over each square to form a triangle. Press edges well together to seal.

(right) Danish Teabread and Teacakes, page 192 *(Danish Agricultural Producers)*

(overleaf) Lardy Cake, page 191 and Hot Cross Buns, page 195 *(Pura Advisory Service)*

5 Brush with lightly beaten egg white then sprinkle with sugar. Put on to wetted baking tray.
6 Bake 20 minutes near top of oven (any position in fan oven) set to 425°F (220°C), Gas 7. Reduce temperature to 350°F (180°C), Gas 4 and continue to bake a further 20 minutes to cook fruit.
7 Serve hot with cream or custard.

Jam Turnovers
makes 6

Make as above but fill each Turnover with 2 tsp jam — cherry, blackcurrant, apricot or strawberry. Bake only 20 minutes at 425°F (220°C), Gas 7, as there is no fruit to be cooked.

Plum Tart

serves 6
(illustrated on page 221)

Pastry
3oz (75g) soft lard
2oz (50g) caster sugar
5oz (150g) plain flour sifted with 1 level tsp cinnamon
1 tsp vanilla essence
A little beaten egg to bind

Filling
1lb (450g) dessert plums
1 Grade 3 egg plus remainder from pastry
2 level tbsp flour
2 level tbsp caster sugar
½ tsp vanilla essence
½pt (275ml) milk
Icing sugar

1 Cream lard straight from the refrigerator with sugar to make a soft mixture, then mix in the sifted flour and cinnamon with the vanilla essence and enough egg to bind the ingredients to a fairly soft pastry. Wrap and chill the pastry for 15 minutes.

(previous page) Pitta Bread, ideal with dips, soups etc, page 196 *(Rank Hovis McDougall)*

(left) Fruit Savarin, page 200 *(Flour Advisory Bureau)*

2 On lightly floured surface, roll out the pastry and use to line a 9in (22.5cm) flan dish.
3 Cut the plums in half, remove the stones, then place the fruit, cut sides down, into pastry case.
4 Beat the egg, and any left from the pastry, to a paste with the flour, sugar and essence then gradually beat in the milk.
5 Carefully pour into the flan dish and bake 35-40 minutes just above oven centre (any position in fan oven) set to 375°F (190°C), Gas 5. At this stage the pastry should be golden and filling set.
6 Sprinkle the top of the tart with sifted icing sugar and serve warm with whipped cream.

Apple Dumplings

makes 4

4 medium cooking apples
1½oz (40g) granulated sugar
1 level tsp cinnamon
½ level tsp finely grated lemon peel
Shortcrust Pastry made with 8oz (225g) plain flour (page 99)
Milk for brushing
Icing sugar for decoration

1 Peel apples then remove cores two-thirds of the way down each. If cut right through, filling will seep out.
2 Mix together sugar, cinnamon and lemon peel and spoon equal amounts into each apple cavity.
3 Cut pastry into 4 equal pieces and roll each out into a round large enough to cover apples completely. For this you need a good eye, rather than a specific measurement.
4 Stand an apple in the middle of each round then dampen edges of pastry with water. Wrap pastry round each apple without stretching, enclosing it completely and pressing all edges and joins well together to seal.
5 Stand Dumplings on greased baking tray and brush each with milk. Decorate with

leaves cut from pastry trimmings. Make 2 slits on top to allow steam to escape then bake 15 minutes in centre of oven (any position in fan oven) set to 425°F (220°C), Gas 7.

6 Reduce temperature to 350°F (180°C), Gas 4. Continue to bake a further 30 minutes when pastry should be golden and apples soft. Sometimes the pastry splits which can be due to 2 things — the type of apples and stretched pastry. To avoid this I have sometimes used Cox's apples which seem to behave in a very dignified fashion.

Baked Jam Roly Poly

serves 4-6

Suet Crust Pastry (page 111)
4 slightly rounded tbsp jam
Icing sugar

1 Roll out pastry into a rectangle measuring about 11 x 9in (27.5 x 22.5cm).
2 Spread to within 1in (2.5cm) of pastry edges with jam. Dampen edges with water.
3 Roll up, starting from one of the longer sides. Put on to greased baking tray.
4 Bake 30 minutes in centre of oven (any position in fan oven) set to 400°F (200°C), Gas 6. Reduce heat to 375°F (190°C), Gas 5 and continue to bake a further 20-30 minutes or until golden brown.
5 Sift icing sugar over the top, cut into portions and serve hot with custard.

Note Baked Roly Poly often splits and this is quite acceptable.

Baked Marmalade Roly Poly

serves 4-6

Made as Baked Jam Roly Poly but use marmalade instead of jam.

Baked Mincemeat Roly Poly

serves 4-6

Make as Baked Jam Roly Poly but use 4oz (125g) mincemeat instead of jam.

Baked Syrup Roly Poly

serves 4-6

Make as Baked Jam Roly Poly but use 4 slightly rounded tbsp golden syrup mixed with 4 level tbsp fresh white breadcrumbs instead of jam.

Baked Apple and Date Roly Poly

serves 4-6

Make as Baked Jam Roly Poly but instead of jam, use 6oz (175g) peeled and chopped apples, 2oz (50g) chopped dates and 1½oz (40g) light-brown soft sugar.

Baked Sausagemeat Roly Poly

serves 4-6

Spread rolled-out pastry with 8oz (225g) sausagemeat instead of jam.

Steamed Suet Pudding

serves 4

4oz (125g) plain flour
1½ level tsp baking powder
4oz (125g) fresh white breadcrumbs
3oz (75g) caster or light-brown soft sugar
3oz (75g) finely shredded suet
1 Grade 2 egg, beaten
About 7-8 tbsp cold milk to mix

1 Sift flour and baking powder into a bowl. Toss in crumbs, sugar and suet.
2 Using a fork, stir to a soft batter with egg and milk.
3 Turn into a 2pt (1.25 litre) well-greased pudding basin.
4 Cover with a double thickness of greased greaseproof paper or single thickness of greased foil.
5 Steam 2½-3 hours, in covered pan, replenishing with extra boiling water once or twice to keep up the level.
6 Turn out and serve with cream or custard.

Variations

Put 2 tbsp jam, marmalade, honey or treacle into basin before adding pudding mixture.

Spotted Dick

serves 4

Make as Steamed Suet Pudding but toss in 4oz (125g) mixed dried fruit, including peel, with the sugar.

College Pudding

serves 4

Make as Spotted Dick, but sift flour with 1 level tsp mixed spice.

Bread and Butter Pudding

serves 4

6 thin slices white bread
2oz (50g) butter, at kitchen temperature
2oz (50g) currants
2oz (50g) caster sugar
2 Grade 2 eggs
1pt (575ml) milk, warmed to blood heat

1 Remove crusts from bread then spread slices thickly with butter. Cut each into quarters.
2 Put half into 2pt (1.25 litre) greased dish, buttered sides uppermost. Sprinkle with all the currants and half the sugar.
3 Top with rest of bread, also buttered sides uppermost, then sprinkle with rest of sugar.
4 Beat eggs and milk well together and pour gently into dish, disturbing ingredients as little as possible.
5 Leave to stand for 45 minutes, then bake 1 hour in centre of oven (any position in fan oven) set to 325°F (160°C), Gas 3, until the custard is set and the top crisp and golden. Serve hot.

Queen of Puddings

serves 4

3oz (75g) fresh white breadcrumbs
5oz (150g) caster sugar
½ tsp vanilla essence
½ level tsp finely grated lemon peel
¾pt (425ml) milk
1oz (25g) butter or margarine
2 Grade 3 eggs, separated
2 level tbsp jam, warmed

1 Put crumbs and 1oz sugar into a mixing bowl.
2 Warm together essence, lemon peel, milk and butter or margarine in a saucepan over a gentle heat.
3 Mix into crumbs then leave to stand for 30 minutes. Beat in egg yolks.
4 Spread smoothly into a 1½pt (850ml) greased pie dish. Bake 30 minutes in centre of oven (any position in fan oven) set to 325°F (160°C), Gas 3.
5 Remove Pudding from oven. Cover top with warmed jam.
6 Beat egg whites to a stiff snow. Gradually beat in 3oz (75g) caster sugar and continue to beat until Meringue is very shiny and stands in firm peaks. Stir in rest of sugar.
7 Swirl the Meringue mixture over pudding on top of jam, then return to oven for a further 40 minutes when Meringue should be crisp and golden on the outside and soft inside. Serve hot with cream.

Fruit Crumble

serves 4-6

1lb (450g) seasonal fruit, prepared according to type
4-6oz (125-175g) caster or light-brown soft sugar, depending on sharpness of fruit
6oz (175g) plain flour
3oz (75g) butter or margarine
3oz (75g) caster sugar

1 Fill a 2pt (1.25 litre) greased heatproof dish with alternate layers of fruit and sugar, finishing with fruit.
2 For crumble, sift flour into a bowl, rub in fat finely then toss in sugar.
3 Sprinkle crumble thickly and evenly over fruit, smoothing with a knife.
4 Bake 15 minutes just above oven centre (any position in fan oven) set to 375°F (190°C), Gas 5. Reduce temperature to 350°F (180°C), Gas 4 and continue to bake for 45 minutes. Serve with cream or custard.

Note If using already cooked fruit or fruit-pie filling, bake Crumble as above, allowing 25 minutes at 375°F (190°C), Gas 5.

Apple Charlotte

serves 4

1lb (450g) cooking apples
4oz (125g) caster sugar
4oz (125g) fresh white breadcrumbs
1 level tsp cinnamon (optional)
1 level tsp lemon peel
4oz (125g) butter, melted

1 Peel, core and slice apples.
2 Toss together sugar, crumbs, cinnamon and lemon peel.
3 Fill a 2pt (1.25 litre) greased heatproof dish with alternate layers of apple and crumb mixture, trickling butter between layers.
4 Finish with a layer of crumbs, trickle more butter over the top then bake 1 hour just above oven centre (any position in fan oven) set to 375°F (190°C), Gas 5.
5 Serve with cream or custard.

Brown Betty

serves 4

The American answer to Apple Charlotte. Make in exactly the same way as Apple Charlotte, but use crushed digestive biscuits instead of breadcrumbs, and dark-brown soft sugar instead of white. Include also ½ level tsp allspice. If liked, sprinkle 2oz (50g) seedless raisins over apples.

Blackberry and Apple Cobbler

serves 4-6

Made with a scone topping and stewed fruit, this is a quick pudding to put together. Any of the scone-mixture recipes in Chapter 8 may be used and any fruit.

1½lb (675g) stewed and sweetened apples and blackberries, cold
Scone mixture
Beaten egg for brushing

1 Put fruit into a 2pt (1.25 litre) greased heatproof dish that is wide and shallow.
2 Roll out Scone mixture to ½in (1.25cm) on floured surface and cut into rounds with a 2in (5cm) biscuit cutter.
3 Arrange Scones in overlapping rings on top of fruit, then brush with egg. Bake 15 minutes near top of oven (any position in fan oven) set to 425°F (220°C), Gas 7.
4 Serve hot with cream or custard.

Baked Vanilla Pudding

serves 4-5

6oz (175g) self-raising flour
3oz (75g) butter or margarine, at room temperature and softened
3oz (75g) caster sugar
1 Grade 2 egg
½ tsp vanilla essence
5-6 tbsp cold milk

1 Sift flour into a bowl. Rub in butter or margarine finely, then toss in sugar.
2 Mix to a softish consistency with egg, vanilla essence and milk, stirring briskly without beating.
3 Spread into greased 2pt (1.25 litre) greased heatproof dish.
4 Bake 45-60 minutes in oven centre (any position in fan oven) set to 350°F (180°C), Gas 4. The pudding is ready when a metal skewer, pushed gently into centre, comes out clean and dry, and pudding is well-risen and golden.
5 Turn out on to a warm dish and serve with cream or custard.

Baked Jam Pudding
serves 4-5
Make exactly as Baked Vanilla Pudding, but spread 2 rounded tbsp jam over base of dish before adding cake mixture.

Baked Syrup Pudding
serves 4-5
Make exactly as Baked Vanilla Pudding but spread 2 rounded tbsp golden syrup over base of dish before adding cake mixture.

Baked Syrup and Ginger Pudding
serves 4-5
Make exactly as Baked Syrup Pudding, but sift flour with 2 level tsp ground ginger before rubbing in the fat.

Baked Marmalade Pudding

serves 4-5

Make exactly as Baked Jam Pudding, but use marmalade instead of jam.

Baked Chocolate Pudding

serves 4-5

Make exactly as Baked Vanilla Pudding but use only 5oz (150g) self-raising flour and ½oz (15g) *each* cocoa powder and corn-flour.

Baked Coconut Pudding

serves 4-5

Make exactly as Baked Vanilla Pudding, tossing in 1oz (25g) desiccated coconut with the sugar, and increasing milk by 1 tbsp.

Baked Fruit and Nut Pudding

serves 4-5

Make exactly as Baked Vanilla Pudding, tossing in 2-3oz (50-75g) mixed dried fruit and 2oz (50g) chopped almonds, peanuts or walnuts with the sugar.

Eve's Pudding

serves 4

1lb (450g) cooking apples
8oz (225g) caster sugar
4oz (125g) self-raising flour
4oz (125g) butter or margarine, at kitchen temperature
2 Grade 3 eggs, at kitchen temperature
2 tbsp cold milk

1 Peel, core and slice apples thinly. Put into 2½pt (1.25 litre) greased heatproof dish in alternate layers with 4oz of sugar. End with a layer of apples.
2 For topping, sift flour on to a plate. Cream butter or margarine and rest of sugar together until light and fluffy.
3 Beat in eggs singly, adding a heaped tsp of flour with each.
4 Fold in rest of flour alternately with milk then spread smoothly over apples.
5 Bake 1-1¼ hours in oven centre set to

325°F (160°C), Gas 3. The pudding is ready when a metal skewer, pushed gently into centre of cake, comes out clean and dry.
6 Serve wth cream or custard.

Note Although apples are traditional, goose-berries, raspberries, plums or damsons may be used instead.

Pancakes

makes 8

4oz (125g) plain flour
Pinch of salt
1 Grade 3 egg
1 tsp melted butter, margarine or salad oil (for velvety texture)
½pt (275ml) skimmed milk (for lightness)
Caster sugar
Lemon juice

1 Sift flour and salt into a bowl.
2 Make a dip in the middle and mix to a thick, creamy batter with egg, melted fat or oil and half the milk. Beat very thoroughly.
3 Gradually stir in rest of milk. Cover batter and refrigerate at least 3 hours or until thoroughly chilled.
4 Brush a smooth, 8in (20cm) frying pan with melted white cooking fat or oil (a very sparing amount or pancakes will stick). Heat until hot.
5 Stir batter round then pour in just enough to cover base of pan thinly (about 2-3 tbsp).
6 Cook until underside is golden, then turn over and cook second side.
7 Turn out on to sugared greaseproof paper, sprinkle with extra sugar and lemon juice and roll up. Serve straight away.

Note Self-raising flour gives a slightly tender batter which is more difficult to handle than batter made with plain flour.

Variations

Fill pancakes with jam, golden syrup, lemon curd, chocolate spread, ice cream and choco-late spread, hot apple purée, bananas and whipped cream, honey, honey and chopped walnuts, or any of the savoury fillings given for Vol-au-Vents (page 120).

Christmas Pudding

makes 2

4oz (125g) plain flour
1½ level tsp mixed spice or allspice
8oz (225g) fresh white breadcrumbs
10oz (275g) finely shredded suet
8oz (225g) dark-brown soft sugar
1½lb (675g) mixed dried fruit including peel
4oz (125g) cooking dates, chopped
2oz (50g) walnuts or brazil nuts, chopped
Finely grated peel of 1 medium washed and dried orange
4 Grade 2 eggs, beaten
1 tbsp black treacle
3 tbsp whisky, brandy or stout
¼pt (150ml) milk

1 Sift flour and spice into a bowl. Toss in all remaining dry ingredients.
2 Work in eggs, treacle, alcohol and milk to give a semi-stiff mixture. Cover. Leave overnight.
3 Divide equally between 2 well-greased 2pt (1.25 litre) pudding basins.
4 Cover as directed for Steamed Suet Pudding (page 214) and steam steadily, in covered pans, for 5 hours, topping up with extra boiling water when necessary.
5 Allow to cool in basins, then turn out and wrap in greaseproof paper when cold. Overwrap in foil and store in a cool, dry place until needed.
6 Re-steam 2 hours before serving.

Plum Cake

serves 12
(illustrated on page 221)

This delicious cake can either be served warm with custard as a dessert, or cold cut into squares for tea-time.

Base
2oz (50g) solid vegetable oil
2oz (50g) light-brown soft sugar
1lb (450g) ripe plums
3 glacé cherries
Cake
3oz (75g) solid vegetable oil
2oz (50g) self-raising flour
3oz (75g) light-brown soft sugar
3oz (75g) digestive biscuits, crushed
2 Grade 3 eggs
¼pt (150ml) milk

1 Melt the oil for the base, stir in the sugar then pour mixture into an 8in (20cm) greased and lined square cake tin.
2 Cut the plums in half, remove stones, then place, cut sides down, into tin. Halve cherries and dot between plums.
3 Using the same saucepan, melt the oil for cake over a low heat then mix in the flour, sugar, biscuits, eggs and milk to make a smooth batter consistency.
4 Pour into the tin over the plums, then bake for 1 hour in oven centre (any position in fan oven) set to 350°F (180°C), Gas 4.
5 Allow cake to cool in tin 10 minutes, then turn out on to a wire cooling rack to cool completely, or serve immediately as a dessert.

Fruited Clafouti

serves 8
(illustrated on page 222)

A cake-cum-pudding made from canned gooseberries, delicious for high tea at any time of year. Clafouti is French — a cross between a Yorkshire Pudding batter and a baked egg custard.

2 cans (each 10oz or 284g) gooseberries
3 level tbsp plain flour
5 level tbsp caster sugar
3 Grade 2 eggs
¾pt (425ml) milk

1 Drain gooseberries and reserve syrup. Spread fruit over base of 2pt (1.25 litre) fairly shallow greased ovenproof dish.
2 Sift flour into a bowl. Add 3 tbsp of sugar. Make a dip in the centre. Break in eggs. Start beating to a batter, gradually pouring in the milk as you do so.

3 Pour batter over gooseberries. Bake 30-40 minutes just above centre of oven (any position in fan oven) set to 425°F (220°C), Gas 7. Clafouti is ready when it is set like an egg custard and golden brown.

4 Sprinkle rest of sugar on top then serve with rest of syrup, heated through until hot, and a bowl of whipped cream.

Apple Toad-in-the-Hole

serves 6

4oz (125g) plain flour
Pinch of salt
1 Grade 3 egg
½pt (275ml) milk
3 tbsp butter or margarine, melted
1lb (450g) dessert apples, peeled, cored and cut into medium-thick slices
3-4oz (75-125g) caster sugar
1 level tsp cinnamon
1 level tbsp caster sugar to decorate

1 Sift flour and salt into bowl. Beat to a thick batter with whole egg and half the milk. Gently stir in rest of milk. Cover and refrigerate for 2 hours.

2 Remove batter from refrigerator, stir in 1 tbsp melted butter or margarine and leave aside for the moment.

3 Heat rest of butter or margarine until hot but not hazy in a 10 x 12in (25 x 30cm) roasting tin. Allow 7-10 minutes near top of oven (any position in fan oven) set to 425°F (220°C), Gas 7.

4 Remove tin from oven and spread apples over base. Sprinkle with sugar and cinnamon. Coat completely with all the batter. Return to oven and bake for 40-50 minutes or until well-puffed and golden. Top with extra sugar.

5 Cut into squares and serve hot with custard.

Plum Toad-in-the-Hole

serves 6

Make as Apple Toad-in-the-Hole, using 1lb (450g) halved and stoned dessert plums instead of apples.

Mince Pies with Walnuts

makes 12

Shortcrust pastry made with 6oz (175g) flour and 3oz (75g) fat etc (page 99).
12oz (350g) mincemeat
2oz (50g) walnuts, finely chopped
1 tbsp port
Beaten egg
Icing sugar

1 Roll out pastry fairly thinly on a floured surface. Cut 12 rounds with a 3½in (9cm) cutter and 12 rounds with a 2½in (6cm) cutter. Re-roll and re-cut trimmings to make required number.

2 Use the larger rounds to line 12 deep, greased bun tins. Fill evenly with mincemeat mixed with walnuts and port. Top with lids, pressing down gently.

3 Brush with egg. Bake 20-25 minutes near top of oven (any position in fan oven) set to 425°F (220°C), Gas 6.

4 Cool for 5 minutes, remove carefully to a wire cooling rack and sift icing sugar over tops (see also Mince Pies, page 102).

Apple Surprise Pie

serves 6-8

Scone Pastry
12oz (350g) plain flour
6 level tsp baking powder
3oz (75g) butter and white cooking fat mixture
3oz (75g) light-brown soft sugar
1 Grade 3 egg, beaten
6 tbsp cold milk
Filling
1lb (450g) Bramley apples, peeled and grated
3oz (75g) light-brown soft sugar
2 level tsp mixed spice
Topping
Beaten egg
Caster sugar

1 For the pastry, sift flour and baking powder into a bowl. Rub in fats then toss in sugar. Using a fork, stir to a soft dough with egg and milk.

219

2 Turn out onto a floured surface and knead lightly until smooth. Cut in half. Roll one piece into a 9in (22.5cm) round and carefully transfer it to a greased baking tray.
3 Mix filling ingredients together. Pile onto centre of pastry round, then brush edges of pastry with water. Cover with a lid rolled from rest of pastry.
4 Press edges well together to seal, then brush with egg and sprinkle with sugar. Bake for 40 minutes near top of oven (any position in fan oven) set to 375°F (190°C), Gas 5. Cut into portions (beware, juices will run) and serve hot with vanilla ice cream.

Baked Bananas with Rum

serves 4

1½lb (675g) bananas
1oz (25g) sliced brazil nuts, lightly toasted
1oz (25g) butter, melted
3 tsp dark rum
2oz (50g) dark-brown soft sugar

1 Peel bananas and cut each in half lengthwise. Place, cut sides down, in a shallow baking dish.
2 Sprinkle with nuts, butter, rum and sugar then bake, uncovered, near top of oven (any position in fan oven) set to 400°F (200°C), Gas 6 until bananas are soft.
3 Spoon onto plates and serve hot with cream.

(right) Plum and Apple Pie, page 208; Plum Tart (front), page 213; and Plum Cake, page 218 *(Pura Advisory Service)*

(overleaf) Fruited Clafouti, page 218 *(Cadbury Typhoo)*

13
Unusual Recipes

There is no rhyme or reason for my choice, no logical sequence but simply the off-loading, if you like, of a happy memorabilia of Cakes and Breads and Flans and Tarts which have gradually crept into my repertoire since I first started out on my cooking and writing career a long, long time ago. A personal collection passed on with pleasure.

German Apple Cake with Brandy

serves 8-10

One of my favourite autumnal cakes, for tea or dessert — a close rival to our apple pie.

Pastry
12oz (350g) plain flour
2 level tsp baking powder
4oz (125g) butter
2oz (50g) white vegetable fat
4oz (125g) caster sugar
1 Grade 3 egg, beaten
1 tsp vanilla essence
2-3 tbsp single cream
Filling
3lb (1.5kg) cooking apples
3oz (75g) caster sugar
3 tbsp brandy
2 level tsp cinnamon
¼ level tsp allspice
1 level tsp finely grated lemon peel
Icing sugar

1 Sift flour and baking powder into a bowl. Rub in butter and fat finely. Toss in sugar. Mix to a stiff paste with egg, essence and cream.
2 Knead lightly, wrap in foil and relax in the refrigerator for 1 hour.
3 Meanwhile, prepare filling. Peel apples and thinly slice. Put into a large mixing bowl and toss in all remaining ingredients. (The apple will brown but this has no adverse effect on the cake.)
4 Roll out one-third of pastry and use to cover the base of an 8in (20cm) well-greased, loose-bottomed deep cake tin. Roll out another third of pastry the same

depth as tin and long enough to go around it, and use to line the inside of the tin. Where they meet at the base, pinch edges of pastry well together to seal. Line with foil to prevent pastry rising as it cooks, then bake 20 minutes just above centre of oven (any position in fan oven) set to 375°F (190°C), Gas 5.
5 Carefully lift out foil and fill with apple mixture. Top with rest of pastry, rolled out into a lid to fit the top.
6 Reduce oven temperature to 350°F (180°C), Gas 4, and return cake to oven. Continue to bake for 45 minutes.
7 Leave to stand 30 minutes then remove sides but leave cake on its metal base. Sift icing sugar thickly over the top, cut into wedges and served cold with whipped cream or ice cream.

German Apple Cake with Rum
serves 8-10
Make as previous recipe but use dark rum instead of brandy.

German Apple Cake with Raisins
serves 8-10
Toss 2oz (50g) seedless raisins in with apple mixture. Use either brandy or rum.

Raspberry Roll Slice

serves 8

Rich and finely flavoured, this is a luxurious cake for tea-time.

Short Pastry made with 6oz (175g) plain flour (see page 99)
1½oz (40g) butter, softened
3 rounded tbsp raspberry jam, at kitchen temperature
1 slightly rounded tsp cinnamon
Beaten egg for brushing
Icing sugar

1 Roll out pastry into a 12 x 10in (30 x 25cm) rectangle and spread with butter to within ½in (1.25cm) of edges. Follow with jam. Dampen pastry edges.

2 Sprinkle with cinnamon, then roll up, starting from one of the longer sides. Press edge well together to seal.

3 Stand the roll on a buttered baking tray, with the join underneath. Brush with egg and bake 25 minutes just above centre of oven (any position in fan oven) set to 400°F (200°C), Gas 6. The roll should be a deep golden brown, so allow a little extra time if necessary.

4 Cool on a wire rack then sift icing sugar thickly over the top. Cut into 8 diagonal slices for serving.

Raspberry and Almond Roll Slice

serves 8

After spreading with jam, sprinkle with 1oz (25g) flaked and toasted almonds, coarsely crushed.

Strawberry and Orange Roll Slice

serves 8

Instead of raspberry jam, use strawberry and sprinkle with 2 level tsp finely grated orange peel instead of the cinnamon.

Chocolate Surprise Cake

serves 12

The surprise element in this American cake is the use of salad cream instead of fat and eggs, resulting in a feather-light texture and rich chocolate flavour. Do not be put off by the curious blend of ingredients — it is well worth trying, and also very easy.

8oz (225g) plain flour
1½oz (40g) cocoa powder
2 level tsp bicarbonate of soda
6oz (175g) caster sugar
7fl oz (200ml) water
1 tsp vanilla essence
7oz (200g) bottled salad cream (I use Heinz)
Chocolate fudge icing
6oz (175g) caster sugar
2oz (50g) butter
3 level tbsp cocoa powder
3 tbsp milk
1 tsp vanilla essence

1 Well-grease and paper-line a medium-sized roasting tin measuring about 11 x 9in (27.5 x 22.5cm) round the top edge and sloping down to about 10 x 8in (25-20cm). The depth should be about 1½in (4cm). Set oven to 350°F (180°C), Gas 4.

2 Sift flour, cocoa powder and bicarbonate of soda into a bowl. Toss in sugar. Mix to a soft consistency with water and essence, then gently stir in salad cream.

3 Spread into prepared tin and bake 45 minutes, one shelf below centre of oven. Leave to stand for 20 minutes then carefully lift out on to a wire cooling rack. Peel away paper when cold.

4 To make fudge icing, put sugar, butter, cocoa powder and milk into a saucepan. Bring slowly to boil, stirring all the time. Boil for 3 minutes only. Stir in vanilla essence.

5 Put saucepan into a sink of cold water and beat for about 2 minutes until icing thickens up to a spreadable consistency. Spread quickly over top of cake (before icing thickens up too much) and leave about 30 minutes before cutting.

Chocolate Mint Surprise Cake

serves 12

Flavour fudge icing with 1 tsp peppermint essence instead of vanilla.

Chocolate Coffee Surprise Cake

serves 12

Add 2 rounded tsp instant coffee powder to icing ingredients before bringing to the boil.

Chocolate Rum Surprise Cake

serves 12

Add 1 tsp rum essence to cake mixture instead of vanilla.

Chocolate Orange Surprise Cake

serves 12

Add 2 level tsp finely grated orange peel to cake mixture instead of vanilla.

Chocolate Velvet Layer Cake

serves 8

With a texture like velvet and as dark as night, here is one of my own special chocolate cakes, easily converted into a special-occasion gâteau for entertaining.

1 bar (3½oz or 100g) plain dessert chocolate
8oz (225g) self-raising flour
1oz (25g) cocoa powder
¼ level tsp bicarbonate of soda
5oz (150g) butter, at kitchen temperature and soft but not oily
7oz (200g) light-brown soft sugar
2 Grade 3 eggs (kitchen temperature)
1 tsp vanilla essence
4 level tbsp natural yoghurt
4 tbsp skimmed milk

1 Break up chocolate and melt in basin standing over pan of hot water.
2 Sift flour, cocoa powder and bicarbonate of soda into a bowl. Add chocolate and all remaining ingredients.
3 Beat steadily for 3 minutes or until ingredients are well blended and all signs of streakiness have disappeared.
4 Transfer to two 8in (20cm) sandwich tins, well-greased and base-lined with grease-proof paper.
5 Bake for 30 minutes in centre of oven (any position in fan oven) set to 350°F (180°C), Gas 4.
6 Leave to stand 5 minutes then turn out on to a wire cooling rack. Peel away paper when cold. Sandwich together with 4 tbsp of double cream, whipped until thick with 2 level tsp caster sugar.

Chocolate Velvet Layer Gâteau

serves 8-10

Whip ½pt (275ml) double cream until thick then fold in 2oz (50g) caster sugar and 1 tsp vanilla essence. Slice each layer in half horizontally then sandwich together with cream. Spread cream over top then decorate by sprinkling lightly with drinking chocolate.

Chocolate Velvet Fudge Gâteau

serves 8-10

Make up icing as given for Chocolate Surprise Cake. Use half to sandwich both layers of cake together and half to cover the top. Decorate with walnut halves.

Short-cut Black Forest Cherry Cake

serves 8-10

Slice layers of Chocolate Velvet Cake in half horizontally. Sprinkle with cherry brandy or kirsch. Sandwich layers together with sweetened whipped cream (about ¼pt or 150ml) and 1 large can of cherry pie filling. Spread another ¼pt (150ml) sweetened whipped cream over the top and sides of cake then press chocolate vermicelli against the sides. Decorate top with a border of halved glacé cherries.

Middle Eastern Crescents

makes 12

Not-too-sweet little cakes which can be served at tea-time or kept for after-dinner petits fours.

Pastry
8oz (225g) plain flour
4½oz (140g) butter
2 level tbsp caster sugar
2-3 tbsp milk
Filling
2oz (50g) flaked and lightly toasted almonds
2 level tsp cinnamon
1½ level tbsp caster sugar
1 egg yolk
Topping
1 egg white from a small egg
Icing sugar

1 For pastry, sift flour into bowl and rub in butter finely. Toss in sugar then mix to a stiffish dough with milk. Turn out onto floured surface and knead lightly until smooth. Divide into 2 equal pieces, roll each into a 10in (25cm) round, then cut into six triangles (total of 12 triangles).
3 To make filling, coarsely crush nuts then mix with rest of ingredients. Place equal

amounts on to widest part of triangles then dampen edge with milk.

4 Roll each up towards the points then curve into crescents on large, greased baking tray. Brush with lightly beaten egg white to glaze then bake 25 minutes just above centre of oven (any position in fan oven) set to 400°F (200°C), Gas 6. Cool on a wire rack and sift icing sugar thickly over top before serving.

Creole Christmas Cake

serves about 50-60

A traditional Christmas cake in Trinidad, where it is called Gâteau Noir, this recipe was passed on to me by Billington's Sugar. I have altered the combination of ingredients slightly to suit personal taste but it still remains a luxurious cross between a cake and a pudding, immensely rich and very moist. The ingredients are plenty for 2 large cakes and 1 medium one.

1 wineglass rum
1 wineglass brandy
1 wineglass port
1 wineglass cherry brandy
1 wineglass water
3 tsp Angostura bitters
1 rounded tsp cinnamon
1 level tsp ground nutmeg
1 level tsp cloves
2 tsp vanilla essence
2 rounded tbsp molasses sugar
1lb (450g) seedless raisins
1lb (450g) sultanas
1lb (450g) currants
4oz (125g) mixed chopped peel
8oz (225g) well-washed dried apricots, wiped dry and scissor-snipped into small pieces
4oz (125g) cooking dates, chopped
1 level tsp grated tangerine peel
2 level tsp grated lemon peel
4oz (125g) chopped walnuts or sliced brazil nuts
1lb (450g) self-raising flour
1½lb (675g) demerara sugar
1lb (450g) butter

10 Grade 3 eggs, at kitchen temperature and well beaten

1 Pour alcohols, water and bitters into a large pan. Add all remaining ingredients except the last four. Bring slowly to the boil, stirring.

2 Simmer 15 minutes. Move pan away from heat and cover. Leave to mature for 24-36 hours.

3 Sift flour into a bowl. Toss in sugar. Rub in butter finely. Stir slowly into fruit mixture with eggs. This is a fairly slow, heavy task and thorough mixing is essential.

4 Divide equally between two 8in (20cm) greased round cake tins and one 7in (17.5cm) tin, all lined with a double thickness of greaseproof paper.

5 Smooth tops with a knife then bake 4-4½ hours in centre of oven (any position in fan oven) set to very cool: 250°F (130°C), Gas ½. Three should fit on one shelf in most modern ovens. If not, they can be baked in 3 positions as the temperature is so low. Positions can be reversed at half time.

6 The cakes are ready when a thin metal skewer, pushed gently into centre, comes out clean and dry. If it remains on the tacky side, bake a further 30 minutes as cakes at this low temperature can come to little harm.

7 Leave in tins for at least 45 minutes then invert carefully onto wire cooling racks. Leave the lining paper on as a protection. When cold, wrap in more greaseproof paper and store in airtight tins.

8 Cut into small pieces and accompany with whipped cream. The cake may also be iced. Follow directions for Christmas Cake (page 40).

Stout Cake

serves 8

Made with Guinness or any other stout, this is an unusual cake with an intriguing flavour. Make and eat within 2 days.

12oz (350g) self-raising flour
6oz (175g) butter, at kitchen temperature
6oz (175g) caster sugar
4oz (125g) cooking dates, chopped
2oz (50g) walnuts, chopped
1 Grade 2 egg, beaten
7 tbsp stout

1 Sift flour into bowl. Rub in butter finely then toss in sugar, dates and walnuts.
2 Mix to a softish consistency with eggs and stout, stirring fairly briskly with a fork.
3 Spread smoothly into a greased and paper-lined 7in (17.5cm) cake tin. Bake 1¼ hours in centre of oven (any position in fan oven) set to 350°F (180°C), Gas 4.
4 Leave 20 minutes then turn out on to a wire cooling rack. Store in an airtight container and peel off lining paper just before serving.

Linz Hazelnut Tart

serves 8-10

From Linz, in Austria, is this marvellous, nut-based jam flan which can be served for elevenses, at tea-time or as an after-dinner sweet with whipped cream.

4oz (125g) plain flour
2 level tsp cinnamon
4oz (125g) light-brown soft sugar
4oz (125g) hazelnuts, very finely ground in blender or food processor
4oz (125g) butter, at room temperature and soft
1 Grade 3 egg yolk
8oz (225g) raspberry jam
Beaten egg for brushing
Icing sugar

1 Sift flour and cinnamon into a bowl. Toss in sugar and hazelnuts.
2 Rub in butter, add egg yolk then knead ingredients together to form a dough. Wrap in foil or cling film and refrigerate until firm enough to manipulate, about 45-60 minutes.
3 Take three-quarters of the pastry and press evenly over base and sides of a 7in (17.5cm) flan ring standing on a greased baking tray. Make a slightly raised border by pinching dough between finger and thumb.
4 Fill with jam. Shape remaining pastry into strips (you can roll with a rolling pin and cut, or roll strips between floured hands) and form into a lattice over top of tart, allowing 3-4 strips each way.
5 Press ends of strips on to pastry edges to seal, then brush with beaten egg.
6 Bake 45 minutes in centre of oven (any position in fan oven), set to 350°F (180°C), Gas 4. Leave to stand for 15 minutes then lift off flan ring. Sift icing sugar over the top of the tart before cutting into wedges and serving.

Linz Almond Tart
serves 8-10
Make as above, substituting ground almonds for hazelnuts.

Sachertorte 1

serves 10

The mystery cake from the Hotel Sacher in Vienna where the recipe for this famous masterpiece remains a highly valued secret. The only thing the rest of us can therefore do is to visit Sacher's, taste the cake and guess at what goes in. With a piece brought home with me, I have worked out two versions which are passable copies of the real thing. I do have to emphasise that a Sachertorte is a rich, shallow cake usually accompanied by scoops of whipped cream.

1 bar (3½oz or 100g) plain dessert chocolate
3oz (75g) unsalted butter, at kitchen temperature and soft
3 Grade 3 eggs, at kitchen temperature and separated

3oz (75g) caster sugar
2oz (50g) ground almonds
2oz (50g) plain flour, sifted
1 rounded tbsp warmed apricot jam
Icing
½ bar (just under 2oz or 50g) plain dessert
  chocolate
½oz (15g) unsalted butter
4oz (125g) icing sugar, sifted
1½ tbsp warm water

1 Brush an 8in (20cm) sandwich tin with melted butter and line base with a round of greaseproof paper.
2 Break up chocolate and put into a basin standing over a saucepan of hot water. Leave until melted, stirring occasionally.
3 Remove basin from saucepan and wipe sides dry. Into the chocolate, beat butter, egg yolks, sugar, almonds and flour.
4 In separate bowl, whip egg whites to a stiff snow. Beat one-third into chocolate mixture then gradually fold in remainder with a large metal spoon or spatula. When smooth and evenly combined and all traces of streakiness have disappeared, spread smoothly into prepared tin.
5 Bake 30-40 minutes in centre of oven (any position in fan oven) set to 350°F (180°C), Gas 4. Stand 10 minutes then turn out and cool on a wire rack. Turn right way up when lukewarm and brush over with apricot jam to hold crumbs in place and to add flavour.
6 For icing, break up chocolate and melt, with butter, in a basin standing over a saucepan of hot water. Stir occasionally.
7 Mix in icing sugar and water. Stir thoroughly. Spread smoothly over top and sides of cake. (Icing will drip through wire rack so it is a good idea to have a plate underneath.)
8 Leave undisturbed until icing has completely set. Cut cake into portions and serve with whipped cream.

Sachertorte 2

serves 10

1 bar (3½oz or 100g) plain dessert chocolate
4oz (125g) unsalted butter, softened
4oz (125g) caster sugar
4oz (125g) ground almonds
2oz (50g) fresh brown breadcrumbs
4 Grade 3 eggs, at kitchen temperature and
  separated
2 rounded tbsp warmed apricot jam

1 Break up chocolate and melt as for Sachertorte 1. Remove basin from pan and cool slightly.
2 Cream butter and sugar until light and fluffy then stir in almonds, crumbs and egg yolks.
3 In clean and dry bowl, beat egg whites to a stiff snow. Beat one-quarter into cake mixture with melted chocolate, then fold in remainder with a large metal spoon.
4 Spread evenly into a 9in (22.5cm) greased sandwich tin, base-lined with a round of greaseproof paper.
5 Bake 45 minutes in centre of oven (any position in fan oven) set to 350°F (180°C), Gas 4. Finish off and ice as directed for Sachertorte 1.

Layered Sachertorte
serves 10
If liked, cut cake in half horizontally and sandwich together with apricot jam. Afterwards brush with more apricot jam as directed, before covering with chocolate icing.

Brown Sandwich Cake

serves 8

This is a sponge-type sandwich cake made with brown flour. It has a nutty flavour and light texture, similar to a Victoria Sandwich cake but sufficiently different to be quite interesting.

6oz (175g) plain wheatmeal flour (*not*
  self-raising)
2¼ level tsp baking powder

6oz (175g) butter or block margarine, at kitchen temperature
6oz (175g) caster sugar
1 tsp vanilla essence
3 Grade 3 eggs, at kitchen temperature
Chocolate spread such as Nutella or Nutch.

1 Toss flour and baking powder into a bowl. In separate bowl, cream butter or margarine, sugar and essence together until light and fluffy.
2 Beat in eggs singly, adding a tbsp of dry ingredients with each. Finally, fold in flour mixture with a large metal spoon.
3 Divide equally between two 7in (17.5cm) sandwich tins and bake 25-30 minutes in oven centre (any position in fan oven) set to 350°F (180°C), Gas 4.
4 Remove from oven, leave to stand 5 minutes then turn out and cool on a wire rack. Peel away paper when cold, sandwich together with chocolate spread and dust top with icing sugar.

Walnut Marzipan Layer Cake
serves 8-10
Make up Brown Sandwich Cake and, while cooling, prepare the walnut 'marzipan'. Grind up 4oz (125g) shelled walnuts in blender or food processor. Combine with 2oz (50g) sifted icing sugar and 2oz (50g) caster sugar. Mix to a firm paste with ½ tsp vanilla essence and a few tsp beaten egg. Roll out into a 7in (17.5cm) round on a sugared surface. Peel paper off cakes, spread with raspberry jam then sandwich together with the walnut marzipan. Dust top lightly with sifted icing sugar before serving.

Chocolate Rose Gâteau
serves 8-10
Make up Brown Sandwich Cake and sandwich layers together with apricot jam when cold. Coat top and sides with chocolate icing given for Sachertorte (opposite). When set, decorate cake with crystallised rose petals.

Coffee Brazil Nut Gâteau
serves 10
Make butter cream by beating 6oz (175g) butter (at kitchen temperature) with 12oz (350g) sifted icing sugar and 3 tbsp very strong cold coffee. Continue beating until light and fluffy and leave 30 minutes in the refrigerator to firm up. Make up Brown Sandwich Cake and peel off paper. Cool completely on a wire rack then cut each layer in half horizontally. Sandwich together with the butter cream then spread remainder over top and sides. Press chocolate vermicelli against sides of cake then decorate top with slices of brazil nuts, arranged in rings. Chill lightly before serving.

Yellow Snow Gâteau
serves 10
Make up Brown Sandwich Cake and leave until cold. Prepare butter cream as above but omit coffee and add one egg yolk beaten with 1 tbsp milk. Also 2 level tsp finely grated lemon peel. Cut cake layers in half horizontally and sandwich together with the butter cream. Swirl remainder over top and sides then decorate top with a shower of hundreds and thousands. Alternatively, decorate with pieces of glacé pineapple and yellow glacé cherries. Chill lightly before serving.

White Snow Gâteau
serves 10
Make up Brown Sandwich Cake and leave until cold. Whip ¾pt (425ml) double cream with 3 tbsp cold milk until thick. Fold in 3 heaped tbsp sifted icing sugar and 2 tsp vanilla essence. Cut cake layers in half horizontally and sandwich together with the whipped cream. Swirl remainder thickly over top and sides then dot here and there with silver balls. Chill lightly before serving.

Boston Cream Pie

serves 8-10

The following traditional American recipes are easily adapted to UK ingredients. Make up Victoria Sandwich Cake (page 28) as directed and fill with half recipe Confectioner's Custard (page 77). Cover top with sifted icing sugar or half quantity of chocolate icing given for Sachertorte 1 (page 230).

Boston Brown Bread

serves 8

Similar to steamed pudding, Boston Brown Bread is traditionally eaten with Boston Baked Beans (a long painstaking dish which is like a strong version of our own beans in tomato sauce) and salted and boiled brisket. The bread is an acquired taste but worth trying for novelty.

4oz (125g) plain white flour
4oz (125g) wholemeal flour
4oz (125g) polenta, cornmeal or semolina
1 level tsp salt
3 level tsp baking powder
6oz (175g) black treacle
¾pt (425ml) buttermilk or half plain yogurt smoothly mixed with half skimmed milk

1 Sift flours into bowl with polenta, salt and baking powder. Mix to a soft consistency with treacle and buttermilk or the yogurt and skimmed milk combination, stirring briskly without beating.
2 Transfer to a 2½pt (1.5 litre) greased pudding basin. Cover with double thickness of foil and stand in a large, fairly deep saucepan. Add sufficient boiling water to come half way up the sides of basin.
3 Cover with lid. Boil gently for 2 hours, topping up pan with boiling water as and when necessary. Unmould bread, cut into wedges and serve warm with butter.

American Apple Pie

serves 8

This one has a lattice top. The apple juices are thickened with cornflour and lemon peel is used to flavour.

Shortcrust Pastry made with 8oz (225g) flour (page 99)
2lb (900g) cooking apples
6oz (175g) caster sugar
2 level tbsp cornflour
1 level tsp cinnamon or allspice
1 level tsp finely grated lemon peel
Beaten egg to glaze

1 Roll out two-thirds of pastry and use to line 9in (22.5cm) well-greased glass pie plate about 2in (5cm) in depth and with a rim. Keep rest of pastry cool for the time being.
2 Peel, quarter and core the apples then cut into very thin slices directly into a large bowl. Stir in sugar, cornflour, cinnamon or allspice and the lemon peel. Mix thoroughly.
3 Put apple filling into pastry case then dampen pastry edges with water. Cut rest of pastry into strips and criss-cross across the top to form a trellis effect.
4 Press edges of strips onto pastry rim to seal, then brush pastry with beaten egg.
5 Bake 45-60 minutes just above centre of oven (any position in fan oven) set to 400°F (200°C), Gas 6. Serve warm with vanilla ice cream or whipped cream.

American Apple and Cranberry Pie
serves 8

Reduce apples by 4oz (125g) and substitute the same weight of fresh cranberries, which are available in Britain during the winter.

Pumpkin Pie

serves 10

Always eaten at Thanksgiving, the last Thursday in November.

3½lb (1.75kg) piece of pumpkin (half a whole one is best)
1 level tbsp black treacle or molasses
6oz (175g) caster sugar
½oz (50g) cornflour
2 level tsp allspice
1 level tsp cinnamon
¼pt (150ml) canned unsweetened evaporated milk (or single cream)
3 Grade 3 eggs, beaten
Shortcrust Pastry made with 8oz (225g) flour (page 99).

1 Remove pips and strings from pumpkin then stand on greased baking tray, skin side up. Cook 1 hour in centre of oven (any position in fan oven) set to 350°F (180°C), Gas 4. The pumpkin is ready when a long thin metal skewer punctures the skin with ease.
2 Scoop out flesh, mash finely, then put into a mesh sieve. Press against sides to remove as much surplus moisture as possible. You should then be left with 1lb (450g) pumpkin pulp.
3 Put into bowl and beat in treacle, sugar, cornflour, allspice, cinnamon, evaporated milk (or cream) and eggs.
4 Roll out pastry and use to line a 10in (25cm) flan ring standing on a greased baking tray (or use a spring-clip tin as recommended for Cheesecakes). Fill with pumpkin mixture.
5 Bake 45 minutes just above centre of oven (any position in fan oven) set to 400°F (200°C), Gas 6.
6 When still warm, cut into wedges and serve with whipped cream.

Lemon Shaker Pie

serves 8

This comes from Ohio and was invented by the Kitchen Sisters of an early nineteenth-century religious sect called the Shakers. The pie is distinctively bitter-sweet and very refreshing. The Vista International Hotel in New York is responsible for the recipe which I have adapted to UK and metric measurements. I appreciate their co-operation in passing it on to me.

2 large lemons, washed and dried
8oz (225g) caster sugar
Shortcrust Pastry made with 12oz (350g) flour (page 99)
3 Grade 2 eggs, beaten
2 tbsp single cream for brushing

1 Slice lemons very thinly and remove pips. Put the lemons into bowl with sugar. Toss well to mix, cover and leave to stand overnight.
2 Roll out just over half the pastry and use to line an 8in (20cm) greased enamel plate. Fill wth lemon mixture mixed with eggs. Dampen pastry edges with water.
3 Cover with lid, rolled from rest of pastry. Press edges well together to seal, brush with cream, then make two slits in the top to allow steam to escape.
4 Bake 15 minutes just above centre of oven (any position in fan oven) set to 450°F (230°C), Gas 8. Reduce temperature to 350°F (180°C), Gas 4 and continue to bake a further 30 minutes. Serve warm or cold, cut into wedges.

Pecan Pie

serves 8-10

As sweet as sweet can be, this is one of my own American treasures, though pecan nuts do make the recipe somewhat costly. It comes from the deep South.

7oz (200g) pecan nuts
Shortcrust Pastry made with 8oz (225g) flour (see page 99)
1oz (25g) butter, melted
8oz (225g) caster sugar
8oz (225g) golden syrup
3 Grade 3 eggs, well-beaten
1 tsp vanilla essence

1 Toast nuts until a warm gold under the grill, arranged in single layer in grill pan. Cool.
2 Line a 10in (25cm) flan ring, standing on a greased baking tray, with pastry.
3 Spread pecans over base. Beat rest of ingredients well together and pour into pastry case over nuts. Bake about 45 minutes just above centre of oven (any position in fan oven) set to 375°F (190°C), Gas 5.
4 Cut into wedges and serve warm with whipped cream.

Pecan Compromise Pie
serves 8-10
Make as above but use walnut halves instead of pecan nuts.

Blue Cheese Flan

serves 8-10

From Iowa (where some Blue Cheese comes from) comes this fabulous flan which I tend to serve as a savoury at the end of a meal.

Shortcrust Pastry made with 6oz (175g) flour (page 99)
2 packets (each 3oz or 75g) Philadelphia Cream Cheese, at kitchen temperature
1 rounded tbsp chopped chives or green part of leek
3oz (75g) blue-vein cheese (I use Stilton or Lymeswold)
2oz (50g) butter, very soft but not runny
2 Grade 3 eggs, well beaten
Salt and pepper to taste
Parsley to garnish

1 Roll out pastry and use to line an 8½in (21.25cm) pie plate.
2 Beat cream cheese until smooth then beat in rest of ingredients. When very well mixed (and, if preferred, use a blender or food processor) pour into pastry-lined plate.
3 Bake 15 minutes near top of oven (any position in fan oven) set to 450°F (230°C), Gas 8. Reduce temperature to 375°F (190°C), Gas 5. Continue to bake a further 30 minutes or until filling is puffy and golden.
4 Cut into wedges and serve warm as a savoury or snack, or cold with salad.

Vanilla Coffee Crumble Cake

serves 10

Many American cakes are called Coffee Cakes — even though coffee never enters their lives — because they are ideally suited to coffee time or a mid-morning 'cuppa'.

8oz (225g) plain flour
8oz (225g) caster sugar
2 level tsp baking powder
½ level tsp bicarbonate of soda
2 Grade 3 eggs
1 tsp vanilla essence
1½ cartons (each 5oz or 142ml) soured cream
Topping
4 level tbsp plain flour
1 level tsp cinnamon
2oz caster sugar
1½oz (40g) butter

1 Sift flour, sugar, baking powder and bicarbonate of soda into bowl.
2 Beat together eggs, vanilla and cream until well-combined. Add to dry ingredients. Fork-stir lightly to mix but on no account beat.
3 Pour into greased and paper-lined roasting tin measuring about 10 x 8in (25 x 20cm).
4 To make topping, sift flour and cinnamon into a bowl. Toss in sugar. Rub in butter. Sprinkle over cake.
5 Bake 30-35 minutes in centre of oven (any position in fan oven) set to 350°F (180°C), Gas 4. The cake is ready when a thin metal skewer, pushed gently into centre, comes out clean and dry. Leave to stand 10 minutes then turn out on to a wire cooling rack. Peel away paper when cake is cool then turn right way up. Cut into squares when cold. Eat fresh.

Lemon Coffee Crumble Cake

serves 10

Omit vanilla and add the finely grated peel of 1 medium washed and dried lemon to the dry ingredients.

Orange Coffee Crumble Cake

serves 10

Omit vanilla and add the finely grated peel of 1 medium washed and dried orange to the dry ingredients.

Almond Chiffon Cake

serves 8

A cake with a satin-like texture made in a ring tin and based on oil. It is fairly time-consuming to put together and needs to hang upside down for about a hour or so before turning out (so that it cools completely and eases away from the tin). But if you do succeed, this is a super cake and one you will want to repeat.

4oz (125g) self-raising flour
5oz (150g) caster sugar
¼ level tsp salt
4 tbsp salad oil
3 Grade 3 eggs, separated
5 tbsp cold water
1 tsp almond essence
½ tsp lemon juice

1 Have to hand an 8in (20cm) ungreased ring tin (called tube pan in the US) and leave *ungreased*.
2 Sift flour, sugar and salt into a bowl. Make a dip in the centre and add oil, egg yolks, water and essence. Stir briskly until mixture is smooth.
3 Beat egg whites and lemon juice to a stiff and peaky snow. Pour one-third of flour mixture on to whites and fold in gently with a metal spoon. Repeat with second portion of flour mixture. Finally, fold in third portion.
4 When smooth and evenly combined, pour into prepared tin and bake 1 hour in centre of oven (any position in fan oven) set to 325°F (160°C), Gas 3.

5 Remove from oven and leave to stand 10 minutes. Afterwards invert tin, through its hole, over a long-necked bottle and leave to hang until cold, about 1 hour. To remove, loosen edges with a knife then tap base of tin sharply.

Vanilla Chiffon Cake

serves 8

Make as Almond Chiffon Cake but add vanilla essence instead of almond.

Lemon Chiffon Cake

serves 8

Make as Almond Chiffon Cake but add 2 level tsp grated lemon peel to dry ingredients before mixing in oil, etc.

Orange Chiffon Cake

serves 8

Make as Almond Chiffon Cake but add 2 level tsp grated orange peel to dry ingredients before mixing in oil, etc.

Chocolate Brownies

makes 24

The last of the American recipes are chewy bars with a rich chocolate flavour. These are one of America's pride and joys and extremely popular for Sunday-morning brunch.

2oz (50g) plain dessert chocolate
3oz (75g) butter
5oz (150g) self-raising flour
1oz (25g) cocoa powder
8oz (225g) caster sugar
2 Grade 2 eggs, beaten
1 tsp vanilla essence

1 Break up chocolate and put, with butter, into a basin resting over a saucepan of hot water. Leave until melted, stirring once or twice.
2 Meanwhile, sift flour and cocoa into a bowl. Toss in sugar. Using a fork, stir to a batter with the melted chocolate and butter, beaten eggs and vanilla essence.
3 Spread into a greased and paper-lined

235

Swiss-Roll tin measuring 11 x 8in (27.5 x 20cm). Bake just above centre of oven (any position in fan oven) set to 350°F (180°C), Gas 4. Allow 20 minutes. Remove from oven (you will notice that mixture falls) then leave to cool in the tin. Cut into bars and store in an airtight container.

Chocolate Walnut Brownies
makes 24
Make as previous recipe, adding 3oz (75g) chopped walnuts with the sugar.

Iced Brownies
makes 24
Coat cooked Brownies with chocolate icing given for Chocolate Eclairs (page 81), or for Chocolate Surprise Cake (page 226) before cutting into bars.

Cornflake Chocolate Crackles

makes 16

Delicious little tea-time cakes which 'cook' in the refrigerator.

3oz (75g) butter
2 level tbsp golden syrup
3 level tbsp cocoa powder, sifted
2 level tbsp caster sugar
1 tsp vanilla essence
3oz (75g) cornflakes

1 Melt butter and syrup together slowly in saucepan. Take off heat.
2 Stir in cocoa, sugar and essence. With a large metal spoon, gently and lightly stir in cornflakes.
3 Transfer mixture to 16 paper cases, stand on a board or baking tray and refrigerate until firm and set.
4 Serve only as many as are needed and keep remainder in a cool place, otherwise they tend to get sticky.

Cornflake Chocolate Rum Crackles
makes 16
Use rum essence instead of vanilla.

Cornflake Chocolate Orange Crackles
makes 16
Omit essence and stir 2 level tsp finely grated orange peel into the melted ingredients.

Refrigerator Chocolate Cake

serves 10-14

A marvellous, devastatingly rich chocolate cake which is the height of luxury. It also lends itself to innumerable variations and needs no baking — just setting in the refrigerator.

2 bars (each 3½oz or 100g) plain dessert
  chocolate
8oz (225g) butter, melted
2 heaped tbsp icing sugar, sifted
2 Grade 3 eggs, beaten
1 tsp vanilla essence
8oz (225g) digestive biscuits, each broken
  into about 12-14 pieces
2oz (50g) walnuts, chopped

1 Line a 7in (17.5cm) loose-bottomed cake tin with non-stick parchment paper.
2 Break up chocolate and put into a large basin over a saucepan of hot water. Leave until melted, stirring occasionally.
3 Take basin out of pan, wipe sides dry, then add butter to chocolate, followed by sugar, eggs and essence.
4 Gently fold in biscuits and nuts. Smooth into prepared tin.
5 Refrigerate about 4-6 hours or until firm and set.
6 Remove sides and carefully ease cake off its base.
7 Transfer to a serving plate and cut into thin wedges. Store leftovers in the refrigerator.

Refrigerator Chocolate Ginger Cake
serves 10-14
Make as Refrigerator Chocolate Cake but add 2oz (50g) chopped preserved ginger (drained of syrup) with the nuts.

Refrigerator Chocolate Tutti Frutti Cake

serves 10-14

Make as Refrigerator Chocolate Cake but add 2oz (50g) chopped glacé cherries, 2oz (50g) chopped dates and 2oz (50g) glacé pineapple with the nuts.

Refrigerator Chocolate Nut Cake

serves 10-14

Make as Refrigerator Chocolate Cake but add 4oz (125g) mixed chopped nuts instead of walnuts.

Refrigerator Chocolate Rum or Brandy Cake

serves 10-14

Make as Refrigerator Chocolate Cake but add 3 tsp dark rum or brandy instead of vanilla essence.

Refrigerator Mocha Cake

serves 10-14

Make as Refrigerator Chocolate Cake but when melting chocolate, add 3 rounded tsp instant coffee powder or granules. Omit vanilla essence.

Festive Refrigerator Chocolate Cake

serves 10-14

When mixture has been spread into tin, stud top with rings of walnut halves, sliced brazil nuts, halved red and green glacé cherries, and blanched and halved almonds.

Potato Chocolate Cake

serves 12-14

I have long since forgotten where I found this recipe but it is a very unusual cake and something to keep people guessing.

1lb (450g) floury potatoes (eg King Edwards, Desirée)
2 bars (each 3½oz or 100g) plain dessert chocolate
6oz (175g) butter, at room temperature and soft
6oz (175g) icing sugar, sifted
2 Grade 3 egg yolks

1 tbsp alcohol such as coffee or orange liqueur, rum, cherry brandy or whisky
Extra icing sugar

1 Line an 8in (20cm) spring-clip tin (the kind used for cheesecake) with non-stick parchment paper.
2 Peel potatoes and cube. Boil in slightly salted water. Drain. Mash finely then work to a purée in food processor or blender. Don't overmix or the potatoes will turn sticky.
3 Break up chocolate and melt in a basin over a saucepan of hot water. Stir occasionally.
4 Cream butter and sugar together until light and fluffy then beat in egg yolks.
5 Beat in potatoes, alcohol and melted chocolate. When very smooth and evenly combined, spread smoothly into tin.
6 Refrigerate 6 hours then unclip and remove sides and lining paper but leave cake on its metal base. Sprinkle with icing sugar before cutting into wedges and serving.

Walnut Torte

serves 8

3oz (75g) plain flour
3 Grade 2 eggs
3oz (75g) caster sugar
1 level tsp finely grated orange peel
4 level tbsp very finely ground walnuts
½pt (275ml) double cream
2 tbsp milk
1 level tbsp caster sugar
Walnut halves for decoration

1 Sift flour twice on to a plate. Put egg yolks and sugar into a bowl and whisk until mixture turns white and paste-like. Stir in peel and walnuts.
2 In clean and dry bowl, beat egg whites to a stiff snow. Fold lightly into egg yolk mixture alternately with flour.
3 When smooth and evenly combined, spoon quickly into 7in (17.5cm) greased and paper-lined round cake tin.
4 Bake 45 minutes in centre of oven (any

position in fan oven) set to 325°F (160°C), Gas 3. Leave to stand for 10 minutes then turn out on to a wire cooling rack covered with a sugar-sprinkled tea-towel, so that the cake does not stick. Peel away paper and leave until cold.

5 Whip cream and milk together until thick. Stir in sugar. Cut cake into 3 layers. Sandwich together thickly with cream then swirl more cream over the top. Stud with walnut halves.

Greek-style Christmas Cake

serves 8

Make as above but leave cake uncut. Cover top with thick glacé icing made from 6oz (175g) sifted icing sugar mixed with a few tsp of brandy. Leave until set then decorate with walnut halves and one or two Christmas novelties.

Cream Cheese Carrot Cake

serves 8-10

This cake with its coating of cream cheese frosting includes ginger and pineapple — an exotic touch of the South Sea islands.

8oz (225g) plain flour
¾ level tsp bicarbonate of soda
1 level tsp baking powder
½ level tsp ground ginger
½ level tsp salt
4oz (125g) granulated sugar
3 almost level tbsp thick (or set) honey
2 Grade 3 eggs
5 tbsp salad oil
4 large carrots, peeled and finely grated
1 can (13¼oz or 376g) crushed pineapple, thoroughly drained
1oz (25g) chopped walnuts
Frosting
1½oz (40g) butter, softened
1½oz (40g) cream cheese
1 tsp vanilla essence
8oz (225g) icing sugar

1 Sift dry ingredients into a bowl, then toss in sugar. Gradually beat in honey, eggs and oil.

2 Stir in carrots, pineapple and walnuts then smooth mixture evenly into a greased and paper-lined 7in (17.5cm) cake tin.

3 Bake 35-40 minutes in oven centre (any position in fan oven) set to 350°F (180°C), Gas 4. To test, push a thin metal skewer gently into centre of cake. If it comes out clean and dry, the cake is ready. If not, return to oven until sufficiently cooked, testing every 10 minutes with a skewer.

4 Leave to stand 10 minutes, then turn out on to a wire cooling rack. Peel away paper and leave cake until cold.

5 To ice, beat together butter, cream cheese and essence. Gradually beat in icing sugar. If too thick and heavy for spreading, work in a few tsp of milk.

6 Swirl the frosting over top and sides of cake then ridge in wavy lines with a fork. Chill for about 30 minutes in the refrigerator before serving.

Christmas Eve Cake

serves 8-10
(illustrated on page 184)

Called 'Dansk Ostekage' in Danish, this is the Scandinavian version of a fruity carrot cake with a cream cheese frosting. Far lighter than anything we make, this is a welcoming cake to offer guests on Christmas Eve with some hot punch or a glass of sherry. It's certainly different.

5oz (150g) Danish butter
7oz (200g) caster sugar
6oz (175g) carrots, peeled and very finely grated
½ level tsp salt
1 level tsp cinnamon
2 Grade 2 eggs
7oz (200g) plain flour
3 level tsp baking powder
4oz (125g) seedless raisins

(right) Iced Fudge Cake (front), page 243 and Crazy-paving Roll, page 244 *(Cadbury Typhoo)*

Frosting

2oz (50g) Danish butter, at kitchen
  temperature and softened
3½oz (90g) cream cheese
4oz (125g) icing sugar, sifted
Finely grated peel of 1 small washed and
  dried lemon or 1 tsp vanilla essence

1 Melt butter in a saucepan and pour into a
  mixing bowl. Beat in sugar, carrots, salt,
  cinnamon and eggs.
2 Sift flour and baking powder directly over
  the top and fold into cake mixture with the
  raisins.
3 Spread smoothly into an 8 x 6½in (20 x
  16cm) buttered tin lined with greaseproof
  paper. Bake 45 minutes in centre of oven
  (any position in fan oven), set to 325°F
  (160°C), Gas 3. Leave to stand 10 minutes
  then turn out on a wire cooling rack.
4 For the Frosting, beat butter and cream
  cheese until smooth, then stir in icing
  sugar and lemon peel or vanilla essence.
  Spread the Frosting over top and sides of
  cake, ridge with a fork and add seasonal
  decorations to taste.

Irish Apple Cake

serves 8

8oz (225g) self-raising flour
3oz (75g) butter
2oz (50g) caster sugar
3 large peeled cooking apples, cored and
  coarsely chopped
1 Grade 3 egg, beaten
About 4-5 tbsp milk
Extra caster sugar

1 Sift flour into a bowl. Rub in butter then
  toss in sugar and apples.
2 Mix to a stiffish consistency with the egg
  and milk. Spread into 7in (17.5cm)
  greased round cake tin and bake in centre
  of oven (any position in fan oven) for 35-45
  minutes at 350°F (180°C), Gas 4 when
  cake should be a warm gold.

(left) Sparkling Chocolate Cherry Cake, page 245
and Thatched Cottage Cake (front), page 245
(Chivers Hartley)

3 Leave in tin 7 minutes then turn out and
  cool on a wire rack. Sprinkle with sugar,
  and cut into wedges and serve freshly
  made.

'Marzipan' Cake

serves 12-14

I was given the recipe for this sweet confection many years ago in Lisbon where spare
eggs for cooking abound, as do almonds.

10oz (275g) caster sugar
¼pt (150ml) water
8oz (225g) ground almonds
8 Grade 3 eggs yolks
1 tsp almond essence
½ level tsp mixed spice
Extra caster sugar

1 Put sugar and water into a saucepan. Heat
  slowly, stirring occasionally, until sugar
  melts.
2 Add almonds. Cook, stirring all the time,
  for about 7 minutes. Cool for 5 minutes.
3 Gradually beat in yolks, essence and spice.
4 Spread into a buttered 10in (25cm) spring-
  clip tin with hinged sides. Bake 15
  minutes near top of oven (any position in
  fan oven) set to 400°F (200°C), Gas 6.
5 Remove from oven and sprinkle top with
  caster sugar. Unclip sides when cake is
  still slightly warm and cut into wedges
  when cold.

Flaky Festival Gâteau

serves 12
(illustrated on page 134)

A very special cake, smothered with chocolate flake bars and unashamedly rich. Lemon
gives the cake an unusual flavour.

Chocolate Sponge baked in deep 7in
  (17.5cm) tin (page 58)
4oz (125g) unsalted butter, at room
  temperature and soft
6oz (175g) caster sugar
Finely grated peel and juice of 2 medium
  lemons, washed and dried
3 Grade 3 eggs, separated

2oz (50g) plain dessert chocolate, melted and cooled but still liquid

½pt (275ml) whipping cream, whipped until thick

10 flake bars from family pack

1 If freshly made, leave cake until completely cold on wire rack. Peel off lining paper if used.
2 For filling, cream together butter and sugar until light and fluffy. Beat in lemon rind and juice, followed by egg yolks. The mixture may look curdled but this has no effect on final result. Beat egg whites to a stiff snow and fold in.
3 Slice cake into 4 layers and return 1 layer to a loose-bottomed, 7in (17.5cm) cake tin. Spread with a layer of lemon butter cream. Continue with rest of cake layers and butter cream, ending with a layer of cake.
4 Place a round of greaseproof paper on top, add a plate, then put a heavy weight on top. Leave to stand in a cool place overnight.
5 Remove cake carefully from tin. Stir chocolate into whipped cream, then spread thickly over top and sides of cake. Cut flake bars into thin strands and arrange in lines over top of cake. Chill lightly before serving.

Frosted Chocolate Layer Cake

serves 8-10

A beautifully moist and dark cake, enveloped in a snow-white frosting. A showpiece of a cake and glorious to eat. The frosting is, when correctly made, crisp on the outside and soft inside.

9oz (250g) self-raising flour
1oz (25g) cocoa powder
7oz (200g) caster sugar
6 tbsp cold milk
1 Grade 2 egg, beaten
1oz (25g) golden syrup, melted
4oz (125g) lard or white vegetable cooking fat, melted
1 tsp vanilla essence

¼ level tsp bicarbonate of soda
3 tbsp boiling water

Frosting
1lb (450g) granulated sugar
¼pt (150ml) water
2 Grade 3 egg whites
¼ level tsp cream of tartar
1 tsp vanilla essence

1 Sift flour and cocoa powder into a bowl. Add sugar, milk, egg, syrup, fat and essence. Mix thoroughly, stirring briskly with a fork. Avoid beating.
2 Mix bicarbonate of soda and water together. Stir into cake mixture. Beat well for 3 minutes. Spread evenly into two 8in (20cm) sandwich tins, greased and base-lined with greaseproof paper.
3 Bake 30-40 minutes in oven centre (any position in fan oven) set to 350°F (180°C), Gas 4. The cakes are ready when well-risen and firm.
4 Turn out on to a wire rack and cool completely. Put into an airtight container and leave 24 hours before icing.
5 To make Frosting, put sugar and water into saucepan. Stir over low heat until sugar dissolves. Bring to boil, cover pan and boil 1 minute. Uncover. Continue to boil, fairly vigorously, for a further 5-7 minutes or until a little of the mixture, dropped into a cup of cold water, forms a soft ball when rolled between finger and thumb.
6 If syrup disappears in the water it needs further boiling so return to heat and continue to boil, testing every 2 minutes, until it forms a ball. If this stage is not reached the frosting will not set.
7 Meanwhile, beat egg whites and cream of tartar to a very stiff snow. Pour syrup on to egg whites in a steady stream, beating continuously.
8 Add vanilla essence and continue beating until Frosting is cool and thick enough to hold soft peaks. This needs a lot of patience and I suggest electric beaters to ease arm-ache.
9 Slice layers of cake in half horizontally,

then sandwich together with Frosting. Spread more Frosting over top and sides of cake in a swirly design.

Frosted Chocolate Peppermint Cake
serves 8-10
Instead of vanilla, use peppermint essence in Cake and Frosting. Tint Frosting pale green.

Pecan Frosted Chocolate Cake
serves 8-10
Make as Frosted Chocolate Layer Cake, then stud top with halves of pecan nuts.

Walnut Layer Cake

serves 8-10

Very fashionable in the Twenties, Thirties and Forties, this elegant cake has somehow fallen by the wayside and is due for a revival. Make a Walnut Torte as directed on page 237. Split into 3 layers when cold. Sandwich together with half of frosting given for Frosted Chocolate Layer Cake then swirl remainder over top and sides. Stud top with walnut halves.

Coffee Walnut Layer Cake
serves 8-10
Prepare as above but when making Frosting, use strong coffee instead of water.

Coffee Fudge Cake

serves 8
(illustrated on page 90)

4oz (125g) soft lard
4oz (125g) light-brown soft sugar
2 Grade 2 eggs, beaten
6oz (175g) self-raising flour
1 level tbsp instant coffee powder or granules
2 tbsp milk
2 level tbsp golden syrup, melted with the milk and cooled
Fudge Icing
2oz (50g) soft lard
3oz (75g) light-brown soft sugar
1 level tbsp instant coffee powder or granules
2 tbsp milk

4oz (125g) icing sugar, sifted
3 level tbsp apricot jam
Chocolate vermicelli
Walnut pieces

1 Cream the lard until soft, beat in the sugar then gradually add the eggs, beating well after each addition.
2 Fold in the flour and coffee powder alternately with the milk mixture.
3 Divide mixture evenly between two 7in (17.5cm) greased sandwich tins, baselined with greaseproof paper.
4 Bake 20-25 minutes just above centre of oven (any position in fan oven) set to 375°F (190°C), Gas 5. Turn out on to a wire rack and leave until cold.
5 For icing, melt the lard over low heat. Add the sugar and, when dissolved, stir in the coffee powder or granules and milk.
6 Gradually beat in the icing sugar to make a smooth, dark icing. Leave to cool and thicken slightly.
7 Sandwich cakes together with jam. Spread icing on top of the cake and ease it to the sides so that it trickles over the edge in places. Decorate centre with chocolate vermicelli and walnut pieces.

Iced Fudge Cake

serves 8-10
(illustrated on page 239)

An iced fantasy of a cake, which is rich without being heavy.

4oz (125g) butter
2 slightly rounded tbsp golden syrup
8oz (225g) Rich Tea biscuits, coarsely crushed but still in small pieces
1oz (25g) seedless raisins
2oz (50g) glacé cherries, quartered
5oz (150g) plain dessert chocolate (1½ large bars), chopped into small pieces
Fudge Icing
2oz (50g) plain dessert chocolate
2 tbsp water
1oz (25g) butter
6oz (175g) icing sugar, sifted
Extra icing sugar

1 Melt butter and syrup slowly in a saucepan. Remove from heat.
2 Stir in biscuits, raisins, glacé cherries and chopped chocolate. Mix well, then press into 2lb (1kg) oblong loaf tin, completely lined with non-stick parchment paper.
3 Leave overnight to harden in the refrigerator. Remove from tin, take off paper and stand cake on a plate.
4 For icing, break up chocolate into squares. Put into pan with water and butter. Heat gently until ingredients have completely melted. Remove pan from heat. Allow to cool.
5 Add icing sugar and beat until icing is thick and fudge-like. Spread over top of cake then cover with sifted icing sugar.

Crazy-paving Roll

serves 6-8
(illustrated on page 239)

3oz (75g) butter
3oz (75g) caster sugar
1 heaped tbsp drinking chocolate
1 Grade 3 egg, beaten
1 packet (about 5oz or 150g) shortbread biscuits, broken up into small pieces
Icing sugar

1 Melt butter in a pan then stir in sugar and drinking chocolate.
2 Stir in the egg and biscuits then leave in pan, in a cool place, until beginning to set.
3 Mould into an 8in (20cm) roll on a piece of foil then wrap round with the foil. Refrigerate until firm. Unwrap, sift icing sugar over the top, then cut into slices.

Austro-Hungarian Caramel Torte

serves 8

From this once-famous Empire, here is a typical cake based on eggs and almonds and cocooned in cream.

3 Grade 3 eggs, separated
4oz (125g) caster sugar
2oz (50g) ground almonds
3oz (75g) semolina
½ level tsp baking powder
Caramel Cream
1oz (25g) caster sugar
2 tsp cold water
½pt (275ml) double cream

1 Beat egg yolks to a thick and white paste with the sugar. Sift in almonds, semolina and baking powder.
2 Whisk egg whites to a stiff snow. Fold into egg yolk mixture with a metal spoon.
3 When evenly combined, spread into two 7in (17.5cm) sandwich tins, greased and base-lined with greaseproof paper.
4 Bake 30 minutes in centre of oven (any position in fan oven) set to 350°F (180°C), Gas 4. Leave to stand 10 minutes then turn out on to a wire cooling rack lined with a piece of foil sprinkled with caster sugar. Leave until cold.
5 For Caramel Cream, put sugar into a saucepan, add water and dissolve slowly over a low heat. Bring to the boil and boil without stirring until mixture turns a deepish gold — rather like a caramel in colour.
6 Add 2 tbsp cream and mix well by stirring quickly. Leave until cold. Whip rest of cream until thick then fold into caramel mixture.
7 Sandwich cakes together thickly with Caramel Cream then spread remainder over top and sides. Chill lightly before serving.

Caramel Hazelnut Torte
serves 8
Make as above but stud top with hazelnuts.

Sparkling Chocolate Cherry Cake

serves 8-10
(illustrated on page 240)

A glamorous cake for any time of year but very pretty for the Christmas tea-table.

6oz (175g) self-raising flour
1oz (25g) cocoa powder
6oz (175g) soft margarine, at kitchen temperature
6oz (175g) light-brown soft sugar
3 Grade 3 eggs, at kitchen temperature
1 tsp vanilla essence
2 heaped tbsp apricot jam
5oz (150g) glacé cherries, halved
2oz (50g) walnut pieces

1 Sift flour and cocoa powder into a bowl. Add margarine, sugar, eggs and vanilla essence.
2 Beat well until all ingredients are thoroughly mixed. Do this either by hand or in a food processor.
3 Spread smoothly into a 7in (17.5cm) round, deep, cake tin, first greased and lined.
4 Bake 1 hour in oven centre (any position in fan oven) set to 350°F (180°C), Gas 4. The cake is ready when a thin metal skewer, pushed gently into centre, comes out clean and dry.
5 Leave to cool for 10 minutes, then carefully invert on to a wire cooling-rack. Remove paper, then turn cake the right way up.
6 For topping, heat jam until just bubbling, then stir in cherries and walnuts. Spoon on top of warm cake, then leave to cool completely before cutting.

Thatched Cottage Cake

serves 8-10
(illustrated on page 240)

6oz (175g) self-raising flour
6oz (175g) soft margarine, at kitchen temperature
6oz (175g) caster sugar
3 Grade 3 eggs
4 rounded tbsp Olde English marmalade
2oz (50g) walnuts, chopped

1 Well grease a 2lb (1kg) oblong loaf tin and line base and sides with greaseproof paper, making sure it protrudes at least 1in (2cm) above edges of tin. Brush paper with melted fat.
2 Sift flour into a bowl, then add margarine, sugar and eggs. Beat well until all ingredients are thoroughly mixed. Do this either by hand or in a food processor.
3 Mix together marmalade and walnuts, then spread half over base of tin. Add cake mixture, smoothing it with a knife.
4 Bake 1¼-1½ hours in centre of oven (any position in fan oven) set to 325°F (160°C), Gas 3. The cake is ready when a metal skewer, pushed gently into centre, comes out clean and dry.
5 Remove cake from oven. Spread rest of marmalade and nut mixture on top. Leave cake to cool in the tin, then with the help of the paper, lift out when cold. Gently ease off paper and cut the cake into slices to serve.

Middle Eastern Orange Cake

serves 8

8oz (225g) self-raising flour
4oz (125g) butter or margarine
4oz (125g) caster sugar
4oz (125g) seedless raisins
Finely grated peel and juice of 1 medium washed and dried orange
1 level tsp finely grated grapefruit peel
2 Grade 3 eggs, beaten
2 tbsp milk

1 Sift flour into bowl. Rub in butter or margarine finely. Toss in sugar, raisins and both fruit peels.
2 Using a fork, mix to a softish consistency with orange juice, eggs and milk.
3 Spread evenly into 7in (17.5cm) greased and lined cake tin and bake 1¼ hours just above centre of oven (any position in fan oven) set to 375°F (190°C), Gas 5.

4 Leave to stand 10 minutes then turn out and cool on a wire rack. Store in an airtight container when cold.

Greek Syrup Cake 1

serves 10

Very typical of Greek cakes, or desserts, this has a fairly delicate texture but uses quite costly ingredients. It has been laced with brandy but you can, if you like the flavour, use Ouzo or Retsina wine.

6oz (175g) butter, at kitchen temperature and softened
6oz (175g) caster sugar
1½ level tsp finely grated orange peel
4 tbsp orange juice
5 Grade 3 eggs, beaten
9oz (250g) semolina
3 level tsp baking powder
6oz (175g) ground almonds

Syrup
6oz (175g) caster sugar
4 tbsp water
1 tbsp lemon juice
2in (5cm) piece of cinnamon stick
3 tbsp brandy, Ouzo or Retsina wine

1 Well grease an 8in (20cm) ring tin and dust lightly with baking powder as this prevents sticking. Set oven to 425°F (220°C), Gas 7.
2 Cream butter and sugar together until light and fluffy. Stir in orange peel and juice. Gradually beat in eggs. (Mixture will curdle but this has no effect on finished cake.)
3 Stir in semolina sifted with baking powder and mixed with the ground almonds. When evenly combined, spread smoothly into prepared tin. Bake 10 minutes in oven centre (any position in fan oven). Reduce temperature to 350°F (180°C), Gas 4 and continue to bake for a further 30 minutes when cake should be firm and golden.
4 Remove from oven and leave to stand for 10 minutes. As the texture is delicate, turn cake out on to a serving dish with great care.

5 Make syrup. Put first four ingredients into a pan and heat slowly until sugar dissolves. Bring to boil then boil, without stirring, until syrup thickens to a tacky consistency and only just begins to turn the palest gold. Cool slightly, stir in alcohol and strain over cake. Cut into wedges and serve cold.

Greek Syrup Cake 2
serves 10
Reduce baking powder to 2 tsp and spread mixture into 7in (17.5cm) square cake tin, prepared as ring mould. Bake in oven centre (any position in fan oven) set to 350°F (180°C), Gas 4. Allow 1 hour 10 minutes. Turn out and coat with syrup as given above.

Spanish Orange Cake

serves 8

A crumbly, beautifully flavoured cake from Spain. It can be glamorized with strawberries and cream for a luscious dessert, or served as it is for afternoon tea.

6oz (175g) butter or block margarine, at room temperature and soft
6oz (175g) caster sugar
Finely grated peel of 1 washed and dried orange
3 Grade 3 eggs, at kitchen temperature
4oz (125g) self-raising flour, sifted
4oz (125g) semolina
1oz (25g) ground almonds
2 tbsp orange juice, strained
½ tsp almond essence
1oz (25g) flaked almonds

1 Cream butter or margarine and sugar together until light and fluffy. Stir in orange peel then beat in eggs singly, adding 2 tsp flour with each to prevent mixture curdling and losing air.
2 Using a large metal spoon, gently fold in rest of flour, semolina, almonds, orange juice and almond essence. When well mixed, spread evenly into a 7in (17.5cm) greased and lined deep cake tin. Sprinkle with almonds.

3 Bake 1½-1¾ hours in centre of oven (any position in fan oven) set to 350°F (180°C), Gas 4. The cake is ready when it is well risen and golden and when a thin metal skewer, pushed gently into centre, comes out clean and dry.
4 Leave in tin 10 minutes then turn out on to a wire cooling rack. Remove paper when cold and store in an airtight tin.

Dutch Ginger Buttercake

makes about 24

Close to a Shortbread, the ginger in this Dutch Buttercake may be omitted if preferred.

8oz (225g) unsalted butter, at kitchen temperature and softened
8oz (225g) light-brown soft sugar
1 level tsp finely grated lemon peel
1 Grade 3 egg, beaten
8oz (225g) plain flour
2oz (50g) stem ginger, well-drained of syrup and chopped (optional)
1½oz (40g) flaked almonds

1 Cream butter, sugar and lemon peel together until light and fluffy.
2 Beat in egg then fold in flour and ginger if used. Spread into a Swiss Roll tin measuring about 12 x 8in (30 x 20cm) then press flaked almonds completely over surface.
3 Bake about 45 minutes in centre of oven (any position in fan oven) set to 350°F (180°C), Gas 4.
4 Remove from oven, cool 10 minutes in tin then cut into about 24 pieces. Remove carefully and cool on a wire rack. Store in an airtight container when cold.

Country Dripping Cake

serves 8-10

Said to come from Wales, this is a typical example of the best in British baking, as is the Teisen Lap (an updated version of Welsh Bakestone Cake) which follows.

12oz (350g) plain flour
4 level tsp baking powder
¼ level tsp ground nutmeg
1 level tsp mixed spice
6oz (175g) beef dripping, at kitchen temperature and softened
2oz (50g) butter
6oz (175g) light-brown soft sugar
8oz (225g) mixed dried fruit, including peel
2 tsp black treacle
2 Grade 2 eggs, beaten
½pt (275ml) cold milk

1 Sift flour, baking powder, nutmeg and spice into bowl. Rub in dripping and butter finely.
2 Toss in sugar and dried fruit then using a fork, mix to a soft consistency with treacle, eggs and milk. Stir briskly without beating.
3 Spread smoothly into an 8in (20cm) round cake tin, well-greased and lined with greaseproof paper.
4 Bake 1¾-2 hours in centre of oven (any position in fan oven) set to 350°F (180°C), Gas 4. When ready, the cake should be well-risen and golden brown. To test, gently push a thin metal skewer into centre. If ready, it should come out clean and dry.
5 Leave cake to stand 15 minutes then turn out and cool on a wire rack. When completely cold, wrap in paper and store in an airtight container.

Teisen Lap

serves 8-10

1lb (450g) self-raising flour
2 level tsp baking powder
½ level tsp salt
½ level tsp ground nutmeg
8oz (225g) mixture of margarine or butter and lard or white cooking fat
6oz (175g) caster sugar
6oz (175g) mixed dried fruit including peel
2 Grade 3 eggs, beaten
¾pt (425ml) milk

1 Sift flour, baking powder, salt and nutmeg into a bowl. Rub in fats finely.
2 Toss in sugar and dried fruit then mix to a thickish consistency with eggs and milk, stirring briskly with a fork. Avoid beating.
3 Spread evenly into a well-greased roasting tin measuring about 11 x 8in (27.5 x 20cm) and bake just above centre of oven (any position in fan oven) set to 375°F (190°C), Gas 5.
4 Cake is ready when a thin metal skewer, inserted into centre, comes out clean and dry.
5 Leave in tin 10 minutes then turn out on to a wire cooling rack. Serve sliced and spread with butter.

Welsh Cakes

makes 16

8oz (225g) plain white flour
1 level tsp baking powder
1 level tsp mixed spice
2oz (50g) white cooking fat or lard
2oz (50g) butter or margarine
3oz (75g) caster sugar
2oz (50g) currants
1 Grade 3 egg, beaten
2 tbsp cold milk
Extra cooking fat or lard for frying

1 Sift flour, baking powder and spice into a bowl. Rub in fat finely. Toss in sugar and currants.
2 Mix to a fairly stiff dough with the egg and milk. Turn out onto a floured surface. Knead until smooth then roll out to about ¼in (75mm) in thickness.
3 Cut into 16 rounds with 3in (7.5cm) biscuit cutter, re-rolling and re-cutting trimmings to make the required number.
4 Brush a large, heavy-based frying pan or griddle with melted fat. Heat until hot. Fry 4-6 cakes for about 5 minutes, turning twice with a knife. Repeat, until all the cakes have been fried.
5 Serve warm or cold with butter. If served without butter, the cakes should be sprinkled with a little caster sugar first.

Index